The Politics of EU
Police Cooperation

The Politics of EU Police Cooperation

TOWARD A EUROPEAN FBI?

JOHN D. OCCHIPINTI

LYNNE
RIENNER
PUBLISHERS

BOULDER
LONDON

Learning Resources
Centre
12526061

Published in the United States of America in 2003 by
Lynne Rienner Publishers, Inc.
1800 30th Street, Boulder, Colorado 80301
www.rienner.com

and in the United Kingdom by
Lynne Rienner Publishers, Inc.
3 Henrietta Street, Covent Garden, London WC2E 8LU

Library of Congress Cataloging-in-Publication Data
Occhipinti, John D., 1967–
    The politics of EU police cooperation : toward a European FBI? /
    John D. Occhipinti.
    Includes bibliographical references and index.
    ISBN 1-58826-118-2 (alk. paper)
    1. Europol—History. 2. Law enforcement—European Union countries—
International cooperation. 3. Police administration—European Union
countries—International cooperation. 4. Transnational crime—European
Union countries. 5. Terrorism—European Union countries—Prevention.
6. Security, International—European Union countries. I. Title.
HV819.A45E876   2003
363.2'06'04—dc21   2003041369

British Cataloguing in Publication Data
A Cataloguing in Publication record for this book
is available from the British Library.

Printed and bound in the United States of America

The paper used in this publication meets the requirements
♾ of the American National Standard for Permanence of
Paper for Printed Library Materials Z39.48-1992.

5 4 3 2 1

For Gina

Contents

Preface

SINCE THE TERRORIST ATTACKS ON THE UNITED STATES ON SEPTEM-
ber 11, 2001, interest in internal security matters in Europe has increased
dramatically. However, when I first began studying Justice and Home
Affairs (JHA) in 1997, few researchers were looking at this aspect of the
EU, especially the area of police cooperation. I was fortunate to be able to
draw on the work of the handful of scholars who were already publishing in
this field, including Cyrille Fijnaut, Monica den Boer, Jürg Monar, Roger
Morgan, and Neil Walker. I rely heavily on their valuable contributions, as
well as those of others. I hope that I have done justice to their pioneering
work.

My examination of JHA and the European Police Office (Europol)
since 1999 is based on official European Union documents obtained largely
through the archives contained within the *Europa* website, as well as on
press articles available through Lexis-Nexis, especially those of *European
Report,* published by the European Information Service. At the later stages
of my research, I was struck by how quickly official EU documents (e.g.,
minutes of Council sessions) started to become available and how press
coverage of JHA matters increased compared to earlier years.

For a variety of reasons, my original plan for this book was to cover
events only through the summer of 2001, but the attacks on the World
Trade Center and Pentagon and the EU's reaction to these caused me to
extend my work on this project by another full year. All along, I had been
arguing that EU cooperation on JHA could be explained, at least in part, by
events taking place outside of Europe, and the events of September 11 sadly
confirmed this. I wish to acknowledge the many lives lost or changed for-
ever on that horrible day.

Many people helped me in various ways to write this book. While an
undergraduate at Colgate University, I took my first classes on European
integration with Charlie Naef, who has continued to serve as a valuable

mentor and friend to me. I am indebted as well to Martin Heisler, who directed my dissertation at the University of Maryland. My doctoral thesis dealt with the transformation of the former Volkspolizei (People's Police) in the new German Länder after 1990 and helped establish my interest in police institutions in the context of European politics, leading to my study of Europol.

More recently, I have benefited from the support of Canisius College, which gave me the opportunity to teach on the European Union, comparative criminal justice institutions, and transnational crime, as well as funded my participation in several academic conferences, where I presented parts of this book. I am also thankful for the encouragement and assistance of my colleagues at Canisius, including the help of several supportive administrators. In addition, over the past six years I have guided my students' participation in the programs of the Transatlantic Consortium for European Union Studies and Simulations (TACEUSS), which has brought me in contact with many new friends from the United States and Europe. Among these, I especially want to thank Roy Ginsberg of Skidmore College, who encouraged and inspired me to write this book.

Several of my past students provided valuable assistance to me on this project, including Tracy Flynn, Nick Mineo, and Michelle McFarland. In addition, Ben Krass and Nathan Shoff provided me with important research assistance funded through the Canisius Earning Excellence Program.

I have enjoyed very much working with my enthusiastic publisher, Lynne Rienner, who first approached me about writing this book several years ago. I would like to express my gratitude to her very professional staff, particularly her assistant, Sally Glover, who has helped me a great deal. I am also thankful for the prompt work of the two anonymous reviewers of my manuscript, as well as their valuable suggestions, which helped to improve my work.

Finally, I would like to acknowledge the support and encouragement of my friends and family as I worked on this and other projects over the past several years. My mother and late father made many sacrifices for my education, and in many ways this project marks both an end to that phase of my academic career and the beginning of the next. I especially want to thank my wife, Gina, for putting up with me while I worked too many long hours at my desk completing this project. I could not have done this without her.

1

Introduction:
Police Cooperation
in the European Union

IT MAY SEEM ODD TO BEGIN A BOOK ON EUROPEAN POLICE COOPER-Ation with reference to the United States, but then these have been unusual times indeed. In the aftermath of the terrorist attacks on the World Trade Center and Pentagon on September 11, 2001, policymakers around the world were forced to rethink matters of internal security. For the United States, this has entailed, among other things, devising new ways to secure its borders from terrorist infiltration, while simultaneously keeping the United States more or less open to trade, immigration, legitimate asylum applicants, and travelers. These often contending concerns of free movement and greater security compelled the United States to hasten ongoing efforts and initiate new strategies to work more closely with foreign governments and police agencies in the sharing of intelligence information and the coordination of antiterrorism efforts. For example, by December 2001, this new approach to internal security resulted in an action plan to create a "smart border" between the United States and Canada, bringing together many existing and new initiatives.

This coordination between the U.S. and Canadian governments reflects, albeit on a smaller scale, the increasingly integrated approach to internal security that has been evident among the countries of the European Union (EU) since the 1970s. At the center of this integration on internal security in the EU, which has been increasing rapidly since 1999, has been cooperation on crime fighting in general and police cooperation in particular. Describing and explaining this aspect of the EU, particularly the development of the European Police Office (Europol), is the main subject of this book.

The official inauguration of Europol in 1998, after years of preparation, debate, and delay, marked a new watershed of EU cooperation in the field of "Justice and Home Affairs." Moreover, it reflects a shift *in the direction* of supranationalism and away from Europe's long-standing intergovernmental approach to international law enforcement. By this, I mean that the individual member states of the EU no longer have total sovereignty over decisionmaking and implementation of policies in matters of internal security (see Chapter 2). In fact, at least in some regards, the EU seems to be on a path toward establishing its own federal police agency, much like the Federal Bureau of Investigation (FBI) in the United States. This is evident in the development of Europol, which was prescribed in the Maastricht Treaty. Europol became a legal reality on October 1, 1998, and took up full operations in The Hague on July 1, 1999, following the entry into force of the necessary protocols to the Europol Convention.

Through its liaison network and computer databases, Europol offers police agencies in the EU a valuable means to exchange information on an increasing variety of transnational crimes. In fact, Europol entails much more than a way for police organizations across Europe to pool and share data. It also assists in the fight against international organized crime by analyzing criminal data, alerting national police forces in the members states about criminal trends and links among crime groups, and helps the police in different EU countries to coordinate their investigations, arrests, and other anti-crime efforts in general. Since its inception, Europol's crime-fighting responsibilities, operational powers, budget, and staff have steadily increased.

For the time being, however, Europol does not enjoy the "executive policing powers" of a true policing organization such as the FBI. That is, Europol personnel are not stationed in branch offices throughout the EU, and they are not empowered to carry out independent criminal investigations in the field, conduct searches, or make arrests. Moreover, there does not seem to be the political will within the EU to transform Europol into a true federal police force for the European Union any time soon, though Germany continues to promote this goal as it has done since the late 1980s.

Despite the limited nature of Europol at this time, a number of recent developments indicate the evolution of a more supranational approach to matters of internal security in general and to police cooperation in particular within the EU. Issues pertaining to internal security, including crime, immigration, refugees, and asylum, were not handled collectively in any formal institutionalized fashion until the Maastricht Treaty (the Treaty on European Union) went into effect in 1993 and with it the creation of the new Third Pillar dealing with cooperation in Justice and Home Affairs (JHA). To clarify this policy area, collaboration on justice deals with both civil and criminal matters, while "home affairs" borrows its terminology from the lexicon of the United Kingdom, where matters of internal security at the national level, including crime fighting and immigration, are handled by the Home Office and its Home Secretary in London. It should be noted that other European states employ terms that translate as "interior minister/ministry" or "minister/ministry for internal affairs" regarding the same kind of agencies dealing with internal security.

In the vocabulary of EU politics, justice and home affairs has come to refer to a variety of policy domains dealing with expanding fields of internal security, including many varieties of crime, public order, policing, terrorism, border control, immigration, and asylum.[1] Similar to other aspects of public policy in Europe, JHA in the member states has come to be influenced by the European Union. As with other issue areas in the EU, cooperation regarding JHA has moved away from pure intergovernmentalism and taken on an incipient supranational character, though the role of the member states in policymaking and administration remains quite strong. That is, national leaders continue to hold most of the decisionmaking and operative authority on matters of internal security, especially compared to EU cooperation in its First Pillar, which deals with the common market and related policies. On First Pillar matters, the EU's supranational institutions—the Commission, the European Parliament, and European Court of Justice (ECJ)—play a much more significant role than they do in the Third Pillar, where the Council of Ministers and the member states hold most of the power.

Turning the reality of a common approach to JHA for the EU into actual policies was initially slow in coming, but progress has quickened in recent years following the entry into force of the Treaty of Amsterdam in May 1999 and its prescribed Area of Freedom, Security, and Justice (AFSJ). Soon after this, in October 1999, a historic meeting of the European Council was held in Tampere, Finland, that established a detailed and ambitious agenda for making the dream of creating an AFSJ for the EU a reality. Since then, progress on JHA has been slow in some areas but quite remarkable in others. The terrorist attacks on the United States on September 11, 2001, only hastened progress in this direction, as did rising concerns over illegal immigration during the spring of 2002.

In the process, it can be argued that dealing with matters of internal security in the EU has gradually taken on a more supranational nature, although it remains correct to characterize EU policy as continuing to be more intergovernmental than not. In other words, the member states of the EU have maintained their predominance in matters of internal security in the EU, but supranational actors, particularly the Commission and, to a lesser extent, the European Parliament (EP), have significantly increased their influence and role in recent years. At the center of this evolution has been various anticrime efforts revolving around Europol.

Although Europol is not nearly as supranational vis-à-vis the member states of the EU as the FBI is relative to the law enforcement agencies of the fifty United States, enduring political forces seem likely to propel EU police cooperation in this direction over the next several years. In addition to Europol, the European Union has gradually been establishing an entire institutional infrastructure of crime fighting to supplement its internal security efforts. This includes the recently created Operational Task Force of

Police Chiefs, the European Police College for high-level officers, and Eurojust, the EU agency that facilitates cooperation among judicial authorities in the member states on criminal matters. In addition, by 2002, there were already initial discussions of creating a common border patrol for the EU, as well as a public prosecutor's office.

To go along with these new institutions, the EU has also begun to establish a common legal infrastructure to fight crime. This has entailed growing mutual recognition of various judicial rulings, as well as the harmonization of some substantive criminal law through agreement on common definitions and minimum sanctions for various forms of serious crimes, such as counterfeiting and terrorism. Concerning procedural criminal law, the EU has agreed, for example, to implement a common European Arrest Warrant that will do away with time-consuming extradition once it takes effect in 2004.

In short, after years of planning and delays, the progress of the EU in building this new institutional and legal infrastructure since 1999 has been quite impressive. In conceptual terms, progress on JHA can thus be characterized in terms of both increased integration, as well as Europeanization. The former refers to increased cooperative decisionmaking on an increasing number of issues, while the latter implies the harmonization of policies, practices, standards, and laws among the member states. This book describes progress in these regards and identifies the key factors that seem both responsible for past developments and likely to drive future integration and Europeanization in the future.

Why has the EU pursued such collaboration on JHA in the first place? The short answer is that the member states of the former European Community (EC), now the EU, have increasingly found it too difficult to combat certain forms of crimes on their own, especially transnational organized crime. Initially, criminal offenses such as terrorism and international drug trafficking provided the impetus for the earliest attempts at European cooperation in this area, leading to the creation of the so-called Trevi Group in 1975. Later, with the creation of Europol, collaborative efforts were expanded to deal with several other forms of organized crime, including automobile theft, the trafficking of human beings, and counterfeiting of the euro.

Before the recent progress noted above, the main problems confronting police organizations in the member states had been the differing national penal codes and their inability to fight crimes across national boundaries. Lacking the authority to operate outside of their territorial jurisdictions and not having institutionalized forms of international cooperation, the police in Europe had to rely on the sharing of some criminal data via Interpol (the International Criminal Police Organization) and informal and mostly sporadic contacts among various police agencies through conferences and clubs (see Chapter 3). Meanwhile, organized crime groups, such as terrorists, the

Italian mafia, and drug traffickers, found it comparatively easy to overcome border controls and operate transnationally.

With the gradual creation of the Schengen free-travel area starting in 1995, the ability of criminals to operate in Europe became even easier. Moreover, this came at the same time that the end of the Cold War had facilitated new forms of crime (e.g., the trafficking of human beings) committed by new criminal gangs based in Central and Eastern Europe (e.g., the Russian mafia). Since the 1970s, European leaders have attempted to deal with this problem of transnational organized crime by increasing their cooperative efforts. Some of this collaboration has taken the form of increased integration, entailing the building of new decisionmaking institutions and common crime-fighting organizations, such as Europol. Over the years, these kinds of cooperative efforts have become more supranational in nature.

Combined with this, the countries of the EU have also experienced increasing Europeanization regarding internal security. Concerning JHA, this has not only entailed the evolving legal infrastructure discussed above, but also the sharing of anticrime strategies and "best practices" among police organizations, as well as efforts to develop a common European culture of policing through organizations such as the new Task Force of Police Chiefs and the European Police College. This book describes this increasing supranationalism and Europeanization regarding JHA in the EU and identifies the variables that seem most significant in explaining these developments.

Examining the evolution of police cooperation in the EU reveals that it has resulted from many of the same factors that fostered the EC's development from a highly intergovernmental international organization in the 1960s and 1970s to one that was much more supranational in nature by the 1990s. As predicted by liberal intergovernmentalism, still the dominant theoretical paradigm in EU studies, collaboration on JHA in the EU is at least partly explainable in terms of the power and motives of the member states, as they simultaneously react to interest formed under the pressure of their respective domestic agendas, as well as bargain with each other, seeking credible commitments for future collaboration. Throughout this book, support for the tenets of liberal intergovernmentalism can easily be identified, notably through the actions of member states at key meetings of the European Council and Council of Ministers (i.e., the Justice and Home Affairs Council).

However, my research should make clear that the evolution of cooperation on JHA in general, and Europol in particular, is attributable to a variety of factors that are overlooked or at least undervalued by liberal intergovernmentalism. For example, a strong case can be made that cooperation on JHA, especially since the mid-1980s, can be explained in terms of "functional spillover," which is a central component of neofunctionalist theory. The concept of spillover, discussed in greater detail in the following chapter, implies that cooperation in one area of European integration leads to cooperation in another. In the case of JHA, for example, it can be shown that the creation of the Schengen free-travel area contributed to the need for a deepening of collaboration on crime fighting in the EU.

In sum, the paradigm of neofunctionalism can help explain the development of cooperation on JHA in the EU. To a lesser extent, collaboration on JHA, including police cooperation and its nature, can also be explained by other "internal factors" found within the member states of the EU. Two of these variables are ideological in nature, namely federalism and concern for democracy. Concerning the first of these, federalist ideology helps explain, at least to some degree, the aspirations of a few European leaders (e.g., in Germany) to create supranational institutions for crime fighting as part of the eventual creation of a true European federation. This book examines the relevance of federalism for JHA, as well as how it has been more than counterbalanced by the enduring significance of subsidiarity, which has served to limit both integration and Europeanization on crime fighting by leaving many aspects of crime fighting to member states or their political subunits. For example, there is no movement underway to replace everyday, uniformed policing with an EU police force. At the same time, it can also be shown, at least to some extent, that a desire to address the so-called democratic deficit in the EU has contributed to the particular shape and form of cooperation on JHA in several regards. This includes, for example, new roles for the European Parliament and attention to civil liberties in areas such as data protection.

Finally, in addition to these internal factors, the development of cooperation on JHA since the 1970s can also be explained by several variables stemming from outside the boundaries of the EU. Important examples of such external factors are international terrorism, drug trafficking, and illegal immigration. Additional external variables include the end of the Cold War and the resulting new sources of organized crime in Central and Eastern Europe and pressure to expand the membership of the EU to include many of the new democracies in this region. The swift reaction of the EU to the terrorist attacks on the United States provides further evidence that EU cooperation on JHA is influenced by external factors.

By serving as a laboratory for examining the salience of these internal and external factors, the study of police cooperation in the EU provides many valuable lessons for students of the EU in general, but especially those interested in JHA. By shedding light on the importance of these variables, this research should be of interest to both specialists on JHA and those with a broader interest in the EU. In doing so, this research entails a test of the major theories of European integration; showing a true picture of integration in the field of JHA requires attention to more than one theoretical framework. This is particularly the case regarding the dominant paradigm of the past, neofunctionalism, and the contemporary champion, liberal intergovernmentalism. While there is clearly evidence from the field of JHA to support the major tenets of the latter theory, the development of police cooperation in the EU since the 1980s supports the prediction of the former, namely that European integration can be partly explained in terms of functional spillover, confirming the expectations of neofunctionalism. Along with these theoretical lessons, my research also shows how external events can help drive both integration and Europeanization in the EU, and how both of these can be shaped by relevant concerns for democracy and limited by the principle of subsidiarity.

On a purely descriptive level, this book offers a highly detailed account of past and recent developments on EU Justice and Home Affairs, which, even after September 11, 2001, remains one of the most underresearched aspects of the European Union. One reason for this, perhaps, is that progress in this policy area had been quite limited until the late 1990s. Even then, cooperation on JHA failed to grab headlines or capture the attention of the public in the same way that the recent cooperation on the Second Pillar on the Common Foreign and Security Policy (CFSP) has done, particularly after the appointment of Javier Solana as high representative for CFSP and planning for the new European Rapid Reaction Force. Of course, all of this changed after the terrorist attacks on the United States, which heightened interest in internal security policy in the EU among the public, press, and politicians. Attention to JHA received a further boost when the popularity of far-right political parties in several member states seemed to rise during spring 2002 in response to increased public attention to the problem of illegal immigration. For those new to the field of JHA, this book should provide a useful introduction to EU policymaking in this area, especially the creation and role of Europol. In general, this book places recent developments on JHA in their proper historical context, as well as juxtaposes these with major events in the recent history of the EU.

In fact, the story of police cooperation in the EU contains many important lessons for the study of the EU beyond the field of JHA. In general, police organizations in any state tend to reflect the major social, political, and financial issues of the societies that they are intended to serve. For example, examining the police in the United States brings to light the importance of race or pressing fiscal issues in U.S. politics, just as the transformation of the police in the young democracies of Central and Eastern Europe helps one to better understand the politics of transition in those countries. In the same way, police cooperation in the European Union reflects many of the main issues that have confronted the EU in recent years, including the changing roles of its major policymaking institutions, enduring concerns for a democratic deficit, and the impact of impending enlargement, to list just a few.

Finally, North Americans might find it both interesting and useful to study the development of police cooperation in Europe, especially after September 11, 2001, as they seek solutions to their own concerns to maintain free movement across international boundaries on the one hand and increase security on the other. It should not be forgotten that U.S. President George W. Bush spent the first months of his new administration exploring the question of how to better facilitate the free movement of people across the United States' southern border, especially Mexican workers, while simultaneously remaining attentive to the problem of drug trafficking. Only after the attacks on the World Trade Center and Pentagon was more attention focused on better securing the United States' northern border from terrorist infiltration, while trying to preserve the flow of goods and people to and from Canada, its largest trading partner.

For many years now, Europeans have been wrestling with the fundamental question of how to protect internal security, while gradually increasing the free movement of people, goods, services, and capital. There are surely many important lessons that North Americans can learn from studying the experiences of the European Union in this regard, since the EU has been working on a common approach to internal security matters since the 1970s. In this context, it is noteworthy to mention that the creation of the Trevi Group, the forerunner to the EU's Third Pillar, came in response to the terrorist killings of Israeli athletes at the 1972 Olympic Games in Munich by the Palestinia group Black September. North Americans will likely look back on September 11, 2001, in a similar way concerning the roots of greater international cooperation on internal security on their own continent. As will be discussed in this book, police cooperation in the EU would eventually focus on other forms of crimes, particularly the trafficking of illicit drugs and human beings (e.g., illegal immigration and prostitutes), before focusing once again on terrorism after September 11, followed by border-control issues in general in 2002. North Americans should find this account of the EU's development in this area to be highly instructive, especially its gradual shift in the direction of supranationalism concerning European police cooperation.

Before examining the historical roots of this recent progress, the following chapter establishes a conceptual framework for evaluating the development of cooperation on JHA in terms of intergovernmentalism and supranationalism. In doing so, it provides a way of understanding how the EU has shifted in the direction of the latter, becoming more and more like a "federal state" in the process. Chapter 2 also spells out the basic elements of the major theoretical models that seek to explain European integration, as well as specifies in more detail the internal and external factors discussed above and how these are related to the progress of European integration.

The next several chapters of the book trace the history of police cooperation in the EU. Chapter 3 describes the earliest foundations of European police cooperation, the progress leading to the creation of the Third Pillar, and the creation of the Europol Drugs Unit, the forerunner of Europol. In Chapter 4, the politics of the Europol Convention and its protocols are examined, as well as the Treaty of Amsterdam and its implications for JHA in general and Europol in particular.

Chapter 5 describes progress achieved at the Tampere European Council of 1999 and the impact of this on efforts to create an institutional and legal infrastructure of crime fighting in the European Union during the Portuguese and French presidencies of the EU during 2000. Chapter 6 provides a detailed account of continuing activity in this direction before the terrorist attacks of September 11, examining progress made under the direction of Sweden during the first half of 2001 and into the early months of the subsequent Belgian presidency. The EU's swift reaction to the terrorist attacks on the United States is covered in Chapter 7, including the negotiations to adopt the European Arrest Warrant and harmonize national penal codes covering terrorism. Chapter 8 covers the entire Spanish presidency of 2002, showing how the EU maintained momentum on JHA, but also how attention began to shift away from counterterrorism to concerns over illegal immigration and border control. The major events covered in each of these historical chapters are noted in the detailed chronology of EU police cooperation found at the end of the book. In addition, the concluding section of each of these chapters provides an evaluation and explanation of EU police cooperation during that time period in terms of the concepts and variables introduced in Chapter 2.

These evaluations are summarized in the final part of the book, Chapter 9, which also spells out some general lessons regarding the internal and external factors that seem to be responsible for progress on JHA in the EU over the years, including the shift in the direction of supranationalism and increased Europeanization. Based on these conclusions, the book closes by speculating on the future of police cooperation in the European Union, entailing the possible creation of an FBI-like organization for the EU. Although Europol presently falls far short of this level of integration, the continued salience of internal and external variables discussed in this book means that future progress in this direction seems likely.

Note

1. D. Biggo, "The European Internal Security Field: Stakes and Rivalries in the Newly Developing Area of Police Intervention," in *Policing Across National Boundaries,* ed. M. Anderson and M. den Boer (London: Pinter, 1994), 161–173.

2

Conceptualizing European Integration

AS NOTED IN CHAPTER 1, THIS BOOK EXAMINES THE INTERNAL AND external factors that have influenced European Union collaboration on Justice and Home Affairs (JHA) since the 1970s, paying special attention to cooperation on policing and crime fighting. It will be shown that past, present, and future development of collaboration concerning internal security can be understood by being attentive to the same sets of internal and external factors that help explain the general evolution of European political and economic integration since World War II. This not only includes those factors that have moved cooperation regarding JHA in the direction of supranationalism, but also those that have contributed to the enduring intergovernmental features of collaboration in this policy domain. As will be elucidated below, this characterization assumes that various forms of collective behavior involving independent states may simultaneously entail elements of both intergovernmentalism and supranationalism. Thus, before proceeding to an examination of cooperation in the area of JHA, the concepts of intergovernmentalism and supranationalism in the context of the EU must be properly developed.

"International" (i.e., "interstate") cooperation regarding the EU may be conceptualized in a number of ways. Viewed through the prism of classic realism, and more recently, neorealism, politics on the world stage can be understood largely in terms of the interaction of sovereign states, such as the fifteen member states of the EU today. From this perspective, the politics and policies of the EU are little more than reflections of the power and interests of the member states (or, for a neorealist, the distribution of power among them).[1]

A neoliberal institutionalist or pluralist would focus on different aspects of international cooperation in Europe. They would not only recognize the significance of states, but also several types of nonstate actors (NSAs) in world politics.[2] Among these NSAs are individuals and international organizations, and among the latter are two types: international nongovernmental organizations (INGOs) and intergovernmental organizations (IGOs). INGOs include lobbying groups or firms that operate in more than one state, such as, respectively, Amnesty International and multinational corporations. IGOs, such as the United Nations or the Council of Europe, are forums for deliberation and/or policymaking formed by two or more states, whose governments are represented by instructed delegates.[3] Although realists would not deny the existence of IGOs, they would tend to focus on the interaction and power of the member states, rather than the impact of IGOs as institutions on the behavior of these states.

The European Union of today may be conceived as an IGO (as well as its various historical manifestations). However, aside from indicating that states are important components of the European Union, the label "IGO" describes very little about the EU. A number of different analytical frameworks have been proposed to explain the development and nature of the European Union.[4] Many of these approaches can be categorized according to the importance they place on the role of the EU's member states in each of these regards.

Paradigms that focus on the power of individual EU member states and reject the relative significance of the European Commission, Court of Justice, or Parliament may be placed in the realist category. Where realists have focused on the EU's institutions at all, this attention has been directed toward the Council of Ministers and European Council, in which the member states are represented. In contrast, regarding both the history of European integration and the nature of policymaking in the EU today, approaches that draw attention to the importance of the EU's governmental institutions, especially those whose significance is denied by realists, can be appropriately classified as being neoliberal institutionalist. In short, the realists have stressed intergovernmentalism in the EU, particularly in new treaty negotiations and in the two councils, while the neoliberal institutionalists have emphasized supranationalism when describing this IGO, mainly given the composition, autonomy, and increasing influence of the Commission, Court of Justice, and European Parliament (EP).

One scholar has argued that this "distinction between intergovernmentalism and supranationalism is losing its relevance in the context of the European Union."[5] In contrast, this book argues these concepts should be retained for the study of the EU.[6] The potential pitfalls of treating the EU as being either intergovernmental or supranational in nature can be avoided if intergovernmentalism and supranationalism are not considered in absolute terms, as is often the case. Rather, these labels should be understood as occupying opposite poles on a "continuum of political authority" regarding the power of IGOs vis-à-vis their member states (or regarding nation-states and their constituent subunits). That is, most IGOs are best

typified as possessing elements of *both* supranationalism and intergovernmentalism, instead of simply being conceived as being one or the other in
nature. Moreover, the same could even be said for federal or confederal
states regarding the degree of political authority possessed by the central
government vis-à-vis the constituent states.

Standing in opposition to this conceptual framework are paradigms that
reject the use of the concept of supranationalism in studying the EU. For
example, Andrew Moravcsik has dismissed supranationalism, arguing that
the development of the EU is best understood as the product of intergovernmental bargaining.[7] In essence, the type of issues falling under the
authority of the EU, along with the role of its governmental institutions in
policymaking concerning these, are reflections of intergovernmental agreements struck upon the signing of the last treaty (e.g., the Single European
Act, Maastricht Treaty, or Treaty of Amsterdam). Rather than focusing on
the impact of these agreements on the nature of policymaking, Moravcsik,
in proposing his paradigm of "liberal intergovernmentalism," has turned to
domestic politics to study the source of the interests each of the member
states bring to the bargaining table.[8]

Although Moravcsik's paradigm seems quite useful for studying the
negotiation of the EU's treaties, intergovernmental paradigms such as his
are not well suited for the study of the changing nature of politics in the
EU. Imagine trying to understand the nature of policymaking in the United
States fifty years after its founding by simply examining the interplay of
power and interests during the negotiations of the Constitutional Congress
of 1787. Even if one were to focus on the post-treaty nature of the EC/EU
at any point in history, the concept of intergovernmentalism alone would be
inadequate to capture the impact of policymaking influences outside of the
Council of Ministers. The concept of intergovernmentalism is especially ill-
suited on its own to elucidate the changing nature of the relationship among
the EC's institutions, although attention to the domestic politics in the
member states is indeed helpful—along with other variables—in explaining
why these changes may have occurred.

Much of the scholarly debate about the nature and development of
European integration from the European Community (EC) of the 1960s to
the EU of today has revolved around explaining this very question. The old-
est and most criticized explanations have been provided by the neofunctionalist theories of Leon Lindberg, Ernst Haas, and others.[9] As is well known,
the core contention of neofunctionalist theory is that international cooperation in one policy area leads to ("spills over" into) new collaboration in
other issue areas. It would not be appropriate here to attempt to summarize
the functionalist scholarship in the context of studying the EC/EU, as well as
criticisms of this. It suffices to say that neofunctionalism has been rejected
as a grand theory for explaining the development of European integration

since the 1950s. This is especially true where functionalism has entailed assumptions of a linear progression of supranationalism and where "spill-over," in its various forms, is purported to be the *only* explanation for this.

It seems, however, that the refutation of neofunctionalist theory in its strongest forms has also entailed the dismissal of what such theories were trying to explain, namely the development of supranationalism. That is, the rejection of functionalist arguments, especially by realists, has been accompanied by a reluctance to employ the very concept of supranationalism to describe the nature of the EC/EU. Although realists/intergovernmentalists seem justified in focusing on the role of state actors in the negotiation of the EU's various treaties and conventions, the rejection of supranationalism as a concept is akin to throwing the baby out with the bath water. As will be demonstrated below, this concept seems to be quite useful for explaining European integration in general, and even progress on JHA.

Before demonstrating the utility of simultaneously employing the concepts of intergovernmentalism and supranationalism, Thomas Risse-Kappen's alternative approach to exploring "the nature of the beast" should be considered.[10] Risse-Kappen has rejected the intergovernmentalism-supranationalism dichotomy, proposing instead a paradigm that views EU policymaking as a network of interlocking politics (i.e., Politikverflech-tung), involving not only state actors, but also several influential trans-national actors (TNAs; e.g., firms and INGOs). Although this depiction indeed captures an aspect of the Union missed by traditional realist or neo-liberal institutionalist approaches, it does not seem appropriate for characterizing the EU as a whole. As Risse-Kappen himself recognizes, the so-called Second Pillar of the EU, concerning Common Foreign and Security Policy (CFSP), is still characterized by intergovernmental bargaining, stem-ming from the role played by centralized political institutions in the member states, a lack of significant social interests, and a relatively low-level of Europeanization of this policy area, although this seems to be changing.[11]

Risse-Kappen's paradigm is also not well suited to examine the nature of policymaking in the EU's Third Pillar on JHA. Although a few member states have decentralized systems of policing (e.g., United Kingdom and Germany), internal security issue-areas such as immigration, asylum, ter-rorism, and organized crime are also handled by centralized domestic polit-ical institutions in the EU. One must also recognize that public (not private) police organizations of any kind are, by their very nature, the apparatus of states. In addition, JHA is characterized by a similarly low degree of Euro-peanization and a lack of involvement of social interests (unless one is pre-pared to treat transnational criminal organizations as "social interests"). Of course, as will be shown in the following chapters, the nature of the EU's Third Pillar has changed significantly since it was first created, especially after 1999.

In sum, Risse-Kappen's paradigm of interlocking politics shaped by TNAs seems most useful when restricted to elucidating the nature of policymaking in the highly economic First Pillar (a.k.a., the Community pillar). However, his paradigm is not well suited to examine the Second or the Third Pillars, and thus, not appropriate for characterizing the Union as a whole. For heuristic purposes, the concepts of intergovernmentalism and supranationalism remain useful points of departure in these regards.

Although it is widely accepted that at least some aspects of the EU can be typified as intergovernmental, there is less agreement that the concept of supranationalism rightly applies to the EC/EU in general. Supranationalism is conventionally defined as "a process of cooperation that results in a shift of authority (and perhaps sovereignty) to a new level of organization that is autonomous, that is above the state, and that has powers of coercion that are independent of the state."[12]

Writing before the entry into force of the Maastricht Treaty, Robert Keohane and Stanley Hoffmann rejected characterizing the EC's nature as supranational, proposing instead the now often-cited metaphor for EU as a "network involving the pooling of sovereignty."[13] This conceptualization implies that the EU "is an experiment in the pooling of sovereignty, not in transferring it from states to supranational institutions."[14]

Perhaps the essence of the EC before 1993 was best captured by focusing on the "pooling of sovereignty" in the Council of Ministers, but, since the implementation of the Maastricht Treaty, it seems that the concept of supranationalism is more appropriate.[15] This has certainly been the case since the Treaty of Amsterdam entered into force on May 1, 1999. Examining whether the EU of today can be properly characterized as being at least somewhat supranational in nature can be accomplished by comparing the nature of the Community to a federation in the capacity of a state.[16]

Because the relationship of the central government of a federation to its constituent "states" (subunits) is generally accepted as being supranational in nature, examining the degree of supranationalism in the United States may serve as a useful point of departure for examining the question of a transfer of sovereignty in the EU. The nature of federalism in the United States has developed such that many federal programs must be administered by the states (e.g., health care), and many state programs are impacted by the role of the central government in terms of guidelines and/or grants (e.g., education, policing, and, recently, welfare). However, in most of the policy areas traditionally controlled by nation-states—foreign relations, defense, customs, immigration, trade, and monetary policy—only the U.S. Congress and president have policymaking authority and/or oversight. These federal governmental institutions have enjoyed similar jurisdiction over many agencies responsible for internal security in the United States, including the FBI, the Drug Enforcement Agency, Secret Service, U.S.

Marshals, Immigration and Naturalization Service (and its Border Patrol), Customs Agency, Coast Guard, and Bureau of Alcohol, Tobacco, and Firearms.

Thus it is not only the predominance of the federal law in general that makes Washington, D.C., supranational vis-à-vis the fifty states, but also the role of the federal government in traditional policy areas of nation-states that makes U.S. federalism supranational. Moreover, since the governments of the states are not represented in the federal government, it is impossible for any one state to dominate policymaking at the federal level to its liking. Finally, concerning any of the policy areas in which it is involved, the federal government in Washington, D.C., has the power to use coercive force to uphold its laws. For all these reasons, the relationship between the government in Washington and the states can thus be characterized as being supranational in nature.

Does this differ from the nature of the relationship between the EU-level policymaking institutions and the governments of the member states to such an extent that the EU should not be regarded as supranational at least to some degree? First, as in the United States, many areas of policy in the EU's member states (e.g., environmental protection, social policy, and transportation) are covered by Community funding or regulations. In addition, just as Washington, D.C., depends on the states (or their subunits) for the administration of many of its programs by states, the EU relies on the governments of the member states to carry out its decisions or directives and enforce its regulations.

However, in the absence of an EU army or a true police force (see below), one might argue that the EU is not supranational vis-à-vis the member states regarding the criterion of coercive power. That is, a member state that does not want to enforce EU law could simply do so, having only to fear a loss of funding. A state could even leave the Union if it chooses to do so in order to avoid following Community law in some regard. In other words, a state could conceivably reclaim its sovereignty from the common EU "pool." Although this seems to make the EU less supranational than federations acting as states, the difference does not seem to be terribly crucial.

For example, had the U.S. federal government lost the Civil War to the South's Confederacy, it would not have been proper to question, retrospectively, the supranational nature of the United States. Likewise, if Quebec were illegally to secede from Canada some day, this would not call into question the supranational nature of the Canadian federation. Viewed from this perspective, a distinction between supranationalism and "pooled sovereignty" does not seem very illuminating, unless the latter is simply synonymous with intergovernmental cooperation and the former implies something much more extensive and permanent.

Thus, the fact that its coercive power is weak vis-à-vis the member states should not disqualify the EU from being considered supranational in nature when compared to federations such as the United States and Canada. As will be discussed below, the fact that no one member state can dominate policymaking in several issue-areas (by at least blocking a decision) means that the EU is at least somewhat supranational in nature. As will be explained below, this assessment is bolstered by the increasing involvement of the EU in many of the traditional areas of nation-state authority, such as monetary policy, foreign and defense policy, and internal security. In sum, although it was perhaps once appropriate to characterize the highly intergovernmental EC as being merely an exercise in the pooling of sovereignty, it seems that this is increasingly less appropriate given the development of many supranational characteristics in the European Union since the 1970s.

The Two Dimensions of the Political Authority Continuum

From the discussion above, we are left with the conclusion that the EU is neither wholly intergovernmental, nor entirely supranational. However, before proceeding to an examination of the latter's development regarding internal security, an important question remains to be considered, namely how to determine whether the central government of a particular IGO such as the EU—or for that matter of a federation or confederation—should be placed on a *continuum of political authority* regarding intergovernmentalism and supranationalism as mentioned above. This kind of classification can be done by considering two dimensions of political authority possessed by central governments. One deals with the scope and type of issues in which the central government is a major policymaker, rather than solely the governments of the constituent parts. The other concerns the ability of any one constituent state in the IGO, federation, or confederation to dominate policymaking at the central governmental level.

Regarding the first set of variables, the higher the number of issues impacted by policymaking at the central governmental level, the more this political entity tends toward supranationalism. More important, however, is the type of issues dealt with by the central government. Monetary policy, foreign and defense policy, border control, and several other internal security matters fall within the traditional policy domain of national governments in countries, rather than regional or local governments. The more a central government of an IGO, federation, or confederation is the primary policymaking institution for these types of issues, the more supranational in nature it is. Conversely, an IGO that leaves dealing with all or most of these issues to the constituent governments should be considered intergovernmental in this regard.

The second set of variables regarding political authority must also be considered, namely the ability of the government of an individual state among the group of states composing the IGO, federation, or confederation to dominate policymaking at the central governmental level. Where any one state has the power to veto legislation at the central governmental level (and regularly exercises this privilege or at least threatens to do so), then the IGO, federation, or confederation should be considered intergovernmental in this regard. In contrast, IGOs, federations, and confederations should be considered supranational concerning this when no single member government can effectively veto legislation at the central governmental level and must consequently submit to the collective will of the other member states or some other policymaking body associated with them (e.g., a type of popularly elected assembly drawn from all of the member states).

Evaluating an IGO according to both sets of variables can be accomplished by establishing a grid in which the x-axis represents the range and type of issues handled by the central government and the y-axis represents the degree to which an individual state can dominate collective decisionmaking at the central governmental level. Central governments that deal with a wide range of policies, including those noted above that are traditionally associated with nation-states, should be plotted to the right of center along the x-axis, while those that deal with a more narrow range of issues, include fewer traditional state issues, should be placed to the left of center. Similarly, central governments that are often dominated by the political desires of any one of its constituent member governments should be positioned near the top of the y-axis (above center), while those central governments that are free of such restrictions should be placed closer to the bottom of the grid. Determining the character of the central government of a particular IGO, federation, or confederation is thus possible by considering its nature on both scales and plotting it at the intersection of the x and y values (see Figure 2.1).

From this, a diagram consisting of four fields can be created. Central governments that deal with a narrow range of issues, including few or no traditional state issues, and that can be dominated by the wishes of any of the constituent governments, would fall in the quadrant at the top left of the diagram. Such central governments are highly intergovernmental in nature. The North Atlantic Treaty Organization (NATO) is a good example of this type of IGO. NATO indeed deals with a traditional state issue, national security, but this is largely its only concern. Thus, it could be placed at the extreme left along the x-axis. Since NATO decisionmaking is done by consensus, any one of its members can essentially block a proposed policy decision (at least in principle). For this reason, NATO could be positioned fairly high along the y-axis. The United Nations, specifically its Security Council, can deal with a somewhat larger range of issues, and therefore could be placed slightly to the right of NATO, yet the veto power of its five permanent members means that it could be in about the same position along

Figure 2.1 Conceptualizing the European Union

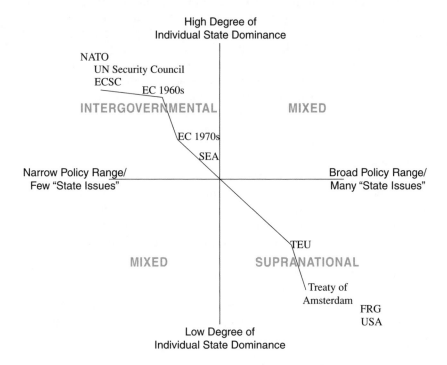

the *y*-axis. Decisions made in these two IGOs may be understood as reflections of the distribution of power and intergovernmental bargaining among its member states. Given the nature of their central governments, NATO and the UN Security Council can thus be characterized as highly intergovernmental IGOs.

Mirror images of this type of intergovernmental organization are provided by the central governments of states or IGOs that reach policy decisions that may not be pleasing to any one of their constituent states *and* deal with a wide range of polices, including those traditionally associated with nation-states. This type of central government, such as that of the United States, could be placed in the lower right, or supranational, quadrant. The central government of the United States deals with a wide range of issues, including national defense, foreign trade and relations, immigration, and monetary policy. Moreover, regarding many other policy areas such as social welfare and transportation, "cooperative federalism" exists, in which the central government supplies funding and regulations, and the state governments provide the execution and administration.

In addition, the central government of the United States operates quite independently from the political wishes of the governments of its constituent states. In fact, these governments are not even represented in Congress. Like the United States, the central government of the Federal Republic of Germany (FRG) also deals with a wide range of policies, including traditional state issues, and its decisionmaking cannot be dominated by any one of the Länder governments. However, the governments of the Länder do have a direct voice in the upper house of the central government (in the Bundesrat). Thus, the FRG could be placed slightly higher along the *y*-axis compared to the United States. However, no single German Länder (state) can veto legislation. In this regard, the EU of today more closely resembles the FRG than it does the United States, as will be explained below.[17]

Although the nature of federalism in Germany and the United States has evolved over the years, the magnitude of these developments pales in comparison to those experienced by the IGO we know today as the European Union. Due to a series of changes taking place concerning the number and type of issues covered by the EU, as well as the inability of any member state to dominate decisionmaking concerning many of these, the EU should no longer be viewed as a highly intergovernmental IGO. Furthermore, the same types of forces that have been significant in this development have also contributed to the development of a degree of supranationalism in the area of police cooperation among EU member states.

Toward a More Supranational EU

The overall historical development of the European Union and its institutional predecessors may be interpreted as consisting of a series of shifts along a continuum of political authority from intergovernmentalism toward supranationalism. This may be understood both in terms of the areas of public policy that have come under the influence of the European Union, as well as the declining ability of individual member states to dominate policymaking at the EU level. Concerning the former, a shift toward supranationalism in the EU can be identified in terms of the number and types of common policies to be made in Brussels, rather than unilaterally in each of the member states. For example, the creation in 1958 of the European Economic Community (EEC) and Euratom by the Treaties of Rome can be thought of as a shift in the direction of supranationalism from the limited jurisdiction of the European Coal and Steel Community (ECSC) created in 1952 by the Treaty of Paris of the previous year. That is, the Treaties of Rome empowered the Community's institutions not only to make common policies regarding the production and sale of coal and steel, but also to create a common market in general, including agricultural policy, a common external tariff, social policy, etc. (notwithstanding the fact that the ECSC's high authority was, in principle, more powerful than the new commission of the EEC).

In this regard, the shift toward supranationalism in terms of policy-making was furthered by the aims of the Single European Act (SEA) to perfect the common market by the end of 1992, including attention to regional economic "cohesion," the environment, and even foreign policy (by giving legal status to European Political Cooperation). Subsequently, the various provisions of the Treaty on European Union (TEU; a.k.a. the Maastricht Treaty) deepened the involvement of Community policymaking in the areas of public health, transportation, consumer protection, social policy (not yet for the UK), and economic and monetary policy after the TEU came into force in November 1993.

Although the shift of policymaking from the capitals of the member states to the EU illustrates a movement toward supranationalism, this change has been made more meaningful by a transfer of decisionmaking authority away from individual interests of the member states within the Council of Ministers. Since the 1980s, the gradual erosion of individual state dominance in the EU, once symbolized by the Luxembourg Compromise, has occurred in two regards. First, beginning with the SEA, the use of qualified majority voting (QMV) in the Council has gradually replaced unanimity in a number of policy areas, making it increasingly difficult for any one or two states to block EU legislation in these areas. Second, the TEU created the "co-decision" procedure, which essentially put the European Parliament on equal footing with the Council in some policy areas by making it impossible for the latter simply to reject the amendments to legislation drafted by the former.[18] Since the entry into force of the Treaty of Amsterdam, most areas of EU policymaking in the First Pillar have come under co-decision procedure, entailing that disputes between the Council and the Parliament must sometimes be resolved in "conciliation committees."[19]

The increasing use of the co-decision procedure is significant due to the nature of the European Parliament. Since the members of the EP are elected directly by the citizens of the Union (not appointed by the member states) and are organized and vote according to transnational party groups (not by their countries of national origin), the increased use of the co-decision procedure must be viewed as a shift toward supranationalism in the EU. That is, the Parliament has effective legislative power and exerts it independently of member-state governments. In the same way, the shifting of authority in many policy areas away from the member states of the EU, along with the loss of individual clout within the Council possessed by their governments due to the use of QMV, means that the European Union is a much less intergovernmental IGO than it was a just over a decade ago. Moreover, neither the actions of the Commission (which proposes EU legislation) nor those of the European Court of Justice (which is empowered to rule on decisions vis-à-vis the treaties and its own growing body of case law) can be viewed as reflections of member states' interests. As always, these institutions continue to provide the EC/EU with a distinct supranational character, but now more than ever.

In sum, the history of the EC/EU can be depicted as a series of shifts to the right along the *x*-axis and down along the *y*-axis of Figure 2.1. Due to its widening policy remit since the ECSC and the declining ability of any one member state to dominate policymaking, the EC/EU can be shown to have shifted from the intergovernmental field in the upper left of Figure 2.1 to the supranational field at the lower right. Not only does this depiction allow one to compare the EC/EU as IGO to federations, confederations, and other IGOs, it also facilitates comparing the EC/EU to itself at different points in time.[20] For example, one can see how the post-Amsterdam EU is much more supranational than the ECSC, but still more intergovernmental than the United States or Germany.

Explaining European Integration

Concerning the question of explaining the development of supranationalism in the EU/EC since the 1950s, the potential independent variables may be categorized into internal factors (stemming from inside the EU and its member states) and external factors (stemming from outside the EU). The former include functional spillover, functionalist ideology, federalist ideology, and concerns for democracy. The latter include global economic competition and external threats to security in Western Europe, such as terrorism, drug trafficking, and illegal immigration.

Internal Factors in History

Among the internal factors that have influenced the development of the EC/EU over the years is the concept of "functionalism." As an explanation for the progress of European integration, functionalism may be viewed to be operating in two ways. In keeping with tenants of neofunctionalism, the first way is that functionalism helps account for the deepening of integration by arguing that "joint action in one area will create new needs, tensions, and problems that will increase the pressure to take joint action in another. For example, the integration of agriculture will only truly work if other sectors (say, transport and agricultural support services) are integrated as well."[21] In this way, functional spillover may actually create the need for further integration.

However, the second way integration may be explained by the concept of functionalism is not by actual spillover, but by the mere perception or belief among policymaking elites that further integration provides solutions to problems that seem to have resulted from previous cooperation. That is, it can be said that the concept of functionalism, combined with the progress of integration itself, has contributed to the development of a "powerful ideological currency."[22] This is a subtle, yet important, distinction. To the extent that policymakers at the subnational, national, and supranational levels come to believe that expanding international collaboration in new areas provides the best solution to new problems, alternative solutions (e.g., traditional domestic strategies) may simply be disregarded, even if no real compelling evidence exists to justify deepening integration.

This is not the only way in which ideology serves as an independent variable for explaining European integration since World War II. The ideology of federalism has also been significant in this regard. The idea of European political unity first began to attract attention among elites in Europe during the interwar years and was nurtured by the Resistance during World War II.[23] Especially since the end of the war, this dream has rested on the belief that "the historic notion of the independent state as the foundation of political organization has been discredited and that it should be abandoned, to be substituted . . . by a comprehensive continental political community."[24]

After 1945, the goal of creating a federal Europe began to attract a wider audience of believers and provided one of the most important motivations for the development of European integration, beginning with the Schuman Declaration of 1950 regarding the ECSC, which stated that "Europe must be organized on a federal basis."[25] Because some policy elites in Europe have come to embrace federalism and reject the nation-state, they have thus been eager to oversee the transfer of public policy-making authority to Community institutions in many areas, including trade, agriculture, and, more recently, monetary policy (at least for most of the member states). In this effort, functionalism, both real and perceived, has provided the means to the end of a federal Europe. That is, functionalist logic provided federalist lobbyists with a compelling explanation of how federalism could be gradually achieved. Moreover, federalists have been successful in gradually shifting political power and authority to the supranational Commission, European Court of Justice, and European Parliament, and away from the intergovernmental Council of Ministers.

Yet another internal factor that has contributed to the development of the EU over the years has been an increasing regard for the democratic nature of the Union. Specifically, as the range and importance of the issues covered by the EU increased in the 1970s, and the role of the Commission in these has become more prominent, many policymakers in the Union came to be concerned with what was perceived to be a growing "democratic deficit" within the Union. In order to ensure that the "citizens" of the Union remained empowered in the expanding policymaking of the Union, the role of the European Parliament was strengthened.

At first, the legitimacy of the Parliament as a representative of the people was simply improved by the establishment of direct popular elections for its members. In doing so, the EP became independent of the governments of the members and more accountable to their own electorate at home and to their party groups in the EP. Later, the strengthening of the European Parliament's role vis-à-vis the Council and Commission via the implementation and expanded use of the cooperation and co-decision procedures represented more tangible means of addressing the perceived democratic deficit.[26] Thus, the concern for democracy ultimately led to a shift toward supranationalism by endowing the EP with more decisionmaking power at the expense of the Council, the legislative protector of intergovernmentalism.

However, the development of supranationalism in the EU, specifically regarding the type of issues with which the EU became involved, has been limited by the principle of "subsidiarity." According to this principle, decisions should be taken as close as possible to the citizens of the member states, and common policies should be developed only when these would be better than policymaking at lower levels in achieving the goals of the Community. In short, subsidiarity means no further integration simply for the sake of making the EU more supranational.

Although mentioned in the SEA's creation of a treaty-based environmental policy (Article 130r[4]), the concept of subsidiary first achieved its present level of prominence at Maastricht, having been espoused most forcefully by the British.[27] Article 3b of the TEU states that policymaking at the EU level should be undertaken only if "the objectives of the proposed action cannot be sufficiently achieved by the member states and can therefore, by reason of scale or effects of the proposed action, be better achieved by the Community."[28]

One view is that this provision means that individual action can be supplanted by collaboration if the latter is comparably more efficient at achieving the same goals.[29] Although this may justify the need for further integration under these circumstances, the inclusion of the principle of subsidiarity in Article 3b of the Maastricht Treaty (as well as the exclusion of direct references to federalism) has enshrined the notion that the EU will only become more supranational if this can better achieve the various goals of the Union. Thus, even as functionalism, federalist ideology, and concerns for a democratic deficit have influenced a shift away from the original intergovernmental nature of the European Community, the principle of subsidiarity serves to limit, or at least brake, the development of supranationalism in the EU.

External Factors in History

Factors stemming from outside the Community also help explain the development of supranationalism in a number of ways. Among these are the onset of the Cold War, and consequently the support of the United States for a unified Europe that would thus be sufficiently strong to resist the Soviet Union. The need to administer Marshall Plan aid to Europe (i.e., the European Recovery Program) led directly to the establishment of the Organization for European Economic Cooperation (OEEC) in 1948, providing an early model of European economic collaboration. Although the OEEC fell far short of the European federalists' political ambitions for a unified Europe, it did help to change the thinking of many skeptical policymakers about the promise of international cooperation and provided many lessons for Jean Monnet and Robert Schuman as they prepared to unveil their plan for the ECSC.[30] The outbreak of hostilities in Korea in June 1950 provided another international factor that shaped the early development of European integration as the United States intervened in negotiations regarding the Treaty of Paris on behalf of West Germany to insure the maintenance of its steel industry and its contribution to the defense of Europe (as U.S. attention was drawn to Asia).[31]

In addition to the impact of the Cold War on the genesis of the Community, another type of international factor played a role in the further evolution of European unity, namely economic competition with the rest of world. For example, the Common Agricultural Policy developed by the Community in the 1960s entailed protectionist measures that were designed not only to regulate the supply and price of food throughout the EEC, but also to benefit the Community's farmers (especially those in France) at the expense of foreign competitors in North America and elsewhere. Another, more compelling, illustration of international factors at work is provided by the motivations behind the drafting and signing of the Single European Act in 1985. According to Moravcsik, the agreement among the twelve Community members on the SEA resulted from a common realization that the purely national strategies of the 1970s and early 1980s had failed and that internal liberalization was necessary in order to compete with the United States and Japan.[32] Similarly, the plans for Economic and Monetary Union that were agreed upon at Maastricht in December 1991 represented an enduring commitment to market liberalization that helped firms in the Community better compete in the world economy.

Furthermore, the political innovations expressed in the TEU were at least partly the result of the end of the Cold War. This was certainly apparent by

December 1990, when the Intergovernmental Conferences leading up to the Maastricht European Council began to meet (one on political reform, and the other on economic and monetary union). On one front, the Cold War's end facilitated the unification of Germany by October 1990, which in turn encouraged both Chancellor Helmut Kohl and French president Francois Mitterrand to accelerate the pace of European political integration to deal with the new "German problem."[33] In another regard, the end of the Cold War unified Europe in general, and it subsequently became apparent to many that the Central and Eastern Europe countries (CEECs) would soon want to apply for Community membership, just as Greece, Spain, and Portugal had done following the consolidation of their new democracies in the 1970s.[34] The impending expansion of the EC's membership consequently added a sense of urgency to the efforts of federalists to complete their task.

In sum, this brief account of the European Community's development has argued that European integration since World War II can be explained by a mix of internal and external variables. The internal factors include actual functional spillover, functionalist and federalist ideology, concerns for a democratic deficit (positively), and subsidiary (negatively). Concerning external variables, European political and economic integration has been impacted by international conditions stemming from the beginning and then the end of the Cold War and aspirations by EU members to compete economically in the world economy. Together, these internal and external factors help explain the increasingly supranational character of the EU. As will be made clear, attention to similar sets of internal and external factors helps to account for a parallel, though not simultaneous, development of EU cooperation in the area of Justice and Home Affairs in the direction of supranationalism.

Notes

1. A. Stone, "What Is a Supranational Constitution," *The Review of Politics,* vol. 56, no. 3, summer 1994, 448–459; see also J. A. Caporaso and J.T.S. Keeler, "The European Union and Regional Integration Theory," in *The State of the European Union: Building a European Polity,* ed. Carolyn Rhodes and Sonia Mazey (Boulder: Lynne Rienner Publishers, 1995), 26–62.

2. See Stone, 459–469.

3. See, e.g., J. McCormick, *The European Union: Politics and Policies* (Boulder, CO: Westview Press, 1996).

4. See, e.g., J. J. Anderson, "The State of the (European) Union," *World Politics,* vol. 47, April 1995, 441–465; see also N. Nugent, ed., *The European Union, Volume I: Perspectives and Theoretical Interpretations* (Brookfield, Vt.: Dartmouth Publishing, 1997), parts I and IV; see also R. E. Breckinridge, "Reassessing Regimes: The International Regime Aspects of the European Union," *Journal of Common Market Studies,* vol. 35, no. 2, June 1997, 173–187.

5. F. Snyder, "Institutional Development in the European Union: Some Implications of the Third Pillar," in *The Third Pillar of the European Union: Cooperation in the Fields of Justice and Home Affairs,* ed. J. Monar and R. Morgan (Brussels: European Interuniversity Press, 1994), 85.

6. See also C. Harding and B. Swart, "Intergovernmental Co-operation in the Field of Criminal Law," in *Criminal Justice in Europe: A Comparative Study,* ed. Fennel et al. (Oxford: Clarendon Press, 1995), 105–106.

7. See, e.g., A. Moravcsik, "Preferences and Power in the European Community: A Liberal Intergovernmentalist Approach," *Journal of Common Market Studies,* vol. 31, 1993, 473–524.

8. Ibid.

9. See, for example, E. B. Haas, *The Uniting of Europe: Political, Social, and Economic Forces 1950–1957,* 2nd ed. (Stanford, CA: Stanford University Press, 1968); L. Lindberg, *The Political Dynamics of European Economic Integration* (Stanford, CA: Stanford University Press, 1963); B. F. Nelsen and A. C.-G. Stubb, *The European Union: Readings on the Theory and Practice of European Integration* (Boulder, CO: Lynne Rienner Publishers, 1994), part II; B. Rosamond, *Theories of European Integration* (New York: St. Martin's Press, 2000), chap. 3.

10. T. Risse-Kappen, "Exploring the Nature of the Beast: International Relations Theory and Comparative Policy Analysis Meet the European Union," *Journal of Common Market Studies,* vol. 34, no. 1, March 1996, 53–80.

11. Ibid., 67–68.

12. McCormick, 11.

13. R. Keohane and S. Hoffmann, "Institutional Change in Europe in the 1980s," in Keohane and Hoffmann, *The New European Community* (Boulder, CO: Westview Press, 1991), 10, fn. 46; see also J. J. Anderson, 460.

14. Keohane and Hoffmann, 277; see also J. J. Anderson; see also McCormick, 14.

15. See A. M. Sbragia, "Introduction," in *Europolitics: Institution and Policymaking in the "New" European Community,* ed. A. M. Sbragia (Washington, DC: Brookings Institution, 1992), 31.

16. See A. M. Sbragia, "Thinking About the European Future: The Uses of Comparison," in *Euro-Politics: Institution and Policymaking in the "New" European Community,* ed. A. M. Sbragia (Washington, DC: Brookings Institution, 1992), 257–292; see also A. M. Sbragia, "The European Community: A Balancing Act," *Publius,* vol. 23, summer 1993, 23–38.

17. See Sbragia, "Introduction," 13. Space limitations preclude detailed explanations of further illustrations for each quadrant, but a few are worth mentioning. In the supranational quadrant, the Organization of Petroleum Exporting Countries (OPEC) could be placed just to the right of NATO. OPEC operates by consensus and deals largely with oil production. The United States under its original Articles of the Confederation could be placed in the supranational quadrant, below and to the left of the EU under the Treaty of Amsterdam. The Internal Labor Organization could be placed in the "mixed" quadrant at the bottom left, as it operates by majority voting and deals only with labor issues. Given its similar decisionmaking procedure but broader policy mandate, the Organization of American States could also be placed in this quadrant. Finally, two German "states" of the past could be placed in the upper-right mixed quadrant. Owing to the de facto dominance of Prussia in its decisionmaking, the German Confederation of 1815–1866 after the establishment of the costumes unions (Zollverein) of 1834 (which excluded Austria) could be placed just to the right of the *y*-axis and above the *x*-axis. The subsequent German Reich

created in 1871 was a federation with a policy remit that included key state issues (e.g., foreign and defense policy), but was dominated constitutionally and in practice by Prussia. It could be placed above and to the right of its predecessor, the confederation.

18. The Council enjoys this power over the EP in both the original "consultation procedure" of the Treaties of Rome and the "cooperation procedure," created by the SEA (though the Council can only do so in the latter regard by a unanimous vote.) The cooperation procedure has been largely eliminated by the Treaty of Amsterdam.

19. See M. Nentwich and G. Falkner, "The Treaty of Amsterdam: Towards a New Institutional Balance," *European Integration online Papers (EIoP)*, vol. 1, 1997, passim.

20. Sbragia, "Thinking"; J. J Anderson, 452–453; and D. N. Chryssochoou, "New Challenges to the Study of European Integration: Implications for Theory-Building," *Journal of Common Market Studies*, vol. 35, no. 4, December 1997, 521–542.

21. McCormick, 16.

22. N. Walker, "Policing the European Union: The Politics of Transition," in *Policing Change, Changing Police: International Perspectives*, ed. O. Marenin (New York: Garland Publishing, 1996), 262.

23. D. W. Urwin, *The Community of Europe: A History of European Integration Since 1945*, 2nd ed. (New York: Longman, 1995), chap. 1.

24. Ibid., 7.

25. Ibid., 46.

26. The increased "transparency" of policymaking, particularly regarding the Council, represents another way the democratic deficit has been addressed.

27. McCormick, 261–262.

28. D. G. Partan, "The Justiciability of Subsidiarity," in *The State of the European Union: Building a European Polity*, ed. C. Rhodes and S. Mazey (Boulder, CO: Lynne Rienner Publishers, 1995), 65–66; see also McCormick, 203.

29. Partan, 65.

30. Urwin, 21 and 43.

31. Ibid., 47–48.

32. A. Moravcsik, "Negotiating the Single European Act," in *The New European Community*, ed. Keohane and Hoffmann (Boulder, CO: Westview, 1991), 72–73. See also Urwin, 231.

33. S. George, *Politics and Policy in the European Union* (New York: Oxford University Press, 1996), 16.

34. Many EU documents refer to the "countries of Central and Eastern Europe," or CCEEs, not CEECs.

3

From the Trevi Group to the Third Pillar

THE NOTION OF A MULTINATIONAL APPROACH TO POLICING IN EUROPE has been around for a century. The idea of cooperation among the sovereign states of Europe in this area can be traced at least as far back as the turn of the last century when the assassination of Empress Elizabeth of Austria in Geneva in 1898 led to a secret international conference of police leaders in Rome on the matter of anarchism in Europe.[1] Initiated by the French in 1914, plans were later developed for an institutionalized form of collaboration, but these efforts were interrupted by World War I.[2] After the war, Austrian ambitions led to the creation in Vienna of the International Criminal Police Commission (ICPC) in 1923, composed of thirty-four nations. Thus, the first permanent international body aimed at coordinating internal security was created.[3] Similar to the influence of the Cold War on the founding of the European Community (EC) in the 1950s, Interpol, as it would become known, was developed in response to "the political instability in Western and central Europe as a result of the First World War and Russian Revolution."[4]

Interrupted by World War II and the Soviet occupation of Austria, nineteen former ICPC states re-formed the agency near Paris in 1946. Ten years later, this organization took the name International Criminal Police Organization (ICPO) or "Interpol," and its membership has grown steadily (especially after the end of the Cold War), currently including 181 states (46 of them European).[5] In 1966, Interpol was moved to a site in Saint Cloud, just outside Paris, where it remained until 1989 when it was relocated to new and larger facilities in Lyons, France. Although its main function has been to promote the global exchange of information and assistance among its members, in practice, 80 percent of all messages that pass through Interpol's system of National Central Bureaus in each member country and its general secretariat in Lyons originate in Europe.[6] Thus for many years Interpol has served as a means of information pooling for European criminal investigations.

29

As an international organization, not only has Interpol not been supranational in character, but it has hardly even been intergovernmental in nature in the normal sense of the concept. Although its governing institutions (General Assembly and its Executive Committee) are composed of national delegates, and nations must apply for membership and pay annual dues, Interpol has never been based on an international treaty or convention.[7] Cyrille Fijnaut has argued that Interpol essentially remains "a more or less private international association of chiefs of police that was set up in 1923."[8] Indeed, the statutes of Interpol are unclear on whether the states or police chiefs are the legal members.[9] Moreover, unlike the Strasbourg-based Council of Europe or the EU, Interpol entails no structure of national representation emanating from the highest governmental levels of its 181 member states (e.g., governmental ministers, officials, or ambassadors). Thus, Interpol seems to be a special kind of transnational actor, rather than a conventional IGO. In this regard, Europol has evolved much differently, although it also began as a European endeavor in the pooling of information.[10]

The Roots of Police Cooperation in the EU

The development of police cooperation on the intergovernmental level in Europe would not really begin until long after Interpol, and even the EC itself, was founded. Until the 1970s, little movement was made toward endowing an IGO in Europe with much competence in the area of policing. Indeed, where the highly intergovernmental Council of Europe has been concerned with criminal justice, it has served largely as a body for drafting conventions regarding human rights and judicial cooperation.[11]

This status of police cooperation in Europe finally began to change in 1969 when George Pompidou succeeded Charles De Gaulle as president of France. Pompidou led the formation of a permanent "Group to Combat Drug Abuse and Illicit Traffic in Drugs" within the Council of Europe, a move De Gaulle never undertook because of his desire to protect French sovereignty in this area and in general.[12] The so-called Pompidou Group was composed of ministers and civil servants and largely concerned itself with studying drug education programs and ways to collect data on drug trafficking and money laundering. Although willing to cooperate with his European neighbors in this manner, Pompidou was careful to maintain his base of support among his fellow Gaulists. He was therefore reluctant to allow European cooperation on internal security to progress beyond this limited form.

Pompidou's death and succession by a non-Gaulist, Valery Giscard d'Estaing, in 1974 led to a general acceleration of European integration, as symbolized by the Paris summit of December 1974 and its decisions to allow direct elections for the European Parliament and to hold regular meetings of the new European Council of heads of state and government.[13] The arrival of Giscard and his willingness to allow the strengthening of the EC facilitated further cooperation in the area of internal security, leading to an agreement forged at the European Council in Rome in 1975 to create a body for cooperation in policing and criminal justice.[14] This initial agreement led to the creation of the so-called Trevi Group, which is the institutional forerunner of the EU's present Third Pillar, home to Europol. The true origin of the name "Trevi Group" has been the subject of some academic debate.[15] Its original derivation seems to be the famous fountain in Rome where the original agreement was struck, as well as a pun on the last name of its first chairman in 1976, A. R. Fonteijn.[16] Later, Trevi came to stand for the first letters of the French words *terrorism, radicalisme, extrémisme et violence internationale.*[17]

The Trevi Group and the Schengen Agreement

Resulting from the desires of Germany and the United Kingdom to deal more effectively with the growing problem of terrorism, the Rome agreement led to the creation of a multilevel intergovernmental forum under the auspices of European Political Cooperation. This body consisted of elected officials (justice and interior ministers), policy experts (i.e., civilian bureaucrats), and practitioners (police officers).[18] Similar to the impetus for Interpol's founding, the establishment of the Trevi Group, which met for the first time after its founding in June 1976 in Luxembourg, came in response to terrorist activities of both European and non-European origin. In general, European police and political leaders had grown impatient with the inability of Interpol and the United Nations to deal with terrorism, which had been on the increase since the late 1960s in the form of numerous skyjackings and hostage-takings, especially the killings at the 1972 Munich Olympic Games.[19]

Thus, parallel to the general development of European integration, the evolution of criminal justice cooperation in the form of the Trevi Group resulted from the coming together of a problem—terrorism—that stemmed at least partly from outside the Community, as well as the increasing perception within the EC that unilateral action would not suffice to deal with it effectively. Nevertheless, the Trevi Group existed outside of the formal institutional structure of the EC, though it included all of the Community's members and mirrored its Council of Ministers and presidency. Trevi was a highly intergovernmental organization, with the EC's court and Parliament playing no role.

The Trevi Group operated on three levels. At the top, the ministers of justice and/or the interior of the EC countries met every six months (i.e., usually at the same site and about the same time as the European Council), chaired by the member holding the EC presidency. The meetings of this ministerial group were prepared by an assortment of senior officials from the ministries involved.

These bureaucrats and top-ranking police chiefs also prepared reports and coordinated the operations of Trevi's third level, its "working groups," which met in the form of seminars and workshops attended by police specialists, detectives, and magistrates. Working Group I, created on May 31, 1977, was the most operational, entailing secure communication links among national authorities for communicating intelligence regarding terrorism.[20] Working Group II was also established in 1977 and dealt with exchanging information on police training, equipment, forensic science, public order, and other general policing topics. In addition, the Trevi Group entailed a number of ad hoc working groups during its existence, including those related to extradition and immigration. A working group on Europol was created within the Trevi structure in 1991.

During its existence, the Trevi Group had no secretariat or headquarters, relying instead upon a troika consisting of the past, present, and next chair of the ministerial group. In 1989, the troika was replaced by a leadership mechanism consisting of the current chair, the two preceding ones, and the next two, which was dubbed a "piatnika." According to Guyomarch, "the effectiveness of the organization was impaired and coordination was difficult in the implementation, monitoring, evaluation, and amendment of decisions."[21] Despite the lack of a permanent central office, the establishment of the Trevi Group was a significant advancement over Interpol in its bringing European cooperation in the area of internal security to the highest level of interstate cooperation.[22]

Although decisionmaking authority in the Trevi Group remained intergovernmental in nature throughout its existence, the scope of its information sharing and policy coordination was eventually expanded. For example, soccer hooliganism was added to the remit of Working Group II in June 1985, following a deadly incident at Heysel Stadium in Brussels when thirty-nine people were killed after British fans initiated violence. In addition, Trevi's Working Group III was added at the same time to handle serious forms of organized international crime, including drug trafficking, the related problem of money laundering, and later, bank robbery and car theft. The aim of this group was to facilitate the exchange of information and expertise, as well as the joint development of research techniques. This working group soon developed guidelines for establishing a system of drug liaison offices posted in each member state, as well as in producer and transit countries.[23] Meeting in Copenhagen in December 1987, the Trevi ministers approved these guidelines, and work on making the plans a reality continued into the early 1990s.[24] These proved to be the initial steps in the creation of Europol.

Explaining Police Cooperation Before the Maastricht Treaty

How can the development of police cooperation in Europe in the form of the Trevi Group be explained? In one regard, external factors in the form of terrorism and drug trafficking must be considered, since both have important sources located outside of Europe (though their sources are clearly not exclusively external).[25] The expansion of the Trevi Group's involvement in coordinating criminal-justice activity in Europe was also impacted by the internal factors of federalism and functionalist ideology. For example, the addition of the third Trevi working group was made following the optimistic Fontainebleau European Council of June 1984 and the publication of the Dooge Report (at the March 1985 European Council in Brussels), which outlined a plan for transforming the EC into a "true political entity."[26] In addition to unveiling the Dooge Report, the Brussels summit was also the occasion of an agreement on the 1992 deadline for perfecting the common market. Thus, even before the Single European Act (SEA) was signed, the spirit of federalism was in the air in Europe, and it was within this political context that the mandate of the Trevi Group was expanded.

Subsequent internal events had a similar impact on the deepening of European integration in the area of criminal justice. By 1984, France and Germany had concluded the Saarbrücken agreement, which called for the eventual elimination of controls on their common border. In June 1985, representatives from France, Germany, and the Benelux countries (which had abolished their mutual border controls in the 1950s) came together at Schengen, Luxembourg, to sign an agreement on the goal of abolishing border checks among them.

The Schengen Agreement recognized that eliminating internal borders necessitated the strengthening and coordination of their borders with non-Schengen states. For this reason, the original agreement in 1985 also called for the creation of a common, central, computer network known as the Schengen Information System (SIS). Thus, by the time the SEA took effect in 1987, its goal of an open market for goods, capital, and labor was already strengthened by parallel developments among the Schengen states, which began drafting a detailed implementation convention and pursued plans to expand its membership.

The goals of the SEA and the original Schengen Group had clear implications for European cooperation in the area of policing.[27] Open borders for tourists, firms, and workers meant open borders for criminals as well. Consequently, a fourth Trevi working group, which became known as "Trevi '92," was created at Athens in December 1988 to study the implications of a Community without borders on policing. Following the reaffirmation of the freedom of movement as a core aspect of the EC at the Paris European Council of December 1989, the Trevi ministers met in Dublin the following June and adopted a program of action that had been prepared by the Trevi '92 working group.[28]

Although the program did not call for creating a much needed permanent secretariat for the Trevi Group, it did launch several important initiatives, including meetings of border patrol officials, plans for allowing police "hot pursuit" across borders, and studies for creating a joint information system.[29] The Trevi ministers' Dublin meeting also approved a plan that had been drafted by Working Group III for the creation of a network of national drugs intelligence units in each member state for the pooling of information.[30] After being approved by the European Council held in Dublin in July 1990, these units were staffed by drug liaison officers and coordinated by a European Drugs Intelligence Unit (EDIU).[31] As will be shown below, the EDIU would serve as an embryonic Europol.

Interestingly, the notion of something like the EDIU was reflected in the Schengen Implementation Convention that had also been agreed upon in June 1990 and covered the complexities of eliminating the internal borders and implementing the common external borders. This convention was much more detailed than the original 1985 agreement, including, for example, specific provisions for creating the SIS (which came to be based in Strasbourg), as well as for police cooperation concerning drug trafficking, illegal firearms, and hot pursuit.[32]

The Maastrict Treaty and the Third Pillar

The parallel and sometimes overlapping developments concerning the Trevi and Schengen Groups reflected a growing consensus on the intergovernmental level that new challenges to internal security in Europe required heightened cooperation. With the Intergovernmental Conference (IGC) on political union already under way in 1991, it was once again the Federal Republic of Germany that pushed for greater cooperation on internal security. As early as 1974, Germany's main trade union for police detectives (Bund der Deutscher Kriminalbeamter) had discussed reforming Interpol and even supplementing it with a European police office, but the idea never received much support outside of Germany.[33] Fifteen years later, Chancellor Kohl found himself leader of a frontline state vis-à-vis the struggling postcommunist societies of the CEECs. He surprised the other eleven EC members at the Luxembourg European Council of June 28–29, 1991, by presenting his plan for the creation of Europol, a pan-European police office.[34] The proposal, which Kohl had first discussed publicly a month earlier in Edinburgh, suggested a two-phase development of Europol, with the first entailing information exchange and the second regarding independent investigative powers (i.e., an organization with true executive policing authority).[35]

The very idea of a common European office for criminal investigation was hardly novel, for, as noted above, similar schemes, though less far-reaching, had already been raised within Trevi's Working Group III in the context of developing the proposed EDIU. However, the timing of Kohl's bold suggestion of executive policing powers for an EU agency was unsettling to some leaders, particularly the British and French. Hoping to win a more positive response from the UK in the future, Kohl ultimately gave in to requests by the new British prime minister, John Major, not to rush the European Council into deciding upon several thorny issues such as this.[36] As the attention of the summit shifted to the erupting conflict in the Balkans, proposals to pursue phase two of the German proposal on Europol (i.e., giving it operative powers) were simply shelved, and an agreement was reached to go forward with just the first phase.[37]

Consequently, plans to create Europol for information pooling and analysis, but without executive policing powers, were incorporated into the deliberation of the 1991 IGC on political reform.[38] In August 1991, the Trevi Group established an Ad Hoc Working Group on Europol (AHWGE). Composed of about fifty members and permanently chaired by a senior British police official, the AHWGE began to plan the development of Europol, including preliminary work on a convention that would decide the specific modus operandi of the new police agency under the expected terms of the new treaty. Thus, the efforts of the Trevi Group and Kohl's bold initiative had come together by the time the two IGCs produced their draft treaty for the European Council at Maastricht in December 1991.[39]

As is well known, the treaty unveiled at Maastricht was officially signed in 1992 and, after a difficult ratification process, took effect by November 1993, creating the European Union that we know today. Since the entry into force of the Treaty on European Union, the EU has consisted of three so-called pillars, the first of which includes the issue- and policy-making institutions of the former European Community created by the Treaties of Rome, which were amended by the SEA and Maastricht Treaty. Given its direct connection to the European Community, the First Pillar is sometimes referred to as the "Community Pillar."

The Second Pillar of the new European Union defines the EU's "Common Foreign and Security Policy." In contrast to the First Pillar, the Second Pillar is intergovernmental in nature, meaning that, in general, the Community's supranational commission, parliament, and court have little authority compared to that of the Council of Ministers.[40] Not only is much of the authority invested in the Council in the Second Pillar, but most decisions require a unanimous vote of the member states, giving each an effective veto that helps to protect their sovereignty in this politically sensitive area.

This is also the case for the EU's Third Pillar, which was first established by Title VI of the TEU, specifying "Provisions on Cooperation in the Fields of Justice and Home Affairs." Its policy domains and structure essentially subsumed and replaced the Trevi Group and its working groups. This original Third Pillar was established in the nine paragraphs of Article K (i.e., K.1–K.9) that make up Title VI of the original TEU agreed upon at Maastricht. Article K.1 identified nine policy domains covered by this pillar, including (1) asylum, (2) external borders, (3) immigration, (4) illegal drugs, (5) international fraud, (6) judicial cooperation on civil matters, (7) judicial cooperation on criminal matters, (8) customs cooperation, and

> (9) police cooperation for the purpose of preventing and combating terrorism, unlawful drug trafficking, and other serious forms of international crime, including if necessary certain aspects of customs cooperation, in connection with the organization of a Union-wide system for exchanging information within a European Police Office (Europol).[41]

Although Article K.4 (2) stated that the Commission "shall be fully associated" with all nine policy domains, it was only empowered to initiate proposals regarding the first six of these (Article K.2). In other words, the Commission was originally not empowered to initiate legislation on judicial cooperation in criminal matters, customs cooperation, and police cooperation. It was therefore entirely up to member states to do so. Nevertheless, the Commission acted quickly to assert its new potential influence, establishing a small Task Force for Justice and Home Affairs (TFJHA) within its secretariat when the Maastricht Treaty was signed on February 7, 1992. However, a directorate-general had yet to be established for JHA at this stage, so the task force's chief reported directly to the commissioner in charge of JHA, Ireland's Pádraig Flynn, who also had responsibility for social affairs and employment, immigration, and JHA between 1993 and 1994.[42] Along with the limitation imposed by the Maastricht Treaty, the fact that the TFJHA was understaffed and overworked limited its influence.[43] It would not be until after the historic Tampere European Council of October 1999 that the Commission would become a highly active and effective actor in the making of EU policy on JHA (see Chapter 5).

In contrast, the Council of Ministers has always played a major role on JHA, as each member state has enjoyed the unilateral power to initiate legislation regarding any of the nine JHA policy domains (Article K.3). As in the Second Pillar, this has reflected the intergovernmental nature of the Third Pillar, which has also been evident in the limited role of the European

Parliament. Under Article K.6 of the original TEU, the EP merely enjoyed the right to be kept informed by the Council and to pose questions to it. As remains the case today, it could not veto the JHA ministers' decisions.

Under Article K.3, decisions taken by the Council on the nine policy areas took the form of "joint positions" and "joint actions." The former refers to unanimous recommendations taken by the Council to which the member states are required to give "full effect" both domestically and in foreign policy.[44] The latter refers to instruments spelling out coordinated activity, where such activity may better achieve the goals of the Union than through the member states acting individually. Neither joint positions nor joint actions required the drafting and ratifying of a new international convention among the member states. However, as today, when the nature of a proposed collaboration was viewed by governmental officials as being politically sensitive in their countries, Article K.3 also provided that the JHA could draft such a convention and submit it to the member states for their signing and ratification. Although Article K.3 specified these three forms of decisions, it was not clear on when one was more appropriate than another, or on which were more legally binding than others.[45] However, given the direct role of the national parliaments in the ratification processes, conventions are often viewed as having more legitimacy, and this was the case regarding policy cooperation under the Maastricht Treaty.

A very significant provision of Title VI was Article K.9, which provided for a potential communitization "bridge" (*passerelle*) for Third Pillar policies to be brought into the First Pillar.[46] This empowered the Council, on the initiative of the Commission or a member state, to shift competence concerning many of the policy domains found in Article K.1, paragraphs 1–6 (i.e., not judicial cooperation in criminal matters, customs cooperation, or police cooperation) from the Third Pillar to the first by unanimous vote. This bridge, though never utilized, permitted the Council to specify the decisionmaking and voting procedure to be applied to any issue that has been transferred to the First Pillar. This created the possibility that the Council could decide at any time to transform the nature of cooperation on JHA from intergovernmental to supranational (e.g., by granting powers of co-decision to the Parliament) without the drafting of a new treaty (although such a decision would still have had be ratified by each member state). Although never implemented during the era of the Maastricht Treaty, the communitization bridge presaged the future movement of some parts of the Third Pillar into the first when the TEU was amended by the Treaty of Amsterdam in 1999.

Mirroring and replacing the structures of Trevi, Article K.4 of Title VI established a coordinating committee to prepare the work of the Justice and Home Affairs (JHA) Council. Thus, this body became known as the "K.4 Committee" and was composed of senior officials from the justice and interior ministries of member states, as well as an observer from the Commission. With its secretariat based in Brussels, the K.4 Committee began to meet monthly in 1993, even before the Maastricht Treaty came into effect in November of that year.[47] The policy proposals of the K.4 Committee were passed along to the JHA Council via the Committee of Permanent Representatives (COREPER), just as the Trevi Group's senior officials once submitted its resolutions to the troika/piatnika before matters were brought to all of the ministers in the group. By contrast, in the EU's First Pillar, COREPER itself prepares Commission proposals for debate and/or vote in the Council of Ministers.

Similar to the former role and composition of the Trevi Group's defunct working groups, the activities of the K.4 Committee were guided by three steering groups, each entailing a number of smaller, policy-specific working groups (a.k.a. "working parties"). The steering groups and their working groups were chaired by officials from the EU member state that held the six-month EU presidency at that time. The following working groups were established:

- Steering Group I on Immigration and Asylum
- Working groups on migration, asylum, visas, external frontiers, and forged documents.
- Steering Group II on Policing and Security
- Working groups on terrorism, police cooperation, drugs and organized crime, customs cooperation, training, scientific matters, crime analysis, combating environmental crime, public disorder, and Europol (taking over for Trevi Group's Ad Hoc Working Group on Europol).
- Steering Group III on Judicial Cooperation
- Working Groups on extradition, international organized crime, criminal and European Community law, mutual recognition, the Brussels Convention (1968; on mutual recognition of judgments), and the transfer of documents.[48]

By creating the K.4 Committee and specifying new, albeit small, roles for the Commission and EP, the Maastricht Treaty changed the nature of police cooperation among the EU's member states. Of course the TEU also called for the creation of Europol in its Article K.1 (9). In fact, Europol was not only referenced there, but also in the Declaration on Police Cooperation that was appended to the final act of the TEU, which explicated its functions in some detail. This declaration recalled the original German proposal from the 1991 Luxembourg summit and specified three main tasks for Europol.[49]

First, it should support national criminal investigations through coordination of investigations and search operations. Europol's second duty is to create a computer database that it can use to provide analyses in the development of investigative strategies. Third, Europol was be charged with analyzing the member states' drug prevention programs, training methods, forensics techniques, and record keeping.

Europol would eventually become a reality through a series of steps following the signing of the TEU. However, this process would prove to be much more difficult and time-consuming than initially imagined. In fact, by the time Europol became fully operational on July 1, 1999, the Maastricht Treaty (TEU) that had spawned it had already been amended by the Treaty of Amsterdam, which entered into force in May 1999.

Meeting in conjunction with the Lisbon European Council of June 1992, the Trevi ministers determined that because establishing a full-fledged European police office entailed the sensitive issues of personal data protection and the role of the Court of Justice, the drafting and ratification of an entire convention would be necessary. Consequently, work began on this as well.[50] Also at Lisbon, the Trevi ministers created a Europol Project Group (PGE) under the jurisdiction of the AHWGE. In July 1992, a staff of fifteen was appointed to the PGE, as well its director, Jürgen Storbeck, an expert in the area of drug criminality. Storbeck, a civil lawyer, was an eighteen-year veteran of Germany's Federal Detective's Office (Bundes-kriminalamt or BKA) in Wiesbaden. His previous career also included work on cases involving the famous Baader-Meinhof gang (domestic terrorism) and Josef Mengele (war crimes). The PGE began to meet in September under the British presidency at a temporary location in Strasbourg that was described as a "shabby hut" or a "porta-cabin."[51] Storbeck's team began work on setting up the proposed EDIU, which was eventually renamed the Europol Drugs Unit (EDU) by the end of the year. The EDU was intended to serve in a limited capacity until the Europol Convention had been drafted, signed, ratified, and entered into force, which would ultimately not happen until October 1, 1998.

Typical of EU politics, the Trevi Group soon began to wrangle over the EDU's initial functions, staffing, accountability, finance, and location.[52] Finally, one year behind schedule, agreements concerning all of these issues, aside from the site of the EDU/Europol, were finally reached by the Trevi ministerial group at Copenhagen in June 1993, resulting in an agreement on the legal establishment of the EDU. In October 1993, the Trevi Group, in one of its last acts before being replaced by the JHA Council under the new Third Pillar, decided to base the EDU (and now Europol) in The Hague, beating out other proposed sites, including Strasbourg, Rome, Wiesbaden, and Lyons.[53] The decision came as part of a much broader compromise concerning the sites of nine new EU agencies to be hosted in eight different member states.

Staffed by about one hundred personnel and headquartered in a building that had first served as the home of a former Jesuit boarding school, and later a convent, Hitler's Gestapo, and, most recently, the Dutch national criminal police (which had recently relocated), the EDU was charged with facilitating the exchange of information among law enforcement officers in the EU's member states. By virtue of the original Trevi ministerial agreement in Copenhagen, the EDU's responsibilities were initially limited to collecting and analyzing information on drug trafficking, related money laundering, and the criminal organizations involved in these. After some delay, the TEU came into force in November 1993, making the Third Pillar a legal reality. Thus, when the EDU officially began operations in The Hague on February 16, 1994, it did so under the oversight of the JHA Council via the new K.4 Committee.

In sum, Title VI of the Maastricht Treaty represented a significant development in European cooperation concerning internal security. By establishing Justice and Home Affairs as one of the pillars of the new European Union, the TEU elevated internal security to an unprecedented level of prominence among the twelve member states (EU membership would grow to fifteen member states in January 1995). Since the entry into force of the Maastricht Treaty, internal security has been an ongoing, not ad hoc, subject of European collaboration. In addition, the secretariat of the K.4 Committee, along with the EDU/Europol, finally gave European cooperation on policing a sense of permanence that it had lacked.

The formal inclusion of the Commission and the Parliament in the area of JHA represented a significant shift away from the pure intergovernmental nature of cooperation in this policy area before the Maastricht Treaty.[54] Nevertheless, as indicated above, the right of the former to initiate policy under the TEU was limited, and the latter enjoyed only the right to be informed of the Council's activities. Still dominated by the Council, and thus still very intergovernmental in nature, cooperation in this area had nonetheless shifted in the direction of supranationalism. Moreover, the inclusion of the communitization bridge in the treaty indicated that the member states were prepared to entertain the possibility of making at least some aspects of their collaboration on matters of internal security even more supranational in the future.

Explaining Cooperation on
Justice and Home Affairs Under the TEU

The development of cooperation in Europe from the Trevi Group to the Third Pillar of the EU may be explained by the same type of factors discussed above that have contributed to the general development of the European Union in the direction of supranationalism. First, the inclusion of the JHA pillar resulted at least in part from functionalism. As the goals of the SEA regarding the free movement of goods, services, and persons became a reality, the governments of the member states came to realize the "logical linkages between economic integration and cooperation and the maintenance of law and order."[55] The European Council had recognized this at its December 1988 meeting in Rhodes, noting in its concluding declaration that the Community's goals were dependent on cooperation in the area of internal security.[56]

One area of growing concern was immigration. Whereas the SEA *facilitated* the free movement of persons, it was the economic recession in Western Europe that *precipitated* the actual migration of people seeking work throughout the EU. Not only were there fears of illegal migration and downward pressure on wages during these tough economic times, but also concern that even legal immigrants who came to new member states looking for work might turn to crime if no jobs were found.[57] In general, the perception was that the increased movement of persons across national boundaries would lead to an increase in transnational criminal activity as well, including drug trafficking, electronic fraud, terrorism, and theft of art and automobiles.[58] Based upon these perceptions, as well as others, the leaders of the member states began to doubt their ability to deal with internal security individually, and became increasingly willing to intensify their collaboration in this policy area.[59]

However, as several authors have pointed out, these perceptions were based more on myth than reality.[60] That is, despite the fact that crime levels in Europe were (and are) much higher than in the immediate postwar years, there is little evidence to support the assumption that the gradual opening of borders in Europe since the late 1980s indeed led to a more rapid increase in crime. In fact, crime rates across Europe had actually leveled off or even decreased in the late 1980s.[61] Although crime was back on the rise by the early 1990s (at the time the 1991 IGC was underway), the increase was largely due to some crimes that do not seem related to the opening of the borders stemming from the SEA, including sexual offense, burglary, and robbery.[62]

Thus, at least concerning crime, actual functional spillover does not adequately explain why cooperation in the area of Justice and Home Affairs grew more supranational when the TEU came into force. However, functionalist ideology seems to have been quite significant in this regard. John Beynon has identified what he refers to as the "functionalist demands" of police practitioners involved in Trevi's working groups, which "arise as the result of perceived law-enforcement requirements."[63] He argues that these have included "claims that organized crime is increasingly transnational and action against it requires a concerted trans-European policing effort."[64]

For Neil Walker, functionalist ideology exemplifies how "public political discourse" has contributed to the development of policing in Europe.[65] He has argued that "the language of political spillover . . . is much more than a theoretical hypothesis purporting to explain change. It is also a powerful ideological currency that taps deep reserves of pro-European thinking, and that, when involved, as in the Euro-policing debate, may actually help to bring about change."[66]

In sum, at least with regard to crime, actual functional spillover does not provide a compelling explanation for why political leaders intensified cooperation in the form of Title VI of the Maastricht Treaty. The crime data at the time would not have justified this. Nevertheless, perceived functional spillover seems to have been an important contributing factor to the development of the Third Pillar.

The idea that further integration was proper and necessary is not the only way ideology played a role in the development of Pillar III, for federalism was also significant in this regard. Alain Guyomarch correctly points out that "justice and policing are particularly sensitive issues as they are traditional 'regalian' functions of the State, and highly symbolic in debates over sovereignty."[67] Eroding the exclusive political authority of the member states in the area of internal security would not only serve to further diminish their sovereignty, but would also be a symbolic victory for federalists who seek to eliminate the European nation-state altogether. It is for this reason that cooperation in the Third Pillar (and Second Pillar for that matter) has been so important to those who hope to strengthen the supranational nature of the European Union.

Walker contends that public political discourse concerning "European integration itself" contributed to the development of cooperation on Justice and Home Affairs.[68] In Benyon's view, the German initiative at the Luxembourg European Council of June 1991 to create Europol must be seen in this light, namely that it has been part of a broader "unionist impetus" to construct further supranational structures to promote European cooperation.[69] At Edinburgh, Kohl asserted that, as a component of political union, cooperation on internal security and judicial affairs was "vital and overdue."[70] Benyon argues that Kohl's proposal for Europol was "a means of promoting further European political integration through another supranational institution. Policing has an important role to play in constructing and consolidating institutions of the European 'state.'"[71] Walker views Kohl's call for a Europol with executive policing powers (in phase two) similarly: "It was intended, and succeeded, as a potent symbol of European Union precisely because it was so audacious, promising to transfer authority in an area that was one of the most jealously guarded preserves of the state."[72]

However, at the same time that Kohl and others (e.g., the Dutch, though more moderately) were pushing for further cooperation on internal security as part of their federalist ideology, the representatives of most member states were reluctant to move toward supranationalism in this area.[73] As is well documented, the British were particularly skeptical of the ambitions of the Dutch presidency in late 1991 and only agreed to include Justice and Home Affairs and Common Foreign and Security Policy in the new treaty in exchange for dropping references to the "F-word" (federalism) in the draft treaty.[74]

Although John Major and the British Euro-skeptics were the most vocal critics of various aspects of the Maastricht Treaty, they were hardly the only opponents of federalist aspirations to transfer sovereignty in internal-security matters over to supranational authorities.[75] This opposition was made more pronounced by the fact that national officials in the member states charged with making policy in this area (the ministers of justice and/or the interior) were much less familiar with calls for deepening integration than their foreign ministry colleagues.[76] Ultimately, even the Commission recognized that cooperation in the area of Justice and Home Affairs must be limited to intergovernmentalism, at least for the time being.[77] Hence, although federalist ideology helped move the nature of collaboration in this area in the direction of supranationalism, particularly because it was embraced by Germany, neither functionalist nor federalist ideology was sufficient to erode the intergovernmental character of European cooperation in Justice and Home Affairs.

Concerns for democracy represent another internal factor that influenced the move to the more supranational nature of collaboration on matters of internal security. The main issue in this regard stemmed from the secrecy in which the Trevi Group met at each of its three levels. As one scholar observed, "The extent of public information about Trevi seems to be in inverse proportion to the importance attached to it by governments and police officers."[78]

The Trevi Group had been criticized by the European Parliament, both for its secrecy and for the evasiveness of representatives of the Council of Ministers to answer parliamentarian questions regarding internal security during plenary sessions' question time. One member of the European Parliament (MEP) described this situation as being "positively dangerous and undemocratic."[79] Malcolm Anderson et al. contend that the intergovernmental nature and secrecy of the Trevi Group meant that "democratic control of its activities had a post hoc character."[80] In recognition of this problem, Jürgen Storbeck, in fact, originally favored keeping the EDU in Strasbourg, having argued in early 1993 that "we need acceptance by the governments and the citizens. We need to show that we are not a secret service."[81]

Although the EDU ended up in The Hague, establishing the Third Pillar within the new European Union nonetheless "brought policing and home affairs into the political daylight."[82] Despite the fact that Title VI granted the EP few powers in the area of internal security, the inclusion of Article K.6 in the TEU may be viewed as a response to the criticisms that a democratic deficit had existed in this area of the European Community.

This, it should be recalled, granted the Parliament the legal rights to be kept informed by Commission, Council, and presidency, as well as the duty of the latter to ensure that the EP's views are "duly taken into consideration." However, compared to its role in the First Pillar after Maastricht, Parliament's role remained quite limited regarding Justice and Home Affairs. Nevertheless, concerns for democracy contributed to a somewhat greater role for the EP in JHA, which must be viewed as a move in the direction of supranationalism, however slight it may be.

External events also helped move cooperation on internal security away from the more extreme intergovernmentalism of the Trevi era. In several regards, recurring and new phenomena originating from outside of the member states triggered calls for closer cooperation on JHA. Among the persistent problems have been drugs and terrorism. Drug trafficking increased in Europe in the 1980s, and although the Italian mafia was responsible for some of this, much of the flow stemmed from criminal organizations located outside of the EC, including the Medellin drug cartel in Latin America and the triads of China.[83] For example, approximately 80 percent of all the illegal drugs confiscated in Germany in the late 1980s and early 1990s were seized at its borders.[84]

The threat of terrorism also remained high on the political agendas in Europe.[85] Of course, the source of this problem has never been entirely non-European in origin, with its notable internal sources enduring into the 1980s, including the Provisional IRA (against the UK), the Basque group ETA (against Spain), the Red Army Faction (Germany), the Red Brigade (Italy), and November 17 (Greece). Other terrorist threats in the 1980s had sources lying outside Community territory, including militant Algerian Islamic fundamentalists and Middle East terrorist groups supported by Libya, Iran, and Syria.[86] There were also concerns about transborder links between terrorist groups of all kinds within Europe. Although terrorism remained an important issue in Europe, there was, at this stage, no single terrorist event comparable to the violence at the 1972 Olympics that propelled the Community to step up its cooperation in this area. In fact, because collaboration potentially entailed the sharing of sensitive information collected by the member states' individual intelligence agencies, there was enduring significant reluctance to deepen cooperation in this area. This is illustrated by the fact that terrorism was not included in the original draft of the Europol Convention, though it was mentioned by Article K.1(9) of the Maastricht Treaty.[87] Of course, the most significant change in the EU's approach to fighting terrorism would eventually result from events stemming from outside of its member states, namely the terrorist attack on the United States on September 11, 2001 (see Chapter 7).

In the early 1990s, perhaps the most important external event of all regarding internal security was the end of the Cold War and its impact on immigration into EU territory. In one regard, the fall of the Iron Curtain seemed to threaten the member states with a flood of economic immigrants from Central and Eastern Europe.[88] A second type of immigration problem triggered by the end of the Cold War was the outbreak of fighting in Yugoslavia in 1991 and the resulting sudden flood of war refugees into some of the member states, seeking political asylum and/or refugee status.

Fears concerning these developments were fueled in part by the ongoing plans to eliminate border controls among the growing number of Schengen states, as well as the belief that increased immigration would also mean higher levels of certain types of crime.[89] Regardless of whether they entered Schengen territory legally or not, "imported criminals" could spread through all of the Schengen states with no border checks to stop them. Although the frontline state of Germany was by far the largest recipient of immigrants and asylum seekers, it was hardly the only member state that perceived a greater threat to its internal security due to the impact of the Cold War's end.[90]

Moreover, by the early 1990s immigration of all kinds replaced drug trafficking and terrorism as the principle perceived threat to internal security in the member states, as it was assumed to be linked to many forms of crime.[91] One consequence of this was the growing belief that increased international cooperation was a necessary and effective alternative way to deal with this, compared to traditional national solutions.[92] In fact, some senior police officials in the EU believed that illegal immigration in particular was the principle reason for increased European police cooperation.[93]

In sum, the same type of internal and external factors that influenced the development of European integration from the highly intergovernmental EC to the more supranational EU of today have also contributed to the evolution of greater supranationalism in police cooperation. Functionalist and federalist ideologies, along with concerns for democracy, shaped this evolution from within the EU, and drug trafficking, terrorism, and increasing immigration into the member states hastened this development from outside of the Union's territory.

However, just as the progress of European integration has been limited by the importance some have placed on subsidiarity, so too has the development of cooperation concerning internal security been checked by adherence to this principle. As discussed above, one of the most notable features of the Maastricht Treaty was the general subsidiarity principle it articulated in its Article 3b. For JHA affairs, this meant that any joint actions taken under Article K.3 of Title VI (or conventions drafted pursuant to it) had to meet the criterion that it achieves the Union's goals better than the member states acting individually.[94] This was spelled out specifically in Article K.3(b), which stated that the JHA Council may "adopt joint action in so far as the objectives of the Union can be attained better by joint action than by

acting individually on account of the scale or effect of the action envis-
aged." Among other things, the inclusion of the subsidiarity principle to
Title VI meant that the "unionist impetus" to make the EU more statelike
by expanding police cooperation would be impeded if the action in question
did not meet the "comparable efficiency" test that the principle of subsidiarity implies.[95]

Of course, even member states that do not share in federalist ideology
may still promote new forms of EU cooperation that may not necessarily be
better than acting alone, if only because doing so may relieve them of the
responsibility and potential domestic criticism involved in handling sensitive matters concerning internal security on their own (e.g., asylum policy).[96] This temptation may be particularly great given that popular perceptions regarding the threat of various kinds of crime often surpass the actual
nature of the crime problem confronting them. Thus, even when crime data
indicates that traditional national solutions are working, the leaders of the
member states may willingly agree to greater supranational cooperation
simply as a way of attempting to address popular perceptions that more
needs to be done.

Notes

1. J. Wright and K. Bryett, "Multilateral Policing and New Conceptions of
Security in the European Union," *Police Studies*, vol. 27, no. 4, 1994, 62; see also
C. Fijnaut, "International Policing in Europe: Its Present Situation and Future," in
Comparisons in Policing: An International Perspective, ed. J. P. Brodeur (Alder-
shot, England: Avebury, 1995).

2. P. Reichel, *Comparative Criminal Justice Systems: A Topical Approach*,
2nd ed. (Upper Saddle River, NJ: Prentice Hall, 1999), 193.

3. A. Guyomarch, "Cooperation in the Fields of Policing and Judicial
Affairs," in *New Challenges to the European Union: Policies and Policy-Making*,
ed. Stavridis et al. (Aldershot, England: Dartmouth Publishing Company Ltd.,
1997), 128–129. See also Reichel, 123.

4. Fijnaut, "International Policing in Europe," 116; for a complete, albeit somewhat dated treatment of Interpol, see M. Anderson, *Policing the World: Interpol and
the Politics of International Police Cooperation* (Oxford: Clarendon Press, 1989).

5. J. Benyon, "The Politics of Police Co-operation in the European Union,"
International Journal of the Sociology of Law, no. 24, 1996, 359.

6. J. Benyon, "Policing the Union: European Supranational Law Enforcement
Co-operation," in *Policing Public Order: Theoretical and Practical Issues*, ed. C.
Critcher and D. Waddington (Aldershot, England: Avebury/Ashgate Publishing Ltd.,
1996), 241.

7. Reichel, 195.

8. C. Fijnaut, "Policing Western Europe: Interpol, Trevi and Europol," *Police
Studies*, vol. 15, fall 1992, 102.

9. Ibid, 102.

10. See J. Storbeck, "Europol: Probleme und Lösungen," *Kriminalistik*, no. 1,
1996, 17–19.

11. J.J.E. Schutte, "Judicial Cooperation Under the Union Treaty," in *The Third Pillar of the European Union: Cooperation in the Fields of Justice and Home Affairs,* ed. J. Monar and R. Morgan (Brussels: European Interuniversity Press, 1994), 186–189; See also C. Harding and B. Swart, "Intergovernmental Co-operation in the Field of Criminal Law," in *Criminal Justice in Europe: A Comparative Study,* ed., P. Fennel et al. (Oxford: Clarendon Press, 1995), 88–93; B. Hebenton and T. Thomas, *Policing Europe: Co-operation, Conflict and Control* (New York: St. Martin's Press, 1995).

12. Guyomarch, 130.

13. D. W. Urwin, *The Community of Europe: A History of European Integration Since 1945,* 2nd ed. (New York: Longman, 1995), 162–179.

14. Guyomarch, 130–131.

15. R. Woodward, "Establishing Europol," *European Journal on Criminal Policy and Research,* vol. 1–4, 1994, 9, note 2.

16. M. Anderson et al., *Policing the European Union* (Oxford: Clarendon Press, 1995), 53.

17. Harding and Swart, 96.

18. M. den Boer and N. Walker, "European Policing After 1992," *Journal of Common Market Studies,* vol. 31, no. 1, March 1993, 6.

19. Fijnaut, "Policing Western Europe," 102; Woodward, 11–12; Hebenton and Thomas, 70; Anderson et al., 53.

20. Woodward, 11; F. Monaco, "Europol: The Culmination of the European Union's International Police Cooperation Efforts," *Fordham International Law Journal,* vol. 19, 1995, 269.

21. Guyomarch, 133.

22. Fijnaut, "International Policing," 117.

23. Woodward, 14.

24. Ibid.

25. J. Peek, "International Police Cooperation Within Justified Political and Judicial Frameworks: Five Theses on Trevi," in *The Third Pillar of the European Union: Cooperation in the Fields of Justice and Home Affairs,* ed. J. Monar and R. Morgan (Brussels: European Interuniversity Press, 1994), 201–208.

26. Urwin, 224.

27. Peek, 203–204; Harding and Swart, 99.

28. Guyomarch, 132–133.

29. Ibid.

30. Fijnaut, "Policing Western Europe," 104.

31. Guyomarch, 131–132.

32. Monaco, 270–271; Guyomarch, 134–135.

33. Woodward, 11–12.

34. Fijnaut, "Policing Western Europe," 105.

35. Woodward, 13; Hebenton and Thomas, 85; Fijnaut, "International Policing," 105.

36. A. Duff, J. Pinder, and R. Pryce, *Maastricht and Beyond* (London and New York: Routledge, 1995), 48.

37. Hebenton and Thomas, 85.

38. Benyon, "The Politics," 366.

39. Woodward, 14.

40. J. Monar and R. Morgan, ed., *The Third Pillar of the European Union: Cooperation in the Fields of Justice and Home Affairs* (Brussels: European Interuniversity Press, 1994).

41. Treaty on European Union, Title VI, Article K.1 (9).

42. Emek M. Uçarer, "From the Sidelines to Center Stage—Sidekick No More? The European Commission in Justice and Home Affairs," *European Integration online Papers (EioP)*, vol. 5, no. 5, 2001, 6–7.

43. Ibid.

44. EU Commission, SCADplus glossary, "Activities of the European Union" (summary of legislation on Justice and Home Affairs): http://europa.eu.int/scadplus/leg/en/s22004.htm, 1998.

45. P.-C. Müller-Graff, "The Legal Bases of the Third Pillar and Its Position in the Framework of the Union Treaty," in *The Third Pillar of the European Union: Cooperation in the Fields of Justice and Home Affairs*, ed. J. Monar and R. Morgan (Brussels: European Interuniversity Press, 1994), 34–36.

46. See R. Bieber, "Links Between the 'Third Pillar' (Title VI) and the European Community (Title II) of the Treaty on the European Union," in *The Third Pillar of the European Union: Cooperation in the Fields of Justice and Home Affairs*, ed. J. Monar and R. Morgan (Brussels: European Interuniversity Press, 1994), 37–48.

47. Hebenton and Thomas, 86.

48. Benyon, "Policing the Union," 245.

49. Monaco, 277.

50. F. Boschi Orlandini, "Europol and the Europol Drugs Unit: A Cooperative Structure in the Making," in *The Third Pillar of the European Union: Cooperation in the Fields of Justice and Home Affairs*, ed. J. Monar and R. Morgan (Brussels: European Interuniversity Press, 1994), 209–211; see also Hebenton and Thomas, 87.

51. Woodward, 17.

52. Ibid., 17–18; Benyon, "The Politics," 366–367.

53. Woodward, 17–19; Walker, 256.

54. See, for example, N. Baxter, "Policing Maastricht," *The Police Journal*, January 1997, 50.

55. Guyomarch, 137.

56. Ibid., 132.

57. Ibid., 138–140.

58. Hebenton and Thomas, 149–150; Guyomarch, 140.

59. Guyomarch, 141.

60. For example, see Hebenton and Thomas, 151–153; Walker, 262; Guyomarch, 140–141.

61. Guyomarch, 140.

62. Ibid.

63. Benyon, "The Politics," 371.

64. Ibid., 372.

65. Walker, 261; Anderson et al., 93–96.

66. Walker, 262.

67. Guyomarch 144. See also Walker, 269–274.

68. Walker, 261.

69. Benyon, "Policing the Union," 248.

70. Cited in Woodward, 12.

71. Benyon, "Policing the Union," 250–251.

72. Walker, 261.

73. Federalist ideology in this sense has also been termed the "general ethos of integration." See den Boer and Walker, 9.

74. D. Dinan, *An Ever Closer Union: An Introduction to European Integration*, 2nd ed. (Boulder, CO: Lynne Rienner Publishers, 1999), 149; Duff, Pinder, and Pryce, 49.

75. Duff, Pinder, and Pryce, 115.

76. Ibid.

77. Ibid.

78. P. J. Cullen of the University of Edinburgh as quoted in Hebenton and Thomas, 78.

79. Hebenton and Thomas, 78–79; Benyon, "The Politics," 363.

80. Anderson et al., 56.

81. Cited in Woodward, 19.

82. Hebenton and Thomas, 86.

83. Guyomarch, 138.

84. Anderson et al., 16.

85. Walker, 270.

86. Ibid., 269.

87. Anderson et al., 65.

88. Benyon, "The Politics," 356; Guyomarch, 139.

89. Benyon, "Policing the Union," 239.

90. See Benyon, "Policing the Union," 239–240; Guyomarch, 140–141.

91. Hebenton and Thomas, 149–150; Benyon, "The Politics," 357.

92. Guyomarch, 139–141.

93. Benyon, "Policing the Union," 357.

94. Harding and Swart, 100.

95. See D. G. Partan, "The Justiciability of Subsidiarity," in *The State of the European Union: Building a European Polity*, ed. C. Rhodes and S. Mazey (Boulder, CO: Lynne Rienner Publishers, 1995), 65–66.

96. den Boer and Walker, 9–10.

4

The Europol Convention
and the Treaty of Amsterdam

POLICE COOPERATION IN THE EU WAS SHAPED BY DEVELOPMENTS IN three main areas following the entry into force of the TEU and its Title VI in November 1993 and the start of the EDU's operations in February 1994. One area of activity was the JHA Council's gradual expansion of the EDU's responsibilities through a series of joint actions, passed in accordance with the provisions of Article K.3 of the TEU. The second was the drafting of the Europol Convention and its related protocols, resulting in controversy as these were debated in the member states prior to their ratification. The third area was the events surrounding the Treaty of Amsterdam, which was signed on October 2, 1997, and entailed several important changes to EU cooperation on internal security, including a few provisions impacting Europol. Collectively, developments in these three related areas moved cooperation in the area of internal security more and more in the direction of supranationalism during the 1990s.

The Europol Drugs Unit and
Its Expanding Role

Although established under the original ministerial agreement of 1993, the specific structure and duties of the Europol Drugs Unit were shaped by another joint action adopted by the JHA Council on March 10, 1995, under the TEU. This joint action specified that each EU country should send liaison officers to the headquarters in The Hague to serve as links between Europol and the member states. These liaison officers, consisting of police and customs agents from each of the member states, were managed by a coordinator, an assistant, and a staff of police experts. The EDU's first and only coordinator was Jürgen Storbeck, who has continued to serve as director of Europol since its formal inauguration on October 1, 1998.

The EDU worked at the request of the member states via its Europol Liaison Officers (ELOs) stationed in The Hague (the working language of the EDU was English).[1] Although each liaison office was legally the sovereign territory of the respective member states, the ELOs were free to interact and collaborate with each other on requests for analysis or assistance from their contact points in their home countries.[2] The work of the EDU was restricted in three significant areas.

First, due to worries about privacy and data protection, the EDU was prohibited from *holding* personal information in any form, and was limited simply to receiving any intelligence of this kind from member states and then returning it. In fact, the EDU was not even permitted to include the names of individuals in the crime analyses it sent to the member state. In this regard, the appropriate data-protection laws of each individual member state applied to the work of its liaison officers, enforced by officials from that state.[3]

A second restriction on the EDU was that it was an entirely nonoperational police agency in the sense that its officers were not allowed to participate in any physical actions. This meant that EDU officials could not engage in a variety of normal policing activities such as surveillance, undercover work, arrests, etc.[4] In fact, it would not be until 2002 that Europol would gain the right to participate in joint investigations teams with member-state officials, though its staff was not empowered to make arrests or use coercive means.

The third way that the EDU was restricted concerned the legal control of its ELOs, which was retained by the home governments and subject to their pertinent legislation, although the joint action creating the EDU specified that the member states were to instruct their liaison officers to follow the orders of the coordinator. Thus, even as the JHA Council retained general oversight over the EDU (e.g., in its right to receive biannual reports), the individual ministers were ultimately in control of their own officers.[5]

Despite these three limitations, the EDU experienced a growing work load. During its first full year of operation, it handled less than four hundred requests for assistance from police agencies in the member states.[6] By 1996, however, this figure had jumped to 2,053 cases, with most of these requests coming from the UK and Germany. This increase came despite the EDU's small staff of 116 personnel (37 ELOs and technical assistants and 79 EDU staff members) and a budget of about ECU 6.397 million.[7]

Indeed, the functions of the EDU were increased several times after it first opened shop in The Hague. This was at least partly the result of the ambitious plans for a true European policing agency proposed by the Germans, who held the EU presidency during the second half of 1994. Building on an agreement reached at the European Council in Essen in December 1994, the JHA Council passed its joint action of March 10, 1995, expanding the remit of the EDU to include the smuggling of nuclear materials, illegal immigration networks, and the trafficking of stolen vehicles.[8] The Germans had also published documents during its presidency, indicating its hope that the EDU's responsibility would eventually be widened to cover as many as twenty-two types of organized crime, including credit-card fraud, product piracy, and the unlawful supply of labor.[9] In some cases, however, expanding the role of the EDU proved to be highly controversial.

For example, in the wake of increasing acts of skinhead violence and attacks on "foreigners" across Europe in the early 1990s, debate had also begun on adding such crimes to the EDU responsibilities. After an agreement reached at its summit in Corfu in June 1994, the European Council announced its approval of a JHA Council plan to combat racism and xenophobia at the Essen summit.[10] However, a British-led dispute over the threat to free speech posed by this proposed cooperation was not resolved until March 1996, when the JHA Council passed a joint action to facilitate police cooperation in the fight against racism and xenophobia.[11] Member states such as the UK and Denmark, which have more liberal hate-speech laws than Germany and Austria, committed themselves to take action only where the speech (e.g., denying the Holocaust) was expected to stir up "racial hatred" (for the British) or was "threatening, insulting or degrading" (for the Danes).[12]

At the time it was hoped that the EDU, and later Europol, would eventually play a role in preventing the export of hate-speech materials from one member state to another. However, enduring controversy over the issue would prevent this from happening until Europol's crime-fighting remit was expanded at the start of 2002 (see Chapters 7 and 8). Nevertheless, after several disappointing years following Europol's incorporation into the TEU, the passage of the joint action on the hate-crime question was one of several indications that progress was finally being made in the area of policing.

Similar to the role of Chancellor Kohl during the German presidency in 1994, Irish Prime Minister John Bruton made crime fighting one of his major priorities during Ireland's leadership in the second half of 1996, contributing to several advancements for Europol. Bruton made no secret of his desire to see an FBI-style police organization created for the EU.[13] At the concluding Dublin European Council, it was agreed, on Franco-German insistence, that giving Europol "operative powers" to conduct investigations along with national authorities should be incorporated into the ongoing Intergovernmental Conference (IGC) that would produce the Treaty of Amsterdam.[14] In addition, with backing from Kohl and President Jacques Chirac of France, Bruton's efforts to hasten anticrime cooperation led to the establishment of a High-Level Group (HLG) of senior police, justice, and customs officials charged with drafting a plan by the following April to recommend ways of intensifying EU cooperation on internal security.[15] Furthermore, as the date of the Amsterdam summit neared, the JHA Council passed a joint action in February 1997 making the fight against the trafficking in human beings part of the EDU/Europol remit. This was aimed at the problems of illegal workers, contract brides, and slave labor, as well as adult and child prostitution and related pedophile crimes. This expansion of the EDU's duties came partly in response to the high-profile pedophile offenses in Belgium around that time, as well as the mishandling of these by the Belgian police.

Soon after this, the HLG had completed its proposals improving cooperation on crime fighting, and these were adopted by the JHA Council in Luxembourg on April 28, 1997. The HLG's Action Plan to Combat Organized Crime included fifteen guidelines and thirty recommendations concerning criminal prosecution and prevention to be implemented by the member states, the Commission, and Europol. In its conclusions on the HLG's recommendations, the JHA Council noted a number of items "of critical importance," including bringing judicial cooperation up to the same level as police cooperation, developing closer ties with EU candidate states and international organizations, and improving prevention programs. The Council also noted the task of enhancing Europol among these critically important areas, including the HLG's guideline (number 10) and recommendation (number 25) to permit Europol's participation in joint operations with national authorities and to empower it to request that national police forces conduct investigations.[16] In addition, the 1997 Action Plan recommended that the EU should examine ways in which judicial and criminal laws could be harmonized and called upon the JHA Council to make specific proposals regarding this by mid-1999.[17] Prior to its adoption by the JHA Council, the HLG adopted its Action Plan on April 9, 1997, and communicated its guidelines and recommendations to the ongoing IGC. As will be discussed below, many of the Action Plan's recommendations were either incorporated into the Treaty of Amsterdam (or had already been included before the HLG had completed its work) or were implemented by the JHA Council after the special summit at Tampere, Finland (see Chapter 5).

The Amsterdam European Council added its endorsement to the Action Plan when it met in June 1997. It also called for the establishment of a multidisciplinary group (MDG) on organized crime to work on the implementation of the Action Plan's thirty recommendations. This MDG subsequently brought together law enforcement practitioners, prosecutors, and policymakers at the senior level in monthly meetings.

In the months that followed, the MDG, K.4 Committee, and the JHA Council oversaw many important developments concerning EU cooperation on internal security. Through joint actions under Article K.3 of the TEU, the JHA Council approved conventions in a number of areas, including corruption involving EC officials, the transmission of judicial and extrajudicial documents in civil or commercial matters, and customs (i.e., the Naples II Convention). In addition, joint actions were passed establishing two new EU-funded programs of personnel exchange, training, and cooperation among the member states, including the Odysseus Program for asylum, immigration, and the crossing of external borders and the Falcone Program regarding organized crime. During the previous year, joint actions had been passed to provide funding for the Oisin Program for law enforcement authorities, the Grotius Program for legal practitioners, the Sherlock Program for officials involved with identity documents, and the Stop Program for combating the trade in human beings and the sexual exploitation of children. In sum, less than a year after the creation of the new Odysseus and Falcone Programs in 1997, the MDG was able to inform the JHA Council that all of the Action Plan's proposals with deadlines at the end of 1997 or mid-1998 had either been completed or were well under way.[18]

Meeting on May 28–29, 1998, the JHA Council noted a number of achievements based on the Action Plan and the work of the MDG (several passed by the Council during that session). These included joint actions on mutual legal assistance in criminal matters, the prosecution of participants in criminal organizations (agreed upon in March 1998), and progress on the creation of a European Judicial Network (EJN). The latter had been approved in principle by the JHA Council in December 1997 and had begun to take shape in 1998, being officially inaugurated on September 25, 1998. The EJN consists of a network of legal practitioners in the member states, who serve as contact points for judicial cooperation and the sharing of legal and practical information.

In addition to these accomplishments, the EU ministers, along with representatives from the CEECs and Cyprus, used the occasion of the May 1998 JHA Council to sign a detailed preaccession pact on fighting organized crime. With the accession negotiations with the six applicant states of the so-called Luxembourg Group having begun on March 31, 1998, the May JHA Council also passed a joint action on the evaluation of applicant states' implementation of the JHA *acquis*.[19] Regarding both of these activities, the European Union emphasized the link between the issues of expanding its membership and making progress on Justice and Home Affairs.

In sum, by the late 1990s, after years of delay following the JHA's unveiling under the TEU, cooperation in the area of policing seemed to be gaining momentum in the European Union. In its *Annual Report* for 1997, the EDU informed the JHA Council that it was being called upon more and more frequently by national law enforcement agencies, indicating that its 1997 case load had increased by nearly 20 percent over 1996.[20] The EDU's *Annual Report* for 1997 showed that it responded to 2,608 requests from member states that year, compared to 2,053 in 1996.[21]

Not only did its work load increase, but, the EDU was determined to be successful in coordinating multinational anticrime efforts and providing analysis to the member states.[22] One example of the EDU's value was its coordination of the simultaneous arrests of two Italians in Lisbon who had smuggled Brazilian drugs into Spain by ship, the couriers who had then brought these drugs to Germany via France, as well as the leader of the ring, who was based in Spain.[23] In another 1996 endeavor, Operation Cocktail, sixty-eight members of a mafia drug ring were arrested after the EDU responded to an Italian police request and then coordinated eighteen months of surveillance, which were followed by simultaneous dawn raids by national authorities in five countries.[24] In 1997, the EDU launched Operation Primo, which began with the investigation of a house in Italy being used to store cocaine and synthetic drugs smuggled in from the Netherlands. Interestingly, the EDU's information pooling and analysis led to the revelation that the gang members related to this drug-storage house were being watched separately, but simultaneously, by national authorities in six different member states. Operation Primo coordinated these investigations, which ultimately culminated in the seizure of drugs, laundered money, a clandestine drug laboratory, and the arrest of twenty criminals from Europe, South America, and Asia.[25]

The EDU's "Work Program" for 1998 gave special emphasis to implementing the measures of the 1997 Action Plan regarding organized crime, indicating that it would focus especially on money laundering, trafficking in human beings, and the tactical coordination between member states' law enforcement agencies.[26] The 1998 Work Program also described the progress it was making setting up "The Europol Computer System" (TECS), which would contain Europol's three main databases.[27] By June 1998, proposals for personnel and budget increases for 1999 became necessary when it finally appeared that the Europol Convention would be able to enter into force in late 1998. This meant that Storbeck's staff would soon be responsible not only for the six types of crime already specified by joint actions regarding the EDU, but also for terrorism (in 1999) and potentially eighteen other types of crime covered in the Convention's annex, should the Council choose to add any of these to Europol's remit.

In light of the EDU's expanding case load, its apparent success, and the impending entry into force of the Europol Convention with its broader remit, the JHA Council agreed to increase the agency's staff from 69 to 119 within a year.[28] Over the next year, however, Europol's staff was increased several more times through the use of regular supplementary budgets, in anticipation of the new police agency finally becoming operational with a remit larger than that of the EDU.

Funding for the EDU (and later Europol) began to increase even more rapidly than the size of its personnel. In June 1998, the UK presidency of the JHA Council proposed to more than double Europol's operational budget from ECU 6.722 million to €14,991,500 for 1999. After being passed by the K.4 Committee, COREPER, this budget was finally approved on September 24, 1998, by the JHA Council in Brussels under the Austrian presidency.[29] Including funding for TECS, Europol's total budget for 1999 was €18.904 million (about US$20.8 million).[30]

In sum, the transformation of the EDU into Europol came as the result of a process that began soon after the Maastricht Treaty took effect in November 1993. Its structure, procedures, responsibilities, and powers were established by the Europol Convention and its protocols, but these were eventually altered somewhat by the Treaty of Amsterdam. Although the entry into force of the Europol Convention legally ended the EDU, Europol would not be fully operational until the last of the Convention's protocols were signed and ratified by the spring of 1999. Consequently, when Europol initiated its full duties under the Convention on July 1, 1999, it did so under the terms of a modified Third Pillar as amended by the Treaty of Amsterdam, which had entered into force the previous May.

The Europol Convention

In June 1992, the European Council, meeting in Lisbon, decided that putting Europol fully into operation necessitated an international convention, as permitted by Title VI of the TEU. This set in motion a series of events over the next six years that would reflect many of the controversies surrounding the establishment of a quasi-federal police agency in the EU. This would not only involve the Europol Convention itself, but also its related protocols, which were negotiated, signed, and ratified separately.

Work on drafting the Europol Convention had begun in the Trevi Group's AHWGE and was then continued in 1993 by the Europol Working Group of the K.4 Committee's Steering Group II. Progress on drafting the convention was initially slow until Chancellor Kohl made it one of his top priorities during the German presidency in 1994. Kohl had hoped to make sufficient headway on negotiations with other member states on the Convention such that it would be ready for signing at the Essen European Council in December 1994.[31]

However, by then, several disputes regarding Europol had come to the fore, including the rights of access to information handled by Europol, the involvement of the European Parliament, and the role of the European Court of Justice (ECJ). Concerning the latter, the Benelux states, in particular, wanted to empower the ECJ to resolve any future disputes citizens or member states may have regarding whether Europol was operating in accord with the terms of its convention.[32] However, the British were adamantly opposed to this, and the German presidency ended before the controversy could be resolved.[33]

The British opposition to the role of the ECJ remained firm throughout the French presidency, which ended with the Cannes European Council in June 1995. However, soon thereafter the United Kingdom was persuaded to allow the ratification process to begin in all of the member states by simply agreeing to resolve the issue of the Court later, specifically by June 1996 in a separate protocol to the convention.[34] This cleared the way for the Europol Convention to be signed on July 26, 1995, and sent to the member states for what would turn out to be a very slow ratification process.[35]

Similar to the way the dispute over the social chapter of the TEU was resolved in 1992 following the Maastricht summit, an accord was reached with the British at the Florence European Council in June 1996 about the Court's jurisdiction regarding Europol. It was agreed that the United Kingdom would be able to opt out of this provision granting the Court powers of interpretation regarding the Europol Convention. Thus, the European Court of Justice would only play this role in the other fourteen member states. A protocol to this effect was signed by COREPER and adopted by the JHA Council on July 23, 1996. Upon signing the protocol, the member states were required to declare which of their national courts would be able to request a preliminary ruling on Europol from the Court.

By 1997, another controversy had erupted in several of the member states regarding a second protocol under the Europol Convention that had been drafted by the JHA Council on June 19, 1997, under Article K.4 of the TEU. The Protocol on the Privileges and Immunities of Europol essentially grants the members of the Europol staff diplomatic immunity from testifying or being prosecuted in any national court for acts performed by them in the exercise of their official functions. The director of Europol can waive his staff members' individual immunity, but only if he believes this would better serve the interests of Europol.[36] Fears that this arrangement would put the officers of Europol above the law drew protests from the British Liberal Democrats and Statewatch, a civil-rights watchdog organization, but this did not prevent the British government from supporting its passage.[37] However, similar protest elsewhere led to the need for debate in several national parliaments, including Germany, Denmark, Sweden, and the Netherlands, delaying passage of the protocol. Combined with the issue of the Court's role, the debate on the immunities protocol (as well as data protection) served to create controversy surrounding the Europol Convention itself, contributing to delays in its ratification in several member states into 1998, including Italy, Luxembourg, Greece, and Belgium.

Yet another controversy regarding the Europol Convention concerned the issue of including combating terrorism among Europol duties. During the history of the Convention's negotiation, the Spanish had been the lone member state pushing for this, hoping to gain assistance in their fight against ETA (Euzkadi Ta Askatusauna), the Basque separatist group.[38] In fact, the Spanish government had long been at odds with the French concerning cross-border activity involving suspected Basque terrorists. More recently, Spain became embroiled with Belgium over the extradition of a Spanish couple from Brussels who had allegedly provided help to ETA.[39] In general, much of the controversy about including the fight against terrorism in Europol's remit stemmed from insufficient agreement on just who should be defined as a "terrorist." Agreement on this issue would not be reached until after the terrorist attacks on the United States on September 11, 2001.

Thus, at a meeting of the JHA Council in Berlin in September 1994, it was agreed that terrorism would not be included in the text of the Europol Convention, but that the issue would also be left open for future consideration.[40] At the JHA Council meeting in March 1995, the French succeeded in brokering a compromise plan agreeable to Spain, entailing that terrorism was to be included in the remit of Europol, but only two years after the Convention had entered into force.[41] However, Spain's patience wore thin as the ratification of the signed Europol Convention was held up in many of the member states' parliaments, and it became apparent that the original January 1, 1998, deadline for its implementation would surely be missed. Consequently, Spain once again began to push for a more rapid inclusion of terrorism among Europol's duties.

Finally, on February 10, 1998, an agreement was reached in the K.4 Committee calling for terrorism to be included in the remit of Europol starting on January 1, 1999.[42] The JHA Council approved the plan at its meeting in Brussels on March 19, 1998, and took the new duties into consideration when considering the 1999 budget for Europol. Even then, doubt remained among Europol leaders that they had the sufficient staffing, resources, and time to begin responding to requests for assistance regarding terrorism by the new deadline.[43]

By May 1998, Belgium was the lone member state not to have ratified the Europol Convention, its consideration having been postponed as the restructuring of its national police forces was deliberated in the wake of several embarrassing blunders. Belgium finally passed the Convention in early June, and, by June 12, 1998, the secretary-general of the Council of Ministers had consequently received the last formal notifications of ratification from the member states. Under the terms of Article 45(3), the Convention could not enter into force until ninety days after the last ratification. Thus, Europol was legally born on October 1, 1998, ending the work of the EDU in the process. However, seven EU countries had still not ratified the Protocol on Privileges and Immunities, including France, Germany, Greece, Italy, Luxembourg, Portugal, and Spain. At the end of 1998, France, Italy, Luxembourg, and Portugal had yet to do so. Finally, by the end of May 1999,

France and Italy became the last member states to ratify this protocol and deposit the instruments of ratification, allowing Europol to become operational on July 1, 1999.

Since then, Europol's mission, under the terms of its convention, has been to enhance cooperation among member states' competent authorities in their fight against the trafficking of illicit drugs, terrorism, and other serious forms of international crimes (Article 2 of the Europol Convention). It has done so by facilitating the exchange of information between member states; obtaining, collating, and analyzing data; notifying member states of any information or analyses pertinent to them; aiding member states in investigations; and maintaining a computerized system of data and analyses (Article 3). Europol's remit under Article 2 of its convention was initially only somewhat more broad than that of the EDU, covering the trafficking of illegal drugs and nuclear and radioactive substances, illegal immigrant smuggling, the trade in human beings (in its various forms), motor vehicle crime, and terrorism. The Convention also empowered Europol to pursue investigations concerning any money laundering or other criminal activity related to these crimes (Article 2) (but not the fight against money laundering in general, which would only be permitted later—see Chapter 5).

In addition to its initial remit, the annex to the Convention lists eighteen other crimes that the JHA Council could have empowered Europol to handle at any time. These crimes are categorized into three types, including crimes against life, limb, or personal freedom (e.g., violent crimes against persons, illicit trade in human organs and tissue, and racism and xenophobia), crimes against property or public goods (e.g., fraud and counterfeiting), and illegal trading and harm to the environment (e.g., the trafficking of endangered species and environmental crime). The expansion of Europol's remit after 1999 on the basis of crimes listed in the annex, as well as beyond this, will be discussed in the next chapter.

Europol's daily operations are led by a directorate officially appointed by a Council Act of April 29, 1999. As already noted, Jürgen Storbeck of Germany continues to serve as Europol's director. He was initially assisted by four deputy directors, including Willy Bruggeman (Belgium), Emanuele Marotta (Italy), David Valls-Russell (United Kingdom), and Gilles Leclair (France).

This directorate operates under the oversight of the JHA Council, which is represented by a Management Board created by the Convention (Article 28). This board is comprised of one representative from each member state and chaired by the state holding the EU presidency.[44] A representative from the Commission is entitled to attend each meeting. The board provides the broad objectives for Europol within the terms of the Convention's provisions. In addition to overseeing the board, the Council may serve to resolve any disputes between a member state and Europol or between two member states regarding Europol activities or staffing.[45] Many of the JHA Council's decisions require unanimity (e.g., regarding finances and the duties of staff members). Europol's daily operations are run by a director, who is appointed for a four-year term by the JHA Council, renewable once. The director, and his/her two deputy directors, are directly accountable to the Management Board and may be dismissed by the Council after consulting with the board.

Similar to the EDU, Europol works through a network of liaison officers. Each member state has created a Europol National Unit (ENU) of officers at home and has sent at least one person from this unit to serve as its ELO and represent it at Europol's headquarters in The Hague. Although covered by the same immunity status as Europol's staff members, the ELOs are only on secondment from their national units and are thus governed by national law in terms of ultimate supervision. In contrast, Article 30 of the Europol Convention specifies that Europol's staff members are not to take orders from any authority outside Europol (they work under the authority of Europol's director or his subordinates).

Working through their ELOs, Europol National Units (ENUs) are supposed be the only direct link between Europol and national police authorities. Through this channel, the ENUs are obligated by the convention to supply criminal information to Europol on their own initiative or by request. However, member states may withhold information when they believe their national security interests outweigh any potential benefits to Europol (Article 4.5).[46] The ELOs are also charged with disseminating information and analyses from Europol to their ENU.

In contrast to the EDU, Europol is not only permitted to analyze information and intelligence, but also to store and organize it in computerized form at its headquarters. The Europol Computer System, known as TECS, entails three major databases. The first is the Europol Information System (EIS), which may only store data related to persons suspected of having committed or who are considered likely to commit an offense covered by Europol's remit.[47] The second database consists of the Analysis Work Files, which may be created by "analysis groups" staffed by ELOs, Europol analysts, and experts drawn from the member states. These files are composed of criminal information obtained from the EIS, as well as other types of intelligence, including data on a wide range of persons who might be called to testify in investigations (i.e., victims, potential victims, contacts and associates of suspects, and anyone who can assist an investigation). The analysis groups of Europol may also request information from the ENUs via their ELOs. In addition, the TECS also contains a third database, consisting of an extensive index system of information stored in the other two databases.

Furthermore, unlike the EDU, the Europol Convention offers the possibility for Europol analysts to seek information from outside sources including, for example, applicant states, Interpol, the FBI, and the recently created European Center for Drugs and Drug Addiction in Lisbon and European Monitoring Center for Racism and Xenophobia in Vienna.[48] These links have to be negotiated by Europol's director at the initiation of the JHA Council and within the guidelines on data protection contained in the Europol Convention. These information-sharing negotiations will be discussed in Chapter 5.

Among the plausible outside sources of information for Europol is the Schengen Information System (SIS), which, among things, contains information on undesirable aliens, wanted criminals, persons under surveillance, and data on firearms and vehicle ownership. However, the flow of information from the SIS, or its successor, SIS II, will likely be severely restricted by the Schengen states' agreements on data protection.[49] Although perhaps politically necessary, this will likely prove to be both costly and inefficient.[50] A link between the two databases or even a replacement of the SIS by the broader EIS (which will gather information from all fifteen member states) is certainly a possibility in the future.[51] Initially, however, the creation of Europol has meant that Europe has, at least temporarily, two parallel databases containing similar (and in some regards, the same) information on international criminals or suspects.

Stemming from the same sets of personal privacy concerns that have surrounded the work of the EDU (as well as the establishment of the SIS), the Europol Convention contains several provisions concerning data protection. Whereas data and analyses that are general in nature may be open to all ELOs and ENUs, information concerning a specific investigative operation is limited to the liaison officers and national units directly impacted by it. A liaison officer from another member state may request this information, and if this is rejected by Europol or a member state, the Management Board may intervene to resolve the conflict (by a two-thirds majority vote).

The Europol Convention also entitles individuals to request that their state's national unit grant them access to data stored about them by Europol (e.g., in the analysis work files). However, Europol or the relevant ENU controlling the data may reject such a request if the dissemination of the information would prevent Europol from properly conducting its duties, compromise the national security of a member state, or jeopardize the rights of third parties.[52] In this regard, the Europol Convention provides a mechanism for upholding national data protection laws and safeguarding individuals' privacy rights by calling upon each member state to create an independent National Supervisory Body to serve as a monitor of its national unit (Article 23). In addition, the Convention calls for the establishment of an international Joint Supervisory Body, consisting of national delegations drawn from each of the national supervisory boards (Article 24). The job of the Joint Supervisory Board is to monitor the activities of Europol, including its data storage and dissemination, and make its findings known to the Management Board.[53]

Despite these provisions, the Europol Convention has been criticized by some for its various democratic shortcomings. For example, concern was expressed that Europol has de facto authority to collect and store "soft data" on virtually anybody, including law-abiding citizens, even if the information takes the form of unverified gossip or slanderous allegations.[54] Since Europol is able to store data on ethnicity, political and religious views, health, and sexuality, there has also been some fear that Europol will eventually target certain groups based on profiles built on truthful information.[55]

Similar concerns have been raised about the accountability of Europol to democratic institutions. One critic in the British media predicted that Europol "will operate in an institutional twilight zone beyond the full control of democratic forces."[56] Indeed, the JHA Council has only indirect oversight via the Management Board, and the European Parliament enjoys only the right to be kept abreast of Europol's activities through its reports and consultations with the JHA Council. In addition, the provisions of the Europol Convention do not make clear whether the National Supervisory Body or the Joint Supervisory Body can override Europol's denial of any citizen's request to access his/her data or to change incorrect information.[57] It may be that this ambiguity in the Convention will only be resolved following a landmark preliminary ruling by the Court of Justice.

Concerns regarding the democratic accountability of Europol have been exacerbated by the immunity of Europol staffers and liaison officers and the exclusive power of the director of Europol to decide whether this should be waived. When Europol began its work, for example, it was not clear whether a Europol staff member would be held accountable for abusing power in some way or misusing personal data (e.g., releasing sensitive information to the media or employers) if doing so would hamper an investigation. These anxieties prompted Thilo Weichert, head of the German Data Protection Association, to declare that "the director of Europol is an absolute monarch."[58] Adding to these worries just prior to Europol becoming fully operational in July 1999 was concern for several provisions of the new Treaty of Amsterdam that altered the way Europol would function.

Internal Security Under the Treaty of Amsterdam

With the aim of creating an "area of freedom, security, and justice" (AFSJ), the Treaty of Amsterdam amended many aspects of the TEU's Third Pillar on Justice and Home Affairs. Some of these provisions impacted Europol directly, while others pertained to the broader effort of the fight against crime in the EU. The Treaty of Amsterdam has been important to Europol in three main regards.

First, the wording of Title VI was changed to "Police and Judicial Cooperation in Criminal Matters," reflecting the fact that a large number of noncriminal areas under the old Title VI would be gradually shifted to the First Pillar as part of a new Title IIIa. More specifically, the Treaty of Amsterdam provides that visas, asylum, immigration, and other polices related to the free movement of persons will eventually be handled by the Community institutions, not by the intergovernmental Pillar III.[59] The treaty also provide that the entire Schengen *acquis* (the Schengen agreement and convention, as well as declarations and decisions of the Schengen executive committee) will be incorporated into the First Pillar of the EU over a period of five years after the new treaty enters into force. Having been foreshadowed all along by the communitization bridge of the old Article K.9, issues relating to the freedom of movement, as well as civil judicial matters, will therefore in the future be dealt with in the First Pillar. Hence, by May 2004, police and judicial cooperation in criminal matters should be all that remains to be handled in the intergovernmental Third Pillar, and thus its new name.

Second, the old Title VI and its Articles K.1–K.9 were amended with new Articles K.1–K.14 (consolidated version of the TEU Articles 29–42), plus a new Title VIa, consisting of Articles K.15–17 (Articles 43–45).[60] The communitization bridge was retained in the new Article K.14 (Article 42), but altered in two significant regards. First, the JHA is *required* under the Treaty of Amsterdam to consult the European Parliament concerning communitization. Second, no police areas are restricted from being shifted to the First Pillar, meaning police cooperation could, at least in principle, be communitized even without the drafting of a new convention or treaty, though such a decision would still have to be ratified in each of the member states.

In addition, Article K.12 (Article 40) facilitates the potential desire of some, but not all, member states to proceed with "enhanced cooperation," using the institutions and mechanism of the EU, even though some members may decide not to participate.[61] The entire JHA Council must decide on the basis of qualified majority voting (QMV) to allow a group of member states to pursue deeper cooperation among themselves in this way. Thus, even as it lays down some specific means of enhanced cooperation (also known as "closer cooperation") concerning policing and criminal justice, the new Title VI also encourages an even higher, and perhaps more supranational, degree of collaboration among some member states that could go beyond the terms of the new treaty.

Despite the possibility of closer cooperation already contained in the Treaty of Amsterdam, the enduring predominance of intergovernmentalism is also present in this area. The second paragraph of Article K.12 (Article 40) states that: "If a member of the Council declares that, for important and stated reasons of national policy, it intends to oppose the granting of an authorization by qualified majority, a vote shall not be taken. The Council may, acting by a qualified majority, request that the matter be referred to the European Council for decision by unanimity." This provision, known as the "Amsterdam Compromise," follows the blueprint from the 1960s by granting a type of veto power to each member state. Unlike the Luxembourg Compromise, however, the important reasons of national policy for the veto must be stated specifically and openly.[62] This makes the European Council, in which each member state has an effective veto, an official "appellate body" for the JHA Council in the matter of allowing a smaller group of states (i.e., less than fifteen) to proceed on their own with deeper integration concerning police and judicial cooperation.[63] The following chapter will discuss how the Treaty of Nice, agreed upon in December 2000, entails some changes regarding the future of "closer cooperation" in the Third Pillar.

The third area of change stemming from the Treaty of Amsterdam is its direct impact on Europol. The new Title VI of the TEU incorporated and expanded upon many of the priorities, objectives, and mechanisms established by the Europol Convention, as well its protocols and the numerous joint actions passed by the JHA Council. New Article K.1 (Article 29) states that the EU's objective in this pillar

> shall be to provide citizens with a high level of safety within *an area of freedom, security, and justice* by developing common action among member states in the fields of police and judicial cooperation in criminal matters and by preventing and combating racism and xenophobia. That objective shall be achieved by preventing and combating crime, organized or otherwise, in particular terrorism, trafficking in persons and offenses against children, illicit drug trafficking and illicit arms trafficking, corruption and fraud.

These goals are to be achieved by promoting closer judicial cooperation, an approximation of rules on criminal matters, and closer police cooperation among the member states both directly and through Europol (new Article K.1; Article 29).

New Article K.2 (Article 30) spells out several forms of common action in the field of police cooperation that are already permitted under the Europol Convention, but its provisions also endow Europol, at least potentially, with a few, new *operative* powers. For example, new Article K.2.2a (Article 30.2a) calls upon the JHA Council, within five years, to enable Europol to physically participate in "joint teams" composed of Europol and national officers, as prescribed in the 1997 Action Plan. Although Europol officers still lack the true executive policing power of arrest, this provision permits the JHA Council to authorize them to take part in a whole range of policing activities (though not without national authorities), including investigations, surveillance, controlled deliveries of drugs, etc. Moreover, new Article K.2.2b (Article 30.2B) permits the Council to adopt measures allowing Europol to ask national authorities to begin investigations in specific cases and to develop expertise that may be put at the disposal of these authorities. These powers are similar to those possessed by the Commission's antifraud unit, Unite pour la Coordination de la Lutte AntiFraude.[64] The JHA Council's activities in granting Europol new operative powers under the terms of the Treaty of Amsterdam will be discussed in Chapter 5.

Although the national authorities of the member states may refuse a Europol request for an investigation or may not want Europol's staff members to participate with its officers in any operations, the terms of the Treaty of Amsterdam have transformed Europol from a police agency charged with simply pooling and analyzing information, to one that can potentially take a proactive and active role in crime fighting regarding a wide range of criminal offenses in all fifteen member states of the European Union. Combined with terms of the protocol on immunity, the unveiling of the provisions of the new Title VI when the Treaty of Amsterdam was agreed upon in June 1997 were alarming to some Europeans who were apprehensive about giving Europol too much authority. Europol officials and JHA ministers tried to downplay the new powers, pointing out that Europol officials could not conduct independent operations or make arrests.[65] Despite this, the innovations of the Treaty of Amsterdam fueled debate on Europol, which contributed to the delay in the ratification of its convention well into 1998.

Europol Under the Treaty of Amsterdam

As the discussion above indicates, gaining a clear picture of how Europol differs from its forerunner, the EDU, requires attentiveness to the terms of the Europol Convention, its protocols, and the new Title VI of the Treaty of Amsterdam. Like the EDU, Europol falls under the policy domain of the JHA Council, but beyond that, several changes have been made. Although some of these are rather superficial, other innovations have been least symbolically, if not tangibly, significant. As before, the main preparatory work of the JHA Council is not to be conducted by COREPER, but rather by the same senior officials from the member states of the so-called K.4 Committee. However, the name of this committee has been changed to the "Article 36 Committee," using the numbering of the post-Amsterdam, consolidated version of the treaties.

More important are the changes to the policymaking mechanisms of the JHA Council. Under the new Article K.6 (Article 34), the JHA Council is permitted to oversee the drafting and adoption of "common positions" to define the consensual approach of the Union to a particular matter, which replaces the "joint position" mechanism but performs roughly the same task. The JHA may also continue to draft "conventions" for policy decisions that seem sufficiently sensitive or seem to go beyond the legal boundaries of the treaty and its provisions.

The Court of Justice will have the power to resolve disputes arising in regard to these two kinds of action (new Article K.7, i.e., Article 35). However, an opt-out provision is provided, allowing states to declare upon signing any convention under this article whether they will recognize the Court's jurisdiction and if so, which national court may request a preliminary ruling from it (new Article K.7.3). Of course, this somewhat diminishes the supranational role of the ECJ in this area by making its role voluntary for individual members states.

Article K.6 of the treaty (i.e., Article 34) eliminates the "joint action" instrument and replaces it with "framework decisions" and "decisions," which are designed to be "more binding and more authoritative."[66] "Framework decisions" do not entail "direct effect" and are intended to be used to help promote the approximation of authority structures to the laws and procedures of the member states in the area of criminal justice (e.g., criminal law) (new K.6.2b, i.e., Article 34.2a). Similar to the "directives" of the First Pillar, which the EU has used to perfect its single market, "framework decisions" are binding on the member states as to the result to be achieved, but leave it up to the states to decide on the form and method of compliance. Ultimately, the drafting of new national legislations based on these framework decisions would lead to the harmonization of some criminal laws and sanctions in the EU after 1999, which would comprise a degree of Europeanization in this area (see Chapter 5). Under the Treaty of Amsterdam, "decisions" (new K.6.2c, i.e., Article 34.2c) are used for any purpose (e.g., setting up a new crime-fighting body or program) other than the approximation of regulations and laws, and thus perform many of the tasks formally conducted by "joint actions" under the original TEU.

In sum, the EU takes action on JHA under the Treaty of Amsterdam by making use of any of four legal instruments, namely common positions, conventions, framework decisions, and decisions. An important innovation of the Treaty of Amsterdam is that its Article 34 grants the Commission power to initiate proposals in these forms regarding any aspect of JHA, including judicial cooperation in criminal matters, customs cooperation, and police cooperation. As before, however, the Commission right of initiative is not exclusive (as it is in Pillar I) but shares it with the Council (any single member state).

Also similar is that the JHA must take any of the four types of actions noted above by unanimous vote. However, in contrast to the terms of the TEU, under which the JHA Council was permitted to decide in advance that

.ing measures" related to joint actions should be taken by quali-
rity voting, the new Article K.6.2.c (Article 34.2c) specifies that
.neasures *must* be taken by QMV (at least sixty-two of the votes cast
. least ten states). Furthermore, by virtue of the new Article K.11 (Arti-
e 39), the Treaty of Amsterdam has strengthened the role of the EP in this
policy area by requiring that "the Council shall consult with the European
Parliament before taking any measures" under new Article K.6 (Article 34)
(e.g., framework decisions or decisions). Under old Article K.6 of the TEU,
the president of the Council was only obligated to keep the Parliament
informed of the discussions in the JHA Council and to see that its views are
"duly taken into consideration."

Although only a small step, these new provisions have moved policymaking on JHA, particularly on police cooperation, in the direction of
supranationalism, for they bring the EP formally into all areas of EU decisionmaking concerning police and judicial cooperation in criminal matters
(via the consultation procedure). This has included, for example, JHA
Council "decisions" since 1999 to expand the remit of Europol to include
crimes contained in the annex of its convention, as well as measures taken
to implement these decisions. Given the direct legitimacy of the EP to the
people of Europe, the Treaty of Amsterdam has made policymaking in this
regard more democratic and, in doing so, has altered the balance of institutional power in this aspect of the Third Pillar in favor of the Parliament
(though the Council will still holds most of the power in this area).

Of course, the EP's victory in this regard is small compared to its winning of co-decision powers via the Treaty of Amsterdam in many aspects of
the First Pillar. As Michael Nentwich and Gerda Falker have argued in their
analysis of the general institutional balance in the EU after the Treaty of
Amsterdam, the next step in granting the Parliament greater powers would
be to endow it with co-decision rights in the Third Pillar wherever QMV is
specified for the Council, as is now the case in many areas of the Community pillar.[67] The Treaty of Nice, which was negotiated and signed in 2000,
supercedes the Treaty of Amsterdam, yet it contains nothing to address this
issue (see Chapter 5).

Europol in an Era of Change

The final events leading up to Europol starting its full duties under its convention, protocols, and the Treaty of Amsterdam took place during the German presidency in the first half of 1999, which would prove to be a chal-
lenging time period for the European Union. On the positive side, the
monetary union based on the euro was implemented at the start of year, cap-
ping decades of trials and tribulations in this area since the 1970s. However,

the creation of the "euro zone" among eleven of the EU members was soon overshadowed by a number of other key events, some of them quite traumatic.

Among these events was a crisis involving the Commission of President Jacques Santer, which had been installed for a five-year term in January 1995 upon the enlargement of the EU. By the start of 1999, the Santer Commission had been involved in a controversy with the European Parliament for over a year concerning the discharging of the 1996 community budget (closing the books). The dispute had been only temporarily resolved at the end of 1998, when a successful EP vote of censure against the Commission was only narrowly avoided after Santer agreed to allow an independent panel of experts to review the Commission's handling of EU finances.

This report was published in March 1999 and revealed several cases of fraud, mismanagement, and nepotism among some members of the Commission. In response, Santer and his whole college of twenty commissioners resigned en masse on March 15, 1999 (though they would remain temporarily in caretaker roles until after their successors took office). Among its findings, the report was critical of Anita Gradin, the commissioner responsible for Justice and Home Affairs, for her mishandling of fraud and financial control, which were in her portfolio as well.

Even before the Commission scandal, many were skeptical of Gradin's ability to carry out her duties.[68] A former Swedish minister of Parliament, Gradin had a background in social work, as well as labor and trade relations. Her only JHA credentials were her terms on the Council of Europe's Committee on Migration, Refugees, and Demography (1978–1982) and as minister responsible for immigrant and equality affairs in Sweden's Labor Ministry (1982–1986). Already hampered by her status as a commissioner from a new member state in a policy area where the Commission had previously had little or no role, Gradin exacerbated her situation by filling her cabinet and staff almost exclusively with fellow Swedes, who were also not sufficiently familiar with the internal workings of the EU.[69] In her study of the Commission and JHA, Emek Uçarer argues that Gradin's inexperience and cautious leadership style, compared to the assertiveness of her predecessor, Pádraig Flynn, also contributed to her inability to make sufficient progress on JHA, even by her own timetables.[70] Thus, the resignation of the Commission and unlikelihood that Sweden would renominate Gradin meant that JHA would potentially be provided leadership from the Commission that it had previously lacked.

The resignation of the Commission in March 1999 marked the start of a period of transition in the EU that would impact police cooperation in many regards. A special European Council was held on March 24–25 to forge an agreement on "Agenda 2000," the budgetary blueprint for the enlargement of the EU. However, it also proved to be the occasion for the heads of states and government to nominate former Italian prime minister Romano Prodi to be the new Commission president.

Much of the spring of 1999 was dominated by the conflict in Kosovo, the human-rights violations there, and the potential for a new wave of refugees into the EU, given the thousands displaced by the violence. With peace negotiations in February and March having failed, NATO's air strikes against Yugoslavia began on the opening day of the Berlin European Council and would continue until June 10. Responding to the crisis, the JHA Council held a special meeting on April 7, which served to highlight the issues of refugees and asylum in the EU under the new Third Pillar.

Soon after this, on May 1, 1999, the Treaty of Amsterdam finally entered into force, with France being the final member state to approve (by constitutional amendment) and deposit the instruments of ratification in late March. In addition to implementing the changes discussed above, the new treaty also brought the *acquis* governing the Schengen states area into the *acquis* of the EU. Later in May, the first meeting of the so-called Mixed Committee was held in association with the implementation and development of the Schengen *acquis*. Consisting of representatives from the Commission, the fifteen member states, Norway, and Iceland, Mixed Committee meetings have since become regular fixtures at most sessions of the JHA Council. At the formal JHA Council meeting, on May 27, the UK and Ireland, which remained outside of the Schengen free-travel area, expressed their interest in participating in the provisions of the Schengen *acquis* on law enforcement and criminal judicial cooperation.

This meeting was also the occasion for the passage of a Council resolution calling for new guidelines to guard against counterfeiting of the euro. With over €130 billion worth of bank notes and coins scheduled to enter circulation on January 1, 2002, this resolution also referred to a possible role for Europol in the anticounterfeiting effort. The idea that the EU's own police agency might be given the power to investigate and even arrest suspected counterfeiters of its currency had been around even before the eurozone went into effect. In the wake of the "disappearance" of a security hologram for the new currency's bank notes, the European Commission had proposed in July 1998, with the support of the EP, that Europol's remit be widened to include the fight against euro counterfeiters (but with no new operative powers).[71] Later, upon the inauguration of Europol the following October, Jürgen Storbeck also came out in support of this, followed in November by Serge Bertholme, the treasurer of the National Bank of Belgium.[72] Thus, even before Europol became fully operation under the terms of the Treaty of Amsterdam, events were already moving in the direction of a widening of its crime-fighting remit, namely protecting the euro, the crown jewel of European integration.

The Cologne European Council on June 3–4, 1999, marked the end of the German presidency. With the conflict in Kosovo still winding down, the summit was dominated by foreign policy. NATO Secretary-General Javier Solana was named secretary-general of the Council and the EU's first high representative for Common Foreign and Security Policy. In addition, plans were established for work on a "Charter on Fundamental Rights," as well as the next IGC, to tackle the issue of institutional reform that was left undone by the Treaty of Amsterdam. Although JHA was not prominent on the agenda for the Cologne summit, the heads of state and government recognized that plans were already under way for a special European Council to be held in Tampere on the topic of Justice and Home Affairs. It was hoped that the EU could accelerate its progress toward establishing the AFSJ called for in the new Treaty of Amsterdam.

Having acquired new legislative powers on this treaty, the European Parliament, fresh from its confrontation with the outgoing Commission, held new elections in mid-June. This marked the first time that elections were held in all fifteen member states at the same time and resulted in a shift of power in favor of the center-right European People's Party (EPP). This set up a conflict between the EP and the Council, which was filled predominately with representatives of center-left governments (e.g., the UK, France, and, since September 1998, Germany). The first dispute in this context was the nomination of the new commissioners, which, for the first time (under the new treaty) was happening under the influence of the new Commission President Prodi, whose own nomination had been approved by the EP in May.

On August 30, 1999, a week of hearings began in the EP for the Commission appointees. Along with other members of the new College of Commissioners, António Vitorino of Portugal was sworn in as the new commissioner for Justice and Home Affairs on September 17. Thus, one chapter in the history of Europol came to end and another began. Fully operational since July 1, 1999, and functioning with the new powers granted to it by the Treaty of Amsterdam, Europol was about to begin a new phase of its young existence. With an expanded legal role for the Commission, a new commissioner in charge of JHA, and heightened attention drawn to it by the upcoming Tampere European Council, Europol, as well as the general nature of European cooperation on internal security, was about to enter a period of rapid development and change.

Explaining the Development of Europol to 1999

By the late 1990s, European integration regarding internal security had moved in the direction of supranationalism, in contrast to its highly intergovernmental beginnings in the 1970s. In the era of the Trevi Group, cooperation took place outside of the legal scope of the EC and totally excluded any meaningful role for the European Commission, Parliament, or Court of

Justice. Although the initial work of the Trevi Group included studies and information exchanges concerning general policing, its main operative focus was limited to secure communication links on terrorism. Gradually, the work of the Trevi Group expanded into several other areas of internal security, yet the nature of its decisionmaking institutions remained purely intergovernmental, and it never established a permanent secretariat. The development of police cooperation in the direction of supranationalism since the Maastricht Treaty was shaped by the same types of internal and external factors that have played a part in the progression of EU integration in general and the earlier evolution of collaboration on internal security in particular.

With entry into force of the Europol Convention and the Treaty of Amsterdam in 1999, the nature of internal security cooperation in the European Union changed significantly. The EU finally had at its disposal formal institutions to help in the fight against organized crime of all kinds, particularly Europol, a permanent, central police agency capable of dealing with crime proactively and without the prior authorization of the JHA Council regarding specific cases. Europol must be considered to be at least somewhat supranational in nature for a number of reasons. It is autonomous to the extent that it will not have to consult with the JHA Council in the course of its daily operations. Moreover, institutional reforms in the Third Pillar under the Treaty of Amsterdam have meant that the EU's supranational institutions—the Commission, Parliament, and Court—have become more important in making policies regarding policing. Explaining why this evolution took place necessitates a consideration of internal factors such as federalist ideology, functionalism, concern for democracy and subsidiarity, as well as external events.

Although federalist ideology seems to have been a salient factor for Chancellor Kohl in his proposal to create a common police agency for the EU, it is less clear that a unionist impetus was influential in the actual development of Europol after the entry into force of the Maastricht Treaty. For example, the decision by fourteen of the member states to allow the European Court of Justice to settle disputes regarding the Europol Convention was based more on a pragmatic solution to deal with expected problems than on a federalist acceptance of the Court's legitimacy and desire to expand its role in the EU. In this regard, it seems that a prediction of liberal intergovernmentalism is correct, namely that the agreement regarding the ECJ stemmed from member states seeking credible commitments about how future matters would be resolved.

Concerning policing issues during this time, the principle of subsidiarity also seemed more important than federalism. Indeed, subsidiarity was embodied in Title VI (new Article K.5) of the Treaty of Amsterdam: "This Title shall not affect the exercise of the responsibilities incumbent upon member states with regard to the maintenance of law and order and the safeguarding of internal security." In other words, the member states agreed that most areas of policing should be left to the member states and their constituent governments. This impact of subsidiary continues to limit the growth of Europol today, meaning that an operative role of any kind for Europol in everyday policing (i.e., uniformed patrolling) should not be expected in the next twenty-five years, or perhaps ever.

The internal factor of functionalism also played a more significant role than federalism in the development of the EU's approach to internal security between 1993 and 1999. The perception existed in Europe that certain types of crime were facilitated by the EU's increasingly open internal borders, at least in the Schengen zone. Moreover, it was assumed in many circles that collective efforts at dealing with these crimes would be more effective than traditional national means. It can be argued that these impressions strengthened support for Europol. In other words, the development of Europol during this phase of its existence can be at least partially explained by functional spillover, in that the cooperation to create free movement of persons led to intensified police cooperation in the form of Europol.

There is some data to support the notion that organized crime in the member states was indeed becoming increasingly international in the mid-1990s. In 1995, for example, Germany's BKA (federal office of criminal investigations) conducted 787 separate investigations of organized crime, involving 8,000 suspects from 80 countries and more than 50,000 separate offenses.[73] Compared to 1994, the share of non-Germans involved in these offenses in 1995 was up 4.0 percent to 63.6 percent.[74] In 1996, the number of investigations had increased to 845, but the number of suspects involved remained about the same and the number of recorded offenses was down to just under 48,000. However, three-quarters of all the cases of organized crime that year had international connections, and the number of non-Germans involved among suspects had risen to about two-thirds.[75]

Increased attention to these statistics may be indicated by the growing number of offenses added to the EDU's remit after 1994 and now included among Europol's present responsibilities. Whether or not crimes in these areas actually increased after implementation of the free-travel zone in 1995 is not as important as the assumption that they did or soon would. By embracing the idea of Europol, expanding its remit, and endowing it with new operative powers, real or potential, European leaders at least hoped to create the impression on their constituencies that they were seeking new solutions to their domestic crime problems.

External factors also help to explain the development of Europol during this time. Organized crime within the EU was increasingly perceived to have sources that were indeed external to the European Union. Although Latin American and Asian sources of Western Europe's drug problem endured, more attention was focused on organized crime in Central and

Eastern Europe, including the Balkans. As an external source of increased police cooperation in recent years, crime in the CEECs was significant in two main regards.

First, these countries were perceived as important sources of crime taking place in the EU. Several areas of Europol's remit were aimed at crimes involving criminal organizations in the CEECs. These include the trafficking of drugs (e.g., via Albania), illegal immigration networks (especially from Romania), and motor vehicle theft. All of the countries in the region, including all of the EU applicant states, experienced increases in illicit drug use and trafficking during this time, with falling prices for cocaine, hashish, and heroin indicating that their supply was increasing.[76] In addition, the new convertibility of local currencies in the CEECs made these countries new centers of money laundering for transnational criminal organizations.[77] The direct impact of organized crime in the CEECs on the EU was demonstrated vividly when the Mercedes sedan belonging to Berlin's chief of police was stolen in broad daylight and later recovered near Moscow, its odometer indicating it must have been flown there, possibly by Russian military aircraft.[78] Thus, in one regard, increased EU police cooperation has been shaped by the perception that individual methods are inadequate to deal with crime problems that have been worsened by organized crime originating outside the EU.

The second way crime in the CEECs fostered collaboration among the member states in the area of internal security during the 1990s was through the influence of the impending accession of several of these states to the EU. At the time the Treaty of Amsterdam was being negotiated, it was expected that as many as five of the CEECs (i.e., Estonia, Poland, the Czech Republic, Hungary, and Slovenia) could join the EU by 2002, bringing into the Union their own criminal organizations, a strong presence of the Russian mafia, and all of the crime problems stemming from these. The expectation in the EU was that the next enlargement, in contrast to the last one in 1995, would bring with it a significant crime problem. While holding the presidency of the JHA Council in 1998, British Home Secretary Jack Straw believed that the explosion of organized crime in Eastern Europe since the fall of the Berlin Wall would mean that judicial and policing issues would play a central role in the EU's membership negotiations with the post-Soviet CEECs (which began in March).[79] French Interior Minister Elizabeth Guigou argued that the EU neglected these issues in its work preparing the candidate countries for membership, and "now we will have to work twice as hard to catch up."[80]

The preparations for the next group of new EU members entailed assisting these countries in improving their criminal-justice institutions, as called for in the 1997 Action Plan (Recommendation 3). To this end, a preaccession pact with the CEECs and Cyprus was signed at the May 1998

JHA Council, outlining fifteen principles of action. These included plans for the applicant states to develop formal ties with Europol (using liaison officers) and, in conjunction with the PHARE (Poland-Hungary: Actions for Economic Reconstruction) program, the extension to these countries of the EU's various training programs (Oison, Falcone, etc.).[81] In sum, police cooperation during this time was not only impacted by crime stemming from the CEECs, but was also shaped by the expected accession of these countries to the EU.[82]

Compared to the pre-Maastricht era, terrorism was not as salient during this period as an external source of Europol's development. To be sure, terrorism was perceived to be a significant problem at the time, contributing to the addition of terrorism to Europol's remit by 1999. However, the perceived terrorist threat in Europe during the 1990s stemmed from the internal matter of Spain's enduring problems with Basque separatist violence. In comparison, terrorism emanating from external sources, including, for example, Turkey, regarding its Kurdish separatists, and Algeria, concerning Islamic fundamentalists, was less influential. The same low level of concern was also true for potential terrorist threats with sources in Iraq, Libya, and elsewhere in Middle East.

Finally, as the pace of police cooperation was hastened by the internal and external factors described above, the actual *form* this cooperation has taken was shaped by concerns for democracy. Just as the work of the Trevi Group was criticized for its secrecy and lack of transparency, the negotiation and ratification of the Europol Convention and its protocols was influenced by concerns for democracy, including the political accountability of Europol and the protection of personal privacy. Various attempts were made to address these concerns, including the establishment of the international management and supervisory boards for Europol and the formalized role for the European Parliament on JHA legislation under the new Article K of the Treaty of Amsterdam. Concerning this, the JHA Council had to wait for the EP's opinion on pending proposals before passing them formally. With this new power won in the 1990s, the EP became much more active in JHA matters after 1999, when the Treaty of Amsterdam took effect. However, as before, the EP's committee reports and final opinions would continue to be ignored by the Council in most instances, leading to enduring concerns for a democratic deficit in the EU's policymaking on Justice and Home Affairs.

Notes

1. In September 1998, the EDU's liaison bureau in Spain began testing an automatic translation software, "T1," developed by a U.S. company, Lernout and Hauspie. It was hoped that this software would eventually speed up the flow of information

on the Europol's liaison network. See *M2 Presswire,* August 5, 1998; *Intelligence Newsletter,* "Automatic Translation: Europol Tests," October 1, 1998.

2. E. Tucker, "Europol Team Is Already on the Case," *Financial Times* (London), February 8–9, 1997.

3. F. Monaco, "Europol: The Culmination of the European Union's International Police Cooperation Efforts," *Fordham International Law Journal,* vol. 19, 1995, 281; J. Benyon, "The Politics of Police Co-operation in the European Union," *International Journal of the Sociology of Law,* vol. 24, 1996, 367.

4. Monaco, 278.

5. Ibid., 281–282.

6. Benyon, "The Politics," 367.

7. Official Report of the Activities of the Europol Drugs Unit in 1996; Tucker, "Europol Team."

8. Benyon, "The Politics," 367.

9. T. Bunyan, "Ministers Agree New Steps Toward Euro-Police Force," *New Statesman & Society,* vol. 8, no. 344, March 17, 1995, 10.

10. N. Walker, "Policing the European Union: The Politics of Transition," in *Policing Change, Changing Police: International Perspectives,* ed. O. Marenin (New York: Garland Publishing, 1996), 268.

11. *The Economist,* March 23, 1996, 52.

12. Ibid.

13. J. Palmer, "Bruton Backs Federal Force," *The Guardian* (Manchester), July 12, 1996, 12.

14. N. Buckley, "EU Leaders Agree Action on Security," *The Financial Times* (London), December 16, 1996.

15. Ibid.

16. E. Tucker, "Closer Links in Crime Crusade," *Financial Times* (London), April 29, 1997.

17. Council of the European Union, *Action Plan to Combat Organized Crime* ("1997 Action Plan"), Brussels, April 28, 1997, No C 251/1–18; Tucker, "Closer Links," 3.

18. JHA Council Meeting, May 28–29, 1998.

19. Ibid.

20. JHA Council Meeting, March 26, 1998.

21. Europol Drugs Unit (EDU), *Annual Report for 1997,* The Hague, 1998.

22. Tucker, "Europol Team"; A. Evans-Pritchard, "The European Police State . . . ," *The Daily Telegraph* (London), February 2, 1998.

23. Tucker, "Europol Team."

24. C. Driessen, "Crime-Busting with a Computer Mouse—Europol Convention Now in Force," Deutsche Press-Agentur, October 19, 1998; A. Evans-Pritchard, "The European Police State," *The Daily Telegraph* (London), February 3, 1998.

25. J. Butler, "New Europe-Wide Bid to Beat Top Crooks," *Press Association Newsfile,* October 1, 1998.

26. JHA Council Meeting, March 26, 1998.

27. While the TECS was being developed, an interim system was in place, along with a secure intranet network at Europol headquarters, along with secure fax gateways and encrypted e-mail connections to link the liaison officers with their national units.

28. JHA Council Meeting, May 28–29, 1998.

29. The Council had opposed a higher budget of ECU 15,852,000 at its meeting in May 1998. See JHA Council Meeting, May 28–29, 1998.

30. *Agence France Presse,* "Europol Misses Deadline to Go Fully Operational," September 24, 1998.

31. Monaco, 283.

32. B. Hebenton and T. Thomas, *Policing Europe: Co-operation, Conflict and Control* (New York: St. Martin's Press, 1995), 87; Benyon, "The Politics," 367.

33. A. Guyomarch, "Cooperation in the Fields of Policing and Judicial Affairs," in *New Challenges to the European Union: Policies and Policy-Making,* ed. S. Stavridis et al. (Aldershot, England: Dartmouth Publishing Company, 1997), 126–127.

34. M. Anderson et al., *Policing the European Union* (Oxford: Clarendon Press, 1995), 65.

35. For Jürgen Storbeck's critical analysis of the Europol Convention, see J. Storbeck, "Europol: Probleme and Lösungen," *Kriminalistik,* no. 1, 1996, 17–21.

36. Evans-Pritchard, "The European Police State." This would, in fact, be done, in June 2000, after a Europol staff member was charged with embezzling funds. See Chap. 5.

37. N. Cohen, "Hold on a Minute . . . ," *The Observer,* December 14, 1997.

38. Walker, 9.

39. *The Economist,* March 23, 1996, 52.

40. Walker, note 9.

41. *The Economist,* March 11, 1995, p. 53.

42. *European Report,* February 14, 1998.

43. Ibid.

44. The United Kingdom, for example, was represented at the time by the director-general of its National Criminal Intelligence Service, John Abbot.

45. Monaco, 286.

46. Ibid., 297.

47. Ibid., 287.

48. Ibid., 288.

49. Ibid., 273–274.

50. Guyomarch, 146–147.

51. The HLG's Action Plan of 1997 recommended (No. 25e) that Europol should have access to the SIS.

52. Monaco, 300.

53. The rules of procedure for the Joint Supervisory Body were still being developed even after the Convention had entered into force, keeping Europol from becoming fully operational.

54. A. Evans-Pritchard, "Europeans Allowed to Keep Files on the Innocent," *The Vancouver Sun,* February 3, 1998.

55. J. Cusack, "McKenna Says Proposed EU Police Force a Threat to Citizen's Rights," *The Irish Times* (Dublin), October 14, 1997.

56. Evans-Pritchard, "Europeans Allowed."

57. Monaco, 301.

58. Evans-Pritchard, "Europeans Allowed."

59. M. Nentwich and G. Falkner, "The Treaty of Amsterdam: Towards a New Institutional Balance," *European Integration online Papers (EIoP)* vol. 1, no. 15, 1997, Table 1; http://eiop.or.at/eiop/texte/1997-0151.htm.

60. In the "consolidated version" of the amended TEU, these are Articles 29–42 and 43–45.

61. This is permitted within the restrictions specified in Article K.12, as well as those found in Articles K.15–K.16.

62. Nentwich and Falkner, 10–11.

63. Ibid, 11.

64. W. A. Tupman, "Supranational Investigation After Amsterdam, the Corpus Juris and Agenda 2000," *Information and Communications Technology Law* (Abingdon), June 1998, 8.

65. Evans-Pritchard, "Europeans Allowed"; J. Dillon, "Row over 'Untouchable' Euro Cops," *Press Association Newsfile,* February 13, 1998.

66. European Commission, SCADplus, "Activities of the European Union" (summary of legislation on Justice and Home Affairs): http://europa.eu.int/scadplus/leg/en/s22004.htm, 1998.

67. Netwich and Falkner, 9.

68. Uçarer, 2001, 7.

69. Ibid., 7–8.

70. Ibid., 8.

71. S. Iskandar," Europol May Be Given Job of Fighting Euro Counterfeiters," *Financial Times* (London), July 21, 1998; Toby Helm, "Call for Action to Stop Euro Fakers," *The Daily Telegraph,* July 23, 1998.

72. Gordan Cramb, "EU's Police Hobbled by Treaty Delays: Europol Launch Replaces Drug Unit," *Financial Times,* October 2, 1998; *Financial Times* (London), "Banknotes Forgery Warning," November 14, 1998.

73. P. Norman, "Germans Look More Co-operation on Crime," *Financial Times* (London), January 3, 1997.

74. Ibid.

75. *Focus Magazin,* "Europol Muss Endlich Richtig Loslegen," March 16, 1998, 99.

76. C. Bobinski, "EU Applicant States Pressed to Close the Door on Drugs," *Financial Times* (London), May 1, 1998.

77. Ibid.

78. B. A. Gilman and C. Cederschiold (MEP), "Co-Operation Against Crime Must Intensify," Letter to the Editor, *Financial Times* (London), June 15, 1998.

79. P. Smyth, "Action Plan on Refugees Likely to Cause Rights Protests," *The Irish Times* (Dublin), January 16, 1998.

80. Ibid.

81. Hungary, the Czech Republic, and Poland were among the first applicant states to do so.

82. See W. Wessels, "The Third Pillar: Plea for a Single Theoretical Research Agenda," in *The Third Pillar of the European Union: Cooperation in the Fields of Justice and Home Affairs,* ed. J. Monar and R. Morgan (Brussels: European Interuniversity Press, 1994), 236–237.

5

Checking the Scoreboard:
Progress After Tampere

THE START OF THE FINNISH PRESIDENCY ON JULY 1, 1999, COINCIDED with Europol becoming fully operational upon the belated entry into force of necessary protocols to the Europol Convention. This marked the end of several years of organizational evolution for Europol since its conception in the Intergovernmental Conference (IGC) of 1991, which had drafted the Maastricht Treaty. However, this juncture also marked the start of a series of events involving the rapid development of the broader environment of police cooperation and crime fighting in the EU, with Europol at its center.

The Prodi Commission and JHA

In contrast to the era of the Maastricht Treaty, the European Commission would begin to play a much greater role in the area of police cooperation. As noted in the previous chapter, Europol's start of full operations was followed by the installation of a new commissioner for Justice and Home Affairs, António Vitorino, who was unique in his combination of a number of key attributes. In one regard, the terms of the Treaty of Amsterdam created an enhanced role for the Commission concerning JHA. Among its new powers, perhaps the most prominent role given to the Commission under the new treaty is its ability to share with the Council the initiation of legislative proposals in all areas of JHA. Combined with the prescription of creating an "area of freedom, security, and justice" (AFSJ), this provision would offer Vitorino more opportunities for making progress on JHA compared to those enjoyed by either of his predecessors.

In addition, Vitorino was also in a much better position than Flynn or Gradin to take advantage of the Commission's new legal role. That is because the commissioner of JHA would have, for the first time, an entire directorate-general (DG) dedicated to his portfolio. This was created by

Romano Prodi soon after he assumed the presidency of the Commission in recognition of the growing importance of the JHA field.[1] Adrían Fortescue, the sitting head of the JHA Task Force in the Council secretariat, was elevated to the position of director general of the new DG, which he would continue to lead into 2002. Fortescue's DG was divided into two main "Directions" (A and B), which were subdivided into nine specialized units, including one for Police and Customs Cooperation (Unit B/1). By the summer of 2000, this DG's staff numbered approximately 180, representing a large increase over the task force's staff of just 46.[2] Thus, unlike commissioners of the past, Vitorino would not face the kinds of institutional and bureaucratic constraints that had inhibited the influence of the Commission in JHA until that point.

However, at about the same time, the European Parliament also re-vamped its Committee on Citizen's Freedom, Rights, Justice, and Home Affairs. Under the direction of British Liberal Democrat MEP, Graham Watson, who was elected chairman, the committee become exceptionally active in monitoring progress on JHA.[3] Along with the Council and the new Commission under Vitorino, the EP would thus offer a third, and increasing audible, voice on JHA.

Finally, in addition to his other attributes, Vitorino possessed several personal traits that seemed to make him uniquely qualified to accelerate cooperation on JHA.[4] Although he was the youngest member of the new Commission, Vitorinio was an expert on constitutional law and justice and came to his new job with a wealth of experience on JHA. This included his service on Portugal's parliamentary committee on European integration (1980–1984) and, more notably, as the past chairman of the EP's Commit-tee on Civil Liberties and Internal Affairs (1994). In contrast to his prede-cessor, Vitorino's strong communication and leadership skills would also provide energetic direction for JHA and its new DG.[5]

In sum, the Treaty of Amsterdam, the new DG, and Vitorino's experi-ence and personal qualities put the Commission in the position of being more influential than ever before in the area of Justice and Home Affairs. When Vitorino assumed office in September, his new DG, along with the Finnish presidency, was already making final plans for the upcoming Spe-cial European Council on JHA, which would be held in Tampere. This sum-mit resulted in measures that not only hastened cooperation on JHA, but also promoted a more prominent role for the Commission in this area. In doing so, this created a further shift in the direction of supranationalism regarding police cooperation in the EU.

The Tampere European Council

The decision to hold an extraordinary European Council devoted to JHA had been made a year earlier after a proposal by the Spanish prime minister, José

María Aznar, at an informal meeting of the heads of state and government at Pörtschach am Wörthersee, Austria, on October 24–25, 1998.[6] This "brainstorming" session, held in the foothills of the Alps, was aimed at planning for the future of the European Union under the Treaty of Amsterdam and beyond. At the time, the decision to conduct the special JHA summit was overshadowed, at least in the media, by other agenda items, namely unemployment and Common Foreign and Security Policy (CFSP). The latter topic took center stage with Britain's Tony Blair's expression of support for a defense arm for the EU, as well as a visit to the meeting by Palestinian leader Yassir Arafat. In fact, the formal announcement of the agreement on the special JHA summit would not come until the Austrian presidency's conclusions from the Vienna European Council in December 1998. The meeting in Pörtschach was also the occasion for the heads of state and government to honor Germany's Helmut Kohl, recently defeated in Bundestag elections, with the title of "Citizen of Europe" for his contributions to the European integration. Thus, even as Europol lost its long-time champion in Kohl, the decision at Pörtschach to hold a special European Council on JHA in 1999 promised further, if not more rapid, EU cooperation on policing.

Preparations for the Tampere summit were made throughout 1999 during the German and Finnish presidencies, starting with a letter of March 18 to the heads of state and government written jointly by Kohl's successor, Chancellor Gerhard Schröder, and Paavo Lipponen, prime minister of Finland. This letter emphasized that the aim expressed in the Treaty of Amsterdam to establish an AFSJ was closely related to the basic goal of bringing Europe closer to its citizens, and that significant "political results" must be achieved at Tampere. Following this letter, the incoming presidency distributed a detailed questionnaire to ministers and senior officials and held extensive talks with many of them during a tour of EU capitals in April 1999.[7]

Thus, by the time the first JHA Council of the Finnish presidency was convened in Luxembourg on October 4, 1999, there was already much consensus on the agenda of the Tampere summit. In anticipation of the new priorities and objectives that would surely result from the Tampere meeting later that month, this JHA Council had a limited agenda. It served as the occasion for the Council's first debate on the Commission's new Action Plan to combat drugs for 2000–2004, as well as the acceptance of the final report from the High-Level Group on Asylum and Immigration. Over lunch, the Council also discussed the state of preparations for the Tampere summit, noting that it would deal with three main themes of JHA, namely immigration and asylum policy, the creation of a European judicial area, and the fight against cross-border crime. Meeting on October 11–12, the foreign ministers later finalized these plans in the General Affairs Council, setting the stage for the historic Tampere summit.

The specific points discussed at Tampere drew on unresolved items named in the action plans agreed upon at Amsterdam in 1997 and Vienna in

1998. More importantly, the Tampere summit was also aimed at implementing a series of measures called upon in the Treaty of Amsterdam, with the ultimate goal of creating the AFSJ. Despite the common goals contained in these documents and the consensus over the summit's agenda, there were some notable differences among the member states about priorities for action.

As a frontline state regarding potential refugees and immigrants, Germany made the development of a common EU policy on asylum and migration a high priority. The system of burden sharing that they proposed was supported by Austria and Italy. However, these proposals were resisted by Denmark, Ireland, and the UK, which were more insulated from migration pressures. Meanwhile, the French stressed the need for the creation of a European judicial area, including the aim of harmonizing national criminal laws throughout the EU and the establishment of a European prosecutor's office.

In contrast, the British at that time supported the less grand idea of improving mutual recognition of judicial standards and judgments.[8] On the issue of crime, the British came out as the main supporters of a Union-wide "Operational Task Force of Police Chiefs" to complement Europol, as well as the establishment of a true European police college, which they hoped to host. In general, there was more agreement among the member states on crime fighting than on crime prevention. Concerning each of the three main themes of the summit's agenda, officials from member states' justice ministries were generally more supportive of deeper forms of cooperation on JHA than their colleagues in interior ministries (where most states' policing policies were determined).[9]

Along with these concerns among and within the member states, a number of concerns related to civil liberties arose as it became clear that the EU was about to embark on progress toward creating the AFSJ. In the run-up to Tampere, the new Commission president, Romano Prodi, attempted to alleviate concerns that this meeting might be viewed as a "summit of repression." In a letter to the summit's host and chair, Prime Minister Lipponen, Prodi argued: "Tampere has clearly to offer our citizens the guarantees they seek in terms of basic rights, and from this point of view, the Charter [of fundamental rights] will be of major importance."[10] In response to these concerns, this extraordinary meeting of the European Council on JHA was linked to work on the charter, serving as a forum for final agreement on the composition and working method of the body charged with drafting the charter.[11]

However, the main outcome of the summit was indeed the establishment of ten so-called milestones toward a "union of freedom, security and justice" in the EU. These ten milestones constituted the main subsections of the Tampere Conclusions, with each section broken into numbered points indicating specific objectives. The first nine points of this document served as an introduction, emphasizing normative rationale for cooperation on JHA. Point 1 expressed the EU's "shared commitment to freedom-based human rights, democratic institutions, and the rule of law." The fight against organized crime was justified by the threat it poses to people's freedom and legal rights (point 6), both for citizens and noncitizens of the EU (point 2).

The remaining Tampere Conclusions consisted of the ten milestones and their concrete objectives grouped into three categories, as well as a fourth section devoted to external action. The Tampere Conclusions, its four sections, ten milestones, and sixty-two points of action (in parentheses), can be summarized as follows:

Introduction (points 1–9)
(A) A Common Asylum and Immigration Policy (points 10–27)
  • Milestone I. Partnership with countries of origin
  • Milestone II. A common european asylum system
  • Milestone III. Fair treatment of third-country nationals
  • Milestone IV. Management of migration flows
(B) A Genuine European Area of Justice (points 28–39)
  • Milestone V. Better access to justice in Europe
  • Milestone VI. Mutual recognition on judicial decisions
  • Milestone VII. Greater convergence in civil law
(C) A Union-Wide Fight Against Crime (points 40–58)
  • Milestone VIII. Reventing crime at the level of the Union
  • Milestone IX. Stepping up cooperation against crime
  • Milestone X. Special action against money laundering
(D) Stronger External Action (points 59–62)

Although the specific objectives contained in each of the four main areas pertain, at least indirectly, to police cooperation in the EU, clearly those contained in part C have had the most significant implications for this aspect of JHA policy. Given their importance, these are worth discussing in some detail.

Point 40 noted that "a balanced development of union-wide measures against crime should be achieved while protecting the freedom and legal rights of individuals and economic operators." Under milestone VIII, "Preventing crime at the level of the Union," point 41 called for the development of national crime-prevention programs. Point 42 prescribed the exchange of "best practices" and strengthening of cooperative networks of national authorities.

Milestone IX, "Stepping up cooperation against crime," called for several noteworthy steps regarding policing, including those that proposed to increase Europol's ability to be involved with operational police work.

Point 43 proposed that the Council should devise rules to allow "joint investigative teams" to be established for combating drug trafficking and terrorism, including participation by Europol in a support capacity as foreseen in the Treaty of Amsterdam. A European Operational Task Force of Police Chiefs was suggested in point 44 to "exchange, in cooperation with Europol, experience, best practices and information on current trends in cross-border crime and contribute to the planning of operative actions." In addition, point 45 called upon the Council to strengthen Europol's ability to initiate, conduct, or coordinate investigations or to create joint investigative teams."

The other points in this section prescribed various measures to strengthen the entire institutional and legal infrastructure of police cooperation surrounding Europol. A European judicial cooperation unit, known as "Eurojust," was proposed in point 46, including a deadline of the end of 2001 for its creation. This was envisioned as an international body of national prosecutors, magistrates, and police officers designed to work with national authorities and Europol to simplify the legal aspects of criminal investigations (e.g., search warrants and surveillance). The idea for Eurojust had long been in the making. Most recently, the idea of a European prosecutor's office was included in the 1997 *Corpus Juris,* produced by several experts on JHA. The idea for this was also raised by the Germans and the French at the 1999 informal JHA Council in Turku, Finland, before being agreed upon at Tampere.

In addition to Eurojust, the European Police College (CEPOL) was proposed in point 47 of the Tampere milestones. This was to begin as a "virtual" institution, entailing a network of training institutes that would also be open to police officers from candidate countries. Eventually, CEPOL (its acronym from its French name, Collège européen de Police) would have a permanent secretariat physically located in one of the member states.

To facilitate the common fight against crime, point 48 called upon the member states to agree on "common definitions, incriminations, and sanctions" for various forms of crime. This was the intended goal for various types of financial crime, including money laundering, corruption, and counterfeiting of the euro. Other crimes mentioned under this heading were drug trafficking, trafficking in human beings (particularly exploitation of women), sexual exploitation of children, high-tech crime, and environmental crime. Point 49 drew attention to "serious economic crime" relating to taxes and duties, and calls upon the members states to provide full mutual legal assistance (MLA) toward investigation and prosecution in this regard. Finally, the last prescription in this section, point 50, highlighted the special importance of the drug problem and called on the Council to adopt the 2000–2004 European Strategy Against Drugs before the upcoming Helsinki summit in December.

The third section in part C of the Tampere Conclusions was milestone X, "Special action against money laundering," containing the next eight related points. Its point 51 noted that money laundering "is at the very heart of organized crime." Point 52 urged the member states to fully implement the provisions of the money-laundering directive, the 1990 Strasbourg Convention, and the Financial Action Task Force recommendations. Point 53 prescribed that the Council and EP should pass a recently revised directive on money laundering proposed by the Commission. In addition, point 54 called upon the Council to adopt necessary measures to allow greater transparency of financial transactions, allowing existing financial intelligence units to expedite the investigations of suspicious activity. Point 55 proposed the approximation of criminal law and procedures on money laundering, including the tracing, freezing, and confiscating of funds.

Point 56 directly impacted Europol. This provision invited the Council "to extend the competence of Europol to money laundering in general, regardless of the type of offence from which the laundered proceeds originate." At that time, Europol's existing mandate to fight money laundering only applied to the specific types of crime that it was already charged with combating.

Point 57 called for the EU and its member states to make arrangements with offshore financial centers in third-party countries to prevent their use in money laundering. Finally, the last article in this section on money laundering, point 58, invited the Commission to draft a report that would identify provisions in banking, financial, and corporate legislation, which would inhibit international cooperation against money laundering. In sum, all of the milestones covered in part C of the presidency's conclusions were aimed at improving the "Union-wide fight against crime," which would help make the proposed AFSJ a reality in the EU under the Treaty of Amsterdam and beyond.

In addition to these internal aspects, the heads of state and government also agreed to take "stronger external action" in the area of JHA, the particulars of which were spelled out in the final four points of the presidency's conclusions in a separate section. Point 59 called for "all competences and instruments at the disposal of the Union," particularly in the area of external relations, to be used to build the AFSJ. Point 60 emphasized the new powers for the EU to act externally under the Treaty of Amsterdam, as well as the possibility to conclude international agreements based on Article 38 of the TEU. Point 61 called upon the Council to work with the Commission to draw up policy objectives by June 2000 concerning the external dimensions of JHA. Finally, in point 62, the European Council expressed its support for regional cooperation against crime involving member states and third-party countries bordering the EU, noting progress made in the Baltic states and plans for a conference regarding the Adriatic region. It is worth noting that the unveiling of these plans at Tampere to develop the external dimension of JHA was soon followed by the installation of Javier Solana as the secretary-general of the Council and the EU's first high representative for CFSP on October 18, 1999.

In addition to the substantive goals agreed upon at the Tampere European Council in the form of the various milestones and objectives, the heads of state and government also agreed on a unique method to help achieve these. The European Council called on the Commission to monitor a timetable of progress with regard to each goal. With the aim of sustaining the momentum generated by the Tampere summit, this so-called Scoreboard was intended to include a timetable for the adoption of measures agreed upon and highlight any delays in implementing these. In addition, it was hoped that the Scoreboard would help to keep the EU's citizens informed of the measures being taken in the field of JHA, increasing the transparency of policymaking and thus reducing the democratic deficit in this regard. Ultimately, the Scoreboard would go beyond the Tampere milestones, serving as a consolidated listing of the EU's goals in JHA, including those still unmet as expressed in the Europol Convention, Treaty of Amsterdam, and the Action Plans of 1997, 1998 (Vienna), and, later, 2000.

In sum, the objectives established at Tampere, along with the Commission's related Scoreboard on JHA, would prove highly influential to subsequent progress by the EU in the building of the AFSJ as proposed in the Treaty of Amsterdam. Many of the Tampere summit's objectives entailed particular changes for Europol, as well as other developments related to police cooperation in the EU. In general, the Tampere European Council marked the start of accelerated progress in these areas, which has lasted well into 2002. The rapid pace of this development is especially impressive when compared to the rather slow movement in the Third Pillar, before the Treaty of Amsterdam took effect (1993–1999).

In the months following the summit in Finland, work on the 1997 Action Plan was concluded and progress made toward reaching the milestones established at Tampere. The JHA Council of October 29, 1999, served merely to follow up on the last European Council, prepare for the next, and set the agenda for the future. More notable were the developments at the next formal meeting of the JHA Council on December 2, 1999. In a public debate on the AFSJ, the Justice and Home Affairs ministers, who had not taken part in the Tampere summit, welcomed the achievements and goals of the special European Council. In doing so, some delegations underlined the role of the present and future candidate countries regarding implementation of the Tampere Conclusions. The JHA ministers also approved, without debate, a report presented by the Article 36 Committee on November 12, 1999, entitled "Finalization and Evaluation of the Action Plan on Organized Crime—Draft Report to the Helsinki European Council." Marking the official end of work on the 1997 Action Plan, this document noted the various areas of progress on JHA that had resulted from its recommendations. The report claimed that its success had been "due to a large extent" to the specificity of, and timetables contained in, the 1997 Action Plan. In those areas where the Action Plan's recommendations required further activity or had yet to be fully implemented (e.g., regarding money laundering), this document referred to the relevant objectives of the Tampere Conclusions.

The December 1999 JHA Council also noted developments on some of the Tampere objectives, including Eurojust, the Operational Task Force of Police Chiefs, and Europol's ability to receive operational data and participate in joint teams. In addition, on the fringes of the Council session, the JHA ministers debated a proposal by Commissioner Vitorino to undertake a preliminary study on creating CEPOL as called for in the Tampere milestones. The study was to examine whether CEPOL could be established in the same progressive manner as the European Monitoring Center for Drugs and Drug Addition, as well as whether it could benefit from the experience of the existing "virtual" police training academies and networks that had been identified by the Article 36 Committee. These included the Association of European Police Schools, the Central European Police School, and the Senior European Police Officers Course.[12]

At their December meeting, the JHA ministers also discussed progress on the Scoreboard, which Commissioner Vitorino pointed out was not a new set of legislative proposals. Instead, the Scoreboard would promote progress by bringing together in one document the various goals and deadlines established in the Actions Plans of 1997 and 1998, as well as those agreed to at Tampere. Similar to the success of deadlines contained in the 1997 Action Plan, the Scoreboard was supposed "to exert pressure on areas where progress is lagging behind, in order to repeat the successful experience made with the White Paper for the Internal Market."[13]

With work on the Tampere milestones and the Scoreboard well under way, the Finnish presidency closed with a meeting of the European Council in Helsinki that was notable in ways not directly related to JHA. For example, agreement was reached to open accession negotiations in 2000 with the six applicant states of Romania, Slovakia, Latvia, Lithuania, Bulgaria, and Malta (the "Helsinki Group"). In addition, Turkey, having made progress on meeting the so-called Copenhagen criteria, was accepted as an official candidate for EU membership. Although not directly related to JHA, the prospect of the EU's membership nearly doubling with the accession of the applicant states made the timely achievement of the AFSJ all the more important. With the preaccession pact on JHA already in place for twelve countries of the Luxembourg and Helsinki groups of applicant states, Turkey would begin receiving similar financial assistance from the EU following the adoption of a Commission proposal by the General Affairs Council in April 2000.

The coming enlargement also influenced the decision reached at Helsinki to open the next IGC in February 2000, which was, in fact, required under the Treaty of Amsterdam. With the intention of addressing matters of institutional reform that were left out of the Treaty of Amsterdam, the new IGC would have a limited agenda focused on institutional reform. Finally, EU leaders also agreed at Helsinki to assemble, by 2003, military and civilian personnel capable of the full range of so-called Petersberg tasks (e.g., peacekeeping) as part of a strengthened Common European Security and Defense Policy (CEDSP). Although not directly connected to internal security in the European Union, the plans for the CEDSP envisioned sufficient police cooperation within the EU to insure the rapid deployment of European police officers in foreign lands in a crisis management role as part of the proposed rapid-reaction force.

Thus, in contrast to its status at the Tampere summit, Justice and Home Affairs took a back seat to other matters at the Helsinki European Council. Nevertheless, the summit took note of the document on the finalization of the 1997 Action Plan, and instructed the Council to follow this up with a new EU strategy on organized crime. The Helsinki European Council also endorsed the newly drafted European Union Drugs Strategy (2000–2004), which COREPER had published on December 1, 1999. This contained a comprehensive plan for dealing with the drug problem in the EU from all angles. This new strategy paper entailed provisions to reduce the demand for drugs, especially among youth, focusing on treatment and rehabilitation. In addition, this document also targeted the supply-demand aspect of the drug problem, noting the potential of the proposed AFSJ, including several of the specific objectives established at Tampere. Going beyond this criminal-justice approach, the new strategy indicated that the EU had a role to play in helping source countries find alternative ways to develop economically rather than relying on the cultivation of drugs. Finally, similar to the Tampere milestones, this new strategy paper concluded by calling for EU action at the international level, noting the global nature of the drug problem.

The Austrian Crisis and JHA

With the start of the new IGC aimed at the next treaty and, in February, the opening of accession negotiations for the six states of the Helsinki group, the first months of 2000 might have been cause for much optimism in the EU. However, European headlines were soon dominated by the "political quarantine" of Austria imposed by the other fourteen member states of the EU. Among other things, the EU viewed the inclusion of the far-right Freedom Party in Austria's new governing coalition as a threat to its efforts to forge common policies on asylum and immigration. Although technically just a collection of bilateral measures, the diplomatic sanctions by the other EU members essentially excluded Austria from some official contacts in the EU.

Eventually, however, enthusiasm for the sanctions among the fourteen waned. In the end, the sanctions were lifted on September 13, 2000, following the publication of a report by a three-member panel giving Austria a clean bill of health concerning the protection of immigrant and refugees, along with its efforts to fight racism and xenophobia. Nevertheless, much of the events of 2000 must be understood in the context of the ongoing crisis over Austria, which arguably was brought on by issues directly related to JHA, namely immigration and asylum. The Austrian crisis also demonstrated how sensitive many issues of JHA continued to be in the domestic politics of several member states. In fact, this would be demonstrated again by the spring of 2002, when concerns over immigration contributed to the rise in popularity of far-right parties in several EU member states (see Chapter 8).

The Portuguese Presidency of 2000

When Portugal took over the presidency of the EU in January 2000, it established a number of key goals, but several of these were only indirectly related to JHA. One was the initiation of accession negotiations with the applicant states of the Helsinki group. Another was the initiation and direction of the IGC on institutional reform, which began in February. A third goal was to examine the possibilities of exploiting new information technologies to promote economic growth in the EU, which became the topic of the Special Lisbon European Council of March 23–24, dubbed the "dot.com summit."

Among its other objectives, Portugal also hoped to use its term as president to launch concrete measures to meet the Tampere milestones required to create the AFSJ. One effort in this regard was to solicit the opinions of the member states on the Tampere Conclusion pertaining to Europol. This was published by the General Secretariat of the Council on February 8, 2000, and contained the views of ten delegations, along with those of the Commission and Europol. Responding to the presidency's questions, the main issues were the nature and relationship of Europol to the proposed joint investigative teams, the Operational Task Force of Police Chiefs, and Eurojust. The ability of Europol to request investigations, receive operational data, and pursue all crimes related to money laundering were also addressed.[14] These issues, especially the potential need to address them with amendments to the Europol Convention, became the main topics of discussion at subsequent JHA Councils in 2000.

From beginning to end, the work of the Portuguese presidency on these matters would be assisted by the Commission under António Vitorino. Hoping to increase backing for his goals and gain input on the Scoreboard, Vitorino toured all of the EU capitals during the first half of the Portuguese presidency. By the informal JHA Council in Lisbon on March 3–4, Vitorino was able to make only a partial and incomplete presentation of the Scoreboard. He used the occasion to build support for the initiatives and deadlines contained in the Scoreboard, reminding the Council that these were based on the Tampere Conclusions and Vienna Action Plan, both of which had already been agreed upon by the member states.

Although Vitorino's report on the Scoreboard was positively received, he was not completely successful at the informal meeting of the JHA Council in hastening and deepening the integration on JHA. On the topic of Eurojust, the ministers failed to embrace the Commission's goal of empowering the new body to conduct preliminary investigations. Instead, there was agreement to limit Eurojust's role to coordinating and facilitating enquiries and to speeding up written procedures.[15] Consensus was also reached on establishment of CEPOL by initially creating a network of training academies for high-ranking officials that would also be open to accession candidates. Many of the final decisions on these new institutions were left to the upcoming French presidency, which began in late June.

The 2000 Action Plan

On March 26, 2000, one day before the next meeting of the JHA Council, Greece put in practice the remaining elements of the Schengen Implementation Agreement, lifting its last travel restriction and joining the other nine states that had already done so.

On the following day, with the free-travel zone expanded, the JHA Council adopted a new Action Plan drafted by the Article 36 Committee, entitled "The Prevention and Control of Organized Crime: A European Union Strategy for the Beginning of the New Millennium." This document brought together many of the unfulfilled goals contained in the Actions Plans of 1997 and 1998, as well as the new objectives established at Tampere. The 2000 Action Plan contained eleven general "Political Guidelines," many laced with references to the Action Plans of 1997 and 1998 or the Tampere Conclusions. These guidelines called upon the EU to:

1. Strengthen the collection and analysis of data on organized crime
2. Prevent penetration of organized crime in the public and the legitimate private sectors
3. Strengthen the prevention of organized crime and strengthen partnerships between the criminal justice system and civil society

4. Review and improve legislation, as well as control and regulatory policies at the national and EU levels
5. Strengthen the investigation of organized crime
6. Strengthen Europol
7. Trace, freeze, seize, and confiscate the proceeds of crime
8. Strengthen cooperation between law enforcement and judicial authorities nationally and within the European Union
9. Strengthen cooperation with the applicant countries
10. Strengthen cooperation with third-party countries and other international organizations
11. Monitor the strengthening of the implementation of these measures for the prevention and control of organized crime within the European Union

For each guideline, the Action Plan provided as many as ten "specific recommendations" (i.e., thirty-nine recommendations in all). Each of these included a priority rating for each (1–5), identification of responsible actors (i.e., various EU institutions and the member states), and a target date.[16] Concerning the latter, some of the recommendations made references to "ongoing activities," and a few had target dates as early as December 31, 2000, or as late as 2010, but most actions contained deadlines of either the end of 2001 or 2002.

In keeping with recommendation 36—to develop closer cooperation with third-party states and international organizations and bodies involved in the prevention and control of organized crime—the JHA Council of March 27, 2000, also formally authorized the director of Europol to begin negotiating with third parties. This would soon set in motion several parallel talks on data-sharing agreements (including those with Interpol), the future, non-EU members of the Schengen free-travel area (Norway and Iceland), and several candidate states (Poland, Hungary, the Czech Republic, Estonia, Lithuania, and Slovenia). In addition, EU ministers of the interior and justice reached a political agreement on a framework decision to improve the criminal protection of the euro from counterfeiting, with an eye toward its physical introduction in January 2002.

Finally, the JHA Council of March 27 also included a presentation by Commissioner Vitorino on the Scoreboard. He noted that it had already undergone some changes in format and content in light of comments that he had received from member states at the informal JHA Council meeting at Lisbon and during his tour of the capitals. Vitorino stressed once again that the Scoreboard was not a new action plan, but rather "an instrument for pro-active monitoring of already existing action plans."[17] He also highlighted the evolving nature of the Scoreboard, indicating that it would be changed during each presidency to include any new objectives, as well as to note progress concerning the "state of play" regarding each of the prescribed actions included in it. With this in mind, the Scoreboard would be further amended to include the comments of national delegation, as well as the matters covered in the 2000 Action Plan, before being formally unveiled at the next JHA Council meeting in late May.

The intervening weeks were marked by several significant events regarding the development of European police cooperation. The Portuguese presidency hosted the first meeting of the new Operational Task Force of Police Chiefs in Lisbon on April 8–9, 2000. At this session, the decision was reached to set up a liaison structure to share information and strategies on a small number of key issues, including trade in human beings, drug trafficking, and terrorism. Although the liaison structure of police chiefs itself would not be used to plan investigations, its work was intended to ensure that activities are effectively coordinated.[18] In addition to the task force of police chiefs, Portugal also hosted a conference on May 3–4 on crime prevention regarding several of the Tampere Conclusions. Finally, on May 26, 2000, the six candidate countries of the Luxembourg group opened negotiations on their JHA chapters of accession, which would continue, for most, until late 2001, and for some into 2002 (see Chapter 7).

These developments were followed by the final JHA Council meeting of the Portuguese presidency on May 29, which took up several key issues concerning police cooperation. For example, meeting as the Mixed Committee with Iceland and Norway, the Council adopted the new Convention on Mutual Assistance in Criminal Matters, designed to supplement the Schengen *acquis* and the existing 1959 Council of Europe Convention. A draft of the new convention had been first proposed in April 1996, but was subsequently amended several times. The convention includes rules covering various ways the signatories had agreed to provide each other with assistance on, for example, data protection issues, hearings by video and telephone conference, and cross-border investigation methods such as controlled deliveries, joint investigations teams, covert activities, and interception of telecommunications. Agreement on the convention initiated a slow ratification process that continued into 2002. In addition, many of the measures prescribed in the convention had to be implemented through legislative acts before taking effect.

On the basis of a UK proposal, the May JHA Council also conducted preliminary discussions on mutual recognition in criminal maters, agreeing that identifying and defining serious crimes may be impossible in some regards, but that conflicting national penal codes might inevitably require eventual harmonization of legal standards. In addition, the council took up debate on the creation of Eurojust, noting the submission of a German proposal on the subject, as well the joint preparation of another by Portugal, along with the next three, namely France, Sweden, and Belgium. Finally, without debate, the council also adopted a framework decision against counterfeiting of the euro. This calls upon the member states to change national legislation to ensure that such an offense is punishable by a period of imprisonment of no less than eight years.

In addition to all of this, the May 2000 meeting of the JHA Council provided Commissioner Vitorino with the opportunity to present the consolidated version of the Scoreboard, which remained in use through 2002. The Scoreboard is designed in the form of a chart with five columns, specifying an "objective," "action needed," "responsibility" (of the pertinent EU institution), "timetable for adoption," and "state of play." Each row represents a different type of action needed, with some actions serving the same objective.

The JHA Scoreboard is divided into seven main sections:

1. A common EU asylum and migration policy
2. A genuine European area of justice
3. Union-wide fight against crime
4. Issues related to internal and external borders and visa policy, implementation of Article 62, the Treaty Establishing the European Communities (TEC), and converting the Schengen *acquis*
5. Citizenship of the Union
6. Cooperation against drugs, and
7. Stronger external action

Each section of the Scoreboard is divided into topical subsections. For example, section three, "Union-wide fight against crime," includes sections:

3.1 Union-wide crime prevention;
3.2 Stepping up cooperation in the fight against crime;
3.3 Fight against certain forms of crime, and
3.4 Special action against money laundering

Table 5.1 illustrates one part of the JHA Scoreboard at this juncture. Most aspects of the Scoreboard came from some part of the Tampere Conclusions or the 2000 Action Plan. Thus, the Scoreboard would be used to monitor progress concerning the goals and deadlines expressed in these documents. After formally unveiling the consolidated version of the Scoreboard at the May JHA Council, the Commission would go on to publish an updated version of this near the end of each presidency, with this happening for the first time in November 2000. In general, each amended version of the Scoreboard has entailed updates to the "state of play" for each of the prescribed actions, leaving the rest of the Scoreboard largely unchanged.

Table 5.1 Section 3.2: Stepping up Cooperation in the Fight Against Crime

Objective	Action Needed	Responsibility	Timetable for Adoption	State of Play
To coordinate and, where appropriate, centralize proceedings	Setting up joint investigative teams as a first step to combat trafficking in drugs and human beings as well as terrorism when investigating cross-border crime	Adoption of the MLA Convention; or Council, on the basis of an initiative by a member state	Without delay	The Council is discussing a proposal presented by the Portuguese presidency
	Setting up a unit composed of national prosecutors, magistrates, or police officers of equivalent competence—Eurojust	Council, on the basis of a Commission proposal or a member-state initiative	End 2001	Preliminary discussions on the basis of papers presented by the Portuguese presidency, Germany, and Italy

The 2000 IGC and JHA

As the Portuguese presidency neared its end, work continued in the IGC on institutional reform, due to be concluded by the Nice summit at the end of 2000. In keeping with its limited agenda, the IGC was focused mainly on issues that would not directly impact JHA, including the weighting of votes in the Council, the size and shape of the Commission, and the allocation of seats in the EP following the accession of new members. On these matters, division between the large and small states of the EU was already apparent, consuming much of the work of the IGC's so-called preparatory group that was meeting regularly to draft the new treaty. However, by the end of the Portuguese presidency two issues related to JHA had arisen in the IGC.

The first was the expanded use of qualified majority voting (QMV) in the Council. Having already discussed matters regarding several areas of the First Pillar, the representatives of the preparatory group met on March 28 to discuss, among other matters, the extension of QMV to Justice and Home Affairs. At stake was the right of member states effectively to veto legislation on Title IV (covering asylum, visas, and freedom of movement) and Title VI (covering cooperation in civil and criminal matters). Concerning the former, some delegations seemed open to the idea of immediately extending QMV to certain articles of Title IV, for which the Treaty of Amsterdam only provided "communitization," as of May 2004 (see Chapter 4). However, the UK, Austria, Ireland, and Denmark remained reluctant to do so.[19] On the matter of extending QMV to parts of Title VI (e.g., matters related to Europol and police cooperation), there was even less support for a change, with only Germany expressing its openness to do so. Thus, in the end, there was agreement to maintain unanimity on Title VI, meaning that cooperation on crime fighting in the EU would remain largely intergovernmental under the Treaty of Nice. However, each delegation pointed out that impending enlargement would eventually require reform of the work of the Council on JHA to insure the proper implementation and management of items covered on the JHA Scoreboard.[20]

In addition to the topic of extending QMV, the IGC raised a second issue related to policymaking on JHA. On April 14 and 15, the representatives of the member states met informally in Sintra, Portugal, to take up the question of "enhanced cooperation." Sometimes referred to as "closer cooperation," this is the mechanism created under the Treaty of Amsterdam that allows a group of member states to pursue closer cooperation in some regards, without compelling all member states to go along. Germany, France, Italy, the Netherlands, Belgium, and Luxembourg pressed for the repeal of the so-called emergency-brake provision that a single member state could utilize in the European Council to veto enhanced cooperation. At this point, Austria, Greece, and Ireland were, in principle, in agreement with the proposal, while Spain, Denmark, and Finland had expressed a new desire to discuss the issue. However, the United Kingdom and Sweden remained, for the time being, opposed to elimination of the emergency brake for JHA.[21]

The Feira European Council of 2000

On June 19–20, the Portuguese presidency closed with the regular summit meeting at Santa Maria da Feira, at which the European Council welcomed the presidency's progress report on the IGC and approved the inclusion of enhanced cooperation as an agenda item for the preparatory group. In the months to follow, during the French presidency, the preparatory group would take up the task of determining how to better facilitate "enhanced cooperation" in the EU, including in its Third Pillar. In addition to a few items related to CFSP and enlargement, most of the Feira European Council followed up on the work of the "dot.com summit" at Lisbon and dealt with the related topics of employment, economic reform, and social cohesion.

Concerning the AFSJ, the Feira European Council endorsed the new EU Action Plan on Drugs for 2000–2004, which was based on the EU's strategy on drugs that had been approved at the Helsinki summit in 1999. The Action Plan transformed the more general principles, objectives, approaches, and targets outlined in the original strategy document into over one hundred concrete measures, organized around five main types of actions. Its first two sections on "coordination" and "information and evaluation" contained, among other measures, several prescriptions for the European Monitoring Center of Drugs and Drug Addiction, located in Lisbon. The third section on "reduction of demand, prevention of drug use, and of drug related crime," specified various actions for the member states, with the support of the Commission. Concerning the fourth section on "supply reduction," the new Action Plan mentioned several tasks for Europol in preventing drug trafficking and the illegal production of synthetic drugs, as well as roles to be played by the proposed European Police College and the Task Force of Police Chiefs. The final, "international," section of the new Action Plan includes several prescriptions for combating drugs at the international level, including for example, the PHARE program, instruments of the CFSP, and agreements with third parties on money laundering.

This last section of the Action Plan on Drugs paralleled the EU's overall efforts to establish the AFSJ by acting outside the boundaries of the Union. The need for an external dimension of policymaking on JHA was highlighted in the final section of the Tampere Conclusions, and "political guidelines" 8 and 9 of the 2000 Action Plan on the Prevention and Control of Organized Crime. In fact, at Feira, the European Council endorsed a document produced by COREPER entitled "European Union Priorities and Policy Objectives for External Relations in the Field of Justice and Home Affairs." This presented a comprehensive overview of all the EU's efforts, actual and potential, to make its "area of freedom, security, and justice" a reality by reaching beyond the boundaries of the European Union. This document also outlined a number of priority areas for cooperation and means and instruments for acting, as well as various international partners and forums for doing so.

In sum, by the time of Feira European Council, the EU had made clear that crime fighting in Europe would not be facilitated solely by an infrastructure of legislation and institutions related to its Third Pillar, such as police cooperation fostered by Europol, Eurojust, etc. Instead, it would also be promoted by activities in the First Pillar (e.g, treating the demand for drugs), as well as the Second Pillar (e.g., using the CFSP to forge international agreements). Thus, the AFSJ would be built on the basis of a cross-pillar approach, linking several different aspects of the EU.

A final notable aspect of the Feira European Council concerning JHA was its expression of shock at the death of fifty-eight Chinese migrants found on June 19, 2000, after suffocating to death in the shipping container of a Dutch-registered truck in the British port of Dover, which had crossed the English Channel aboard a ferry from Zeebrugge, Belgium. Detectives from the UK, Belgium, and the Netherlands took the crime under investigation, and, working with the assistance of Europol, the crime was solved. The Dutch driver of the truck, contracted by a criminal gang based in China, was convicted of fifty-eight counts of manslaughter and sentenced in April 2001 to nearly fourteen years in prison (four months for each death). A Chinese interpreter was also sentenced to six years in jail for her role in the crime, which had been organized by a criminal gang based in China known as the Snakeheads.[22] The tragic incident highlighted the nature and severity of the crime of illegal trafficking of human beings, and led to renewed talks on dealing with the problem.

Worldwide, over 70 million migrants are estimated to be on the move, with Europe viewed as an easy target. Criminal networks facilitate their entry via an illicit business valued at $3 billion per year. Reflecting on the deaths at Dover, Willy Bruggeman, deputy director of Europol, noted that "there is a problem of saturation in Europe . . . The difference between rich and poor countries are such that people are going to move and we cannot stop them. But open borders amounts to mission impossible."[23]

The trafficking of human beings not only includes the kind of migrants found dead in Dover, but also women, and sometimes children, caught up in the sex trade. Typically, women are promised jobs as waitresses or maids in Central or Western Europe, particularly Germany, but they are then forced into prostitution until their "debt" is paid off and their identity papers are returned to them. Conservative estimates put the number of woman smuggled into Central Europe and the EU at about 300,000 annually, but not all of these are involved in the sex trade.[24]

The French Presidency of 2000

With the tragedy at Dover still making headlines, the Portuguese handed the presidency of the EU over to France. Almost immediately, the French started work on a draft framework decision on the trafficking of human beings, including a precise definition of "people-trafficking," severe sanctions for traffickers, as well a notable exemption for people who help family members enter the EU, facilitating their testimony against the traffickers.[25] This initiative would be the first of many regarding the AFSJ in the French presidency, as the EU worked toward meeting some of the goals endorsed by the European Council in the Tampere Conclusions and the 2000 Action Plan. Adding to France's desire to achieve these was the first formal review of progress on JHA via the Commission's Scoreboard, which was due in November.

In preparation for the full slate of activities regarding the AFSJ, including three planned meetings of the JHA Council, the French presidency hosted an informal gathering of the JHA Council in Marseilles on July

28–29. In addition to preparing for the upcoming formal sessions of the Council, the ministers also discussed illegal immigration, Internet crime, and the external dimensions of JHA, especially in the Euro-Mediterranean region. The informal JHA Council at Marseilles also took up the important issue of mutual recognition, which had been the subject of a Commission communication to the Council on July 26.

Looking ahead, the French were particularly interested in reaching agreements on creating Eurojust and dealing with financial crime, especially money laundering. Concerning the latter, Portugal had already tabled a proposal to adopt a protocol under the Europol Convention to extend the competence of Europol to money laundering, regardless of the type of offense from which the laundering proceeds originated, as had been prescribed in the Tampere milestones. At that time Europol was limited to combating money laundering only as it was related to the particular crimes already included in its mandate.

The French presidency also had to oversee the successful completion of the ongoing IGC by December, with the aim of signing the resulting draft treaty at the planned Nice European Council in December. In this regard, several contentious issues needed to be resolved, especially concerns over a "two-speed Europe" that were connected to the debate on enhanced cooperation, as well as outstanding disputes between large and small states on various aspects of institutional reform. By the summer of 2000, many of these issues were embedded in two broader debates concerning the future of the European Union.

The first dealt with the ongoing accession negotiations with the twelve candidate states and expectations for when and how many of these would be formally admitted to the EU.[26] The second debate concerned the contending public proposals for the future of Europe, beyond the IGC. This discussion had been initiated by Germany in May 2000, when Foreign Minister Joschka Fischer presented his federalist vision for the EU. By July, the British and the French had presented their own alternative blueprints for the future of the European Union, leading to a wide-ranging debate on the matter that would continue into 2003.

In addition to questions surrounding enlargement and the future of Europe, the French presidency also inherited the lingering problem of Austria's Freedom Party. Along with Belgium, France had originally taken a hard line on the issue. However, by this time the political will in the EU to continue the informal sanctions had softened, and Austria accepted a plan proposed by the outgoing Portuguese presidency to have its human-rights record evaluated by a panel of three experts, including former Finnish president Martii Ahtsaari. Published in early September, the panel's report gave Austria a clean bill of health on human rights and, with the threat of an Austrian veto looming at the end of the IGC on institutional reform, France and the other member states relented, ending the sanctions on September 13.[27]

Many citizens in smaller countries, especially in the Nordic region, had come to see the sanctions against Austria as a potentially threatening precedent of the EU dominating the internal affairs of member states. In this regard, Denmark's referendum on adopting the euro, set for later in the month, provided additional pressure to lift the political quarantine of Austria. However, this failed to save the Danish government, which saw its voters reject the holy grail of European integration, the common currency (the euro), on September 28. This, in turn, cast some doubt on the willingness of all of the EU's member states, present and future, to progress at the same pace of integration.

These kinds of concerns were reflected in the negotiations within the ongoing IGC regarding enhanced cooperation. The experience of the euro, which would be extended to Greece in January 2001, served as a model for allowing some member states to make progress on some aspects of European integration ahead of others. On the other side of the issue were the concerns of some member states about being left behind in a "two-speed" Europe.

A more direct impact of the Austrian crisis on the IGC was evident in the negotiations regarding Article 7 of the TEU, created under the Treaty of Amsterdam. This provision, which had been under discussion in the IGC since June, allows the Council to take action against any member state where breaches of liberty, democracy, and respect for fundamental rights have taken place. The debate in the IGC concerned supplementing this measure with provisions allowing the Council to take preventive actions before any breaches had actually occurred.

In sum, all of these issues shaped the broader political context of developments regarding EU crime fighting during the French presidency in the second half of 2000. France had established some of its agenda regarding police cooperation in a document provided to the Police Cooperation Working Party of the Article 36 Committee. Concerning the Mixed Committee (the EU fifteen plus Iceland and Norway), France proposed extending cross-border surveillance under Article 40 of the Schengen agreement beyond the particular suspects involved to the offenses at issue.

Among other matters, the document also contained items on hooliganism at sports events, counterfeiting of bankcards, cooperation with the candidate states on meeting the JHA *acquis,* police training on environmental crime, planning sessions on CEPOL, and technology. A formal proposal for the latter had been made by Portugal in the last days of its presidency on June 27, 2000, and by the end of September work in the Article 36 Committee on a plan for CEPOL was nearly complete without much change to the original blueprint.[28] Along with its work on CEPOL, the French presidency also hosted the second meeting of the Operational Task Force of Police Chiefs in Paris on September 14–15, which included the participation of the Commission, General Secretariat, and Europol.

The first formal meeting of the JHA Council under the French presidency was held on September 28, resulting in several areas of progress toward the goals of the 2000 Action Plan, including items mentioned in the Tampere Conclusions' section on a Union-wide fight against crime. In this regard, the Council took up the issue of protecting the environment through criminal law. This initiative was based on a 1999 Danish proposal for a framework decision to harmonize criminal law among the member states on this issue.[29] Although no final decision was reached, the presidency noted that the ministers were in agreement on the need for an approximation of criminal law in this area before the next enlargement. However, subsequent progress on the protection of the environment through criminal law would prove be slow, as work on EU legislation in this area would continue into 2002.

The September 2000 JHA Council also took up the problem of money laundering, which the heads of state and government at Tampere had recognized as being "at the very heart of organized crime." In keeping with this rationale, the JHA ministers, after some debate, also reached a political agreement on the protocol to the Europol Convention to extend the competence of Europol to all forms of money laundering, not just when it was related to other crimes in its mandate. After waiting for the EP's opinion on this in October, the act drawing up the protocol was formally passed as an "A-point" (i.e., without debate) at the JHA Council meeting of November 30–December 1, 2000.

At its September 2000 session, the JHA Council also debated Eurojust, which had been prescribed in the Tampere Conclusions. A political agreement was reached on setting up a provisional version of Eurojust that would eventually become known as "Pro-Eurojust." The provisional judicial-cooperation unit's objectives were to improve cooperation among various national authorities in the member states regarding investigation and prosecutions in relation to "serious crime, particularly when it is organized, involving two or more states." In addition, it was decided that the Commission would be "fully associated" with the activity of Pro-Eurojust, including work projected for 2001 on setting up a permanent Eurojust unit. Work on this would continue over the next year, with the goal of the putting the permanent unit into operation by the end of 2001.

The September 2000 meeting of the JHA Council also included a few noteworthy formal decisions reached without debate, having been resolved at previous Council sessions or within the Article 36 Committee. One such matter concerned the creation of the European Refugee Fund, designed to help member states cope with sudden mass influxes of refugees. Concerning matters more closely related to police cooperation, the Council adopted two key items regarding Europol. One authorized Europol to enter negotiations with Interpol, with the aim of allowing the two agencies to share data. The other matter was a formal recommendation that member states should deal with any request from Europol to initiate, conduct, or coordinate investigations in specific cases, giving such requests due consideration. This was explicitly based on Tampere Conclusion number 45, which prescribed that Europol should be authorized to ask member states, among other things, "to initiate, conduct, or coordinate investigations." Moreover, the recommendation prescribed that member states are to keep Europol informed as to how the request was being handled and the reasons for this. However, as this measure took the form of a "recommendation," it would not be binding on member states and also fell short of Europol's hope that it would be able to participate in joint investigative teams, which were also prescribed in point 45 of the Tampere Conclusion.[30] Nevertheless, this act lent normative pressure to Europol's efforts to initiate criminal investigations, rather than simply having to react to requests from member states. In fact, this would contribute to the passage of more binding legislation during the Spanish presidency of 2002 covering these areas of Europol's power (see Chapter 8).

Progress on the 2000 IGC

By the end of September 2000, there had already been significant progress on several JHA matters as discussed above. Of course the highest priority for the French presidency was the completion of the IGC, which was still deadlocked on several issues regarding institutional reform, including the size and shape of the Commission and reweighting of votes in the Council. With the aim of facilitating a high-level airing of views, the French presidency hosted an informal meeting of the European Council in the Atlantic coastal resort town of Biarritz on October 13–14, 2000.[31]

The Biarritz summit revealed consensus on some issues, but not on others. On the positive side, agreement was solidified on the need for enhanced cooperation when the UK declared itself open to this in principle. Although opposed to a clear-cut two-speed Europe across the board, British Prime Minister Tony Blair noted that "there may be circumstances in which Britain wants to go with other countries further forward—for example in fighting organized crime."[32] There was also growing support for a revision of Article 7 of the TEU that, following on the experience of the Austrian crisis, would allow the EU to take preventive action concerning the human-rights practices of a member state.

However, on other matters it was clear that much discord remained. This was the case for the question of extending QMV to social policy, taxation, and JHA, as well as on the issues of the future reweighting of votes in the Council and composition of the Commission. The heads of state and government did manage to approve the content of the Charter of Fundamental Rights and planned to make a formal declaration to this effect at Nice.

Thus, virtually every central issue of the IGC remained unresolved past the midpoint of the French presidency of 2000. Many of the issues on institutional reform were held up by disputes between the EU's smaller and larger states, with the latter mindful that they would be outnumbered in this regard following the next enlargements. However, other questions revolved around the more traditional dispute among those member states favoring movement toward supranationalism (i.e., greater federalism) and those that supported intergovernmentalism.

The issue of enhanced cooperation provided an interesting twist on the latter dichotomy. On the one hand, removal of the member states' ability to veto enhanced cooperation meant that a smaller group of states could more easily pursue deeper integration. On the other hand, this would take place outside of the "community method," which entails prominent roles for the supranational Commission and EP.

Following Biarritz, the IGC's preparatory group began the busy final two months of negotiation and planning leading up to the Nice European Council. Some of these issues were related to the field of Justice and Home Affairs, which figured prominently at the session of the IGC's preparatory group of October 30, 2000. That meeting entailed discussions on extending QMV to matters related to visas, asylum, immigration, and judicial cooperation in civil matters.

In addition, the October meeting of the IGC's preparatory group also entailed discussion of Eurojust, which included a declaration by the French delegation that it would soon table a proposal to include a reference to this in the draft treaty. It eventually did so on November 19, 2000, proposing an amendment to Article 30, which covers Europol. The French argued that including a similar reference to Eurojust would "ensure a balanced and consistent approach to judicial cooperation and police cooperation in the legal basis."[33] Consequently, this matter was discussed at the first of two "conclave" negotiating sessions of the IGC held in Val Duchesse (Brussels) on November 24–25, along with several other outstanding issues in the draft treaty.

Fighting Financial Crime

As the pace of the ICG picked up following the Biarritz European Council, work continued under the French presidency toward realization of the goals of the Tampere Conclusion and the 2000 Action Plan on organized crime.

In the week following the informal summit, two important Council meetings dealing with crime fighting, particularly money laundering, were held on October 17, 2000. The first was a regular meeting of the JHA Council, which reached a political decision on a framework decision on "money laundering, the identification, tracing, freezing, seizing, and confiscation of instrumentalities and the proceeds of crime." Among other measures, this entailed a four-year minimum prison sentence for convictions on money laundering. The Council also reached a political agreement on part of the draft convention on improving mutual assistance in criminal matters, namely that rights to secrecy on banking and tax reporting may not be invoked in response to requests by judicial authorities from other member states. Based on this agreement, work on this issue would continue in the Council in the following months, culminating in protocol to the convention, which would be finalized during the Belgian presidency in the second half of 2000.

The importance of these agreements during the French presidency was recognized on the same day as the regular JHA Council of October 2000 by the first-ever joint meeting of the Councils of Economic and Finance Ministers (ECOFIN) and JHA. This unprecedented "financial crime summit" involved more than forty-five EU ministers of economics, finance, justice, and the interior. At the time, the scope of the money-laundering problem was pointed out by the British home secretary, Jack Straw, who noted International Monetary Fund (IMF) estimates indicating that over US$590 billion is laundered worldwide. According to Straw, "Depriving crooks of their ill-gotten gains is a worthy aim in itself, but money laundering is the Achilles heel of international crime. When unearthed . . . it can lead back to the major criminals themselves."[34]

Overall, the joint Council meeting highlighted the importance of recent EU actions on money laundering, including the new framework decision, the extension of Europol's mandate to money laundering, the adoption of a decision facilitating cooperation and information exchange among financial intelligence units in the member states, and work on a directive requiring various professions (e.g., lawyers) to report any money-laundering activity that they may identify.[35] This Council session also reviewed a collection of EU strategies to combat money laundering, including common and stiffer sanctions, measures directed at non-EU states, mutual recognition concerning freezing of assets, and the Internet. In sum, the activities discussed at the joint meeting of the ECOFIN and JHA Councils highlighted the EU's strategy to deal with the problem of money laundering through international coordination (via Europol), harmonization of national law (through the framework decisions), and attention to the external sources of the problem. Following the terrorist attacks on the United States on September 11, 2001, the problem of money laundering as related to international crime would gain even greater prominence, with many of the issues raised during the French presidency being definitively resolved on the occasion of the next joint meeting of the JHA and ECOFIN Councils held in October 2001 (see Chapter 7).

Although the focus of the day was on money laundering and the joint Council session, the regular JHA Council of October 17, 2000, was also significant for a few unrelated accomplishments. The Council took note of the two past meetings of the Chiefs of Police Operational Task Force, as well as a statement from the British delegation indicating their desire to institutionalize this forum by making it a formal, legal EU entity. In addition, an important "A-point" of the JHA Council was the decision, based on an initiative of the preceding Portuguese presidency, to establish a single secretariat for the joint supervisory data-protection authorities established in three treaties, namely the Europol Convention, the Schengen Implementation Agreement, and the Convention on the Use of Information Technology for Customs Purposes. As well as being a cost-saving measure, some member states hoped that this would be a first step toward an eventual linkage and information sharing among the data systems of the three institutions, which, among other things would require a revision of the Schengen Implementation Convention.[36]

Concluding the French Presidency

Several additional issues remained on the French presidency's agenda for the JHA Council meeting of November 30–December 1, 2000. The highlight of the session was the expected formal decision to extend the Schengen area to the Nordic states of Denmark, Sweden, Finland, Norway, and Iceland on March 25, 2001, allowing time for the installation of the Schengen Information System (SIS) and training of border-control personnel. At this meeting, the Council also reached political agreement on a draft regulation listing of which third-country nationals need a visa to enter the Schengen zone (the so-called blacklist) and which do not (the "white list"). Due to changes in the original text, the draft regulation was then resubmitted to the EP for consultation before being formally adopted by the JHA Council in March 2001 under the Swedish presidency.

The November-December JHA Council of 2000 also adopted two important sets of conclusions. With the tragic death of Chinese immigrants at Dover still in mind, one of these concerned cooperation between member states in combating illegal immigration networks, including a prescription that the Center for Information, Discussion, and Exchange on the Crossing of Frontiers and Immigration should share information on its proceedings with Europol and the Chiefs of Police Operational Task Force. These con-

clusions also called for a revamped rapid-alert system and reinforced cooperation between immigration liaison officers. The other set of conclusions
contained detailed guidelines on the conditions for the reception of asylum
seekers. Although vague on some matters, such as freedom of movement
and employment for applicants, the conclusions did specifically permit the
use of "waiting zones" for asylum seekers at border posts.[37] In the end,
more significant progress on these and related issues dealing with border
control would have to wait until the Spanish presidency of 2002 (see Chapter 8).

Concerning police cooperation, the ministers discussed two items submitted by France related to the protection of the euro. One called for the
creation within Europol of a unit to combat counterfeiting of the euro,
while the other concerned the need for a framework decision to facilitate
mutual judicial assistance between member states to fight counterfeiting.
Both items would be developed further in the Article 36 Committee. Also
discussed but unresolved at the November JHA Council was the creation of
a European Crime Prevention Network. Proposed by France and Sweden
(which would assume the presidency in January 2001), this would consist
of contact points in the Commission, Europol, and member states that
would work together with local authorities to develop crime prevention
strategies, especially regarding urban, juvenile, and drug-related crime.
However, on November 29 the Commission adopted a communication
describing a crime prevention strategy of its own. Much broader than the
one proposed by France and Sweden, this was directed at a long list of
crimes, including organized crime, rape, fraud, and violence in schools and
sports stadiums. The Commission's plan not only envisioned roles for local
law enforcement agencies, but also for schools, social services, banks, and
researchers. Along with their plan, the Commission called for the establishment of a new "European Forum" for various public- and private-sector
actors, aimed at cyber-crime, corruption, financial crime, and environmental crime. In addition, the Commission proposed the creation of a new program called "Hippocrates" to provided funding for training, exchanges,
seminars, and cooperation for crime prevention projects involving at least
three member states or two member states and one applicant country. Managed by the Commission, the Hippocrates program would operate with a
budget of €2 million, which would provide funding of up to 70 percent for
projects in the member states for 2001–2002.

The strategies of the French/Swedish initiative and the Commission
would ultimately be discussed at the conference on crime prevention organized by Sweden in February 2001 in Sundvall. Based in part on the conclusions of these discussions, the JHA Council reached an agreement on European crime prevention policy at its meeting in March 2001. This consisted
of the network proposed by France and Sweden, as well the new European

Forum and Hippocrates program initiated by the Commission.[38] In addition to the new Hippocrates program on crime prevention, the Swedish presidency oversaw the allocation of €18 million in funding for the second generation of three other EU-cofinanced programs administered by the Commission, facilitating exchanges, training, and cooperation for officials engaged in various aspects of JHA in the member states. This included funds for the Stop II (the program on the trafficking of human beings and the sexual exploitation of children), Oisin II (for law enforcement in the area of police and customs), and Grotuis II-criminal (for legal practitioners on criminal matters).

Along with contributing to the debate on crime prevention, another major accomplishment of the November-December JHA Council under the French presidency was political agreement on the establishment of the European Police College. As discussed above, the idea for CEPOL originated in the Tampere Conclusions and had been formally proposed by Portugal. CEPOL provides education and training to senior police officers by encouraging and optimizing cooperation among the various training academies of the member states. This is intended to increase mutual knowledge about Europol, national police systems, and the various means of cross-border police cooperation now available in the EU. CEPOL is also charged with establishing relations with training institutes in the applicant states, as well as in Norway and Iceland (despite initial Spanish reservations about including these two non-EU, Schengen participants).

CEPOL is funded by intergovernmental contributions on the basis of gross national product and run by a governing board consisting of the directors of the national training academies in each member state (chaired by the country holding the EU presidency). The first task of this governing board was to create a permanent secretariat to assist CEPOL with administration and planning. Before being established as a physical entity that could actually be visited by police officials, CEPOL would begin as a "virtual" academy, consisting of information networks connecting the various national training academies. The politically sensitive issue of the permanent location for the college was not decided at that time, and eventually became caught up in the imbroglio over sites for various EU agencies that led to the abrupt ending of the Laeken European Council at the end of the Belgian presidency (see Chapter 7).

In light of what would happen less than a year later on September 11, 2001, the November-December meeting of the JHA Council during the French presidency of 2000 is also notable for its debate on terrorism. The Council discussed the nature of the terrorist threat to Europe, especially stemming from ETA, the Basque separatist group in Spain. In addition, the Commission announced its plans to send proposals to the Council on the harmonization of penal codes and penalties regarding terrorism, the simplification of extradition procedures, and a European arrest warrant. Work on these matters would continue in the Article 36 Committee and the Commission throughout 2001, but would gain greater significance and relatively swift resolution after September 11 (see Chapter 7).

Along with the formal decision discussed above on Europol's ability to combat money laundering, a noteworthy item passed without debate at this JHA Council meeting was the recommendation for the member states to include the assistance of Europol in "joint investigative teams" formed by two or more member states. Like the recommendation of the September 2000 JHA Council for member states to respond to requests from Europol for investigations to be conducted, this decision also stemmed from Tampere Conclusion number 45. As was the case with the September proposal, however, this recommendation was not binding on member states and would only be strengthened by measures adopted during the Spanish presidency of 2002 (see Chapter 8).

Finally, the November-December 2000 meeting of the JHA Council provided Commissioner Vitorino with his first opportunity to present a full biannual update on the JHA Scoreboard, noting that "considerable progress" had been achieved since he presented the first version of the Scoreboard. By updating the "state of play" column, the Commission demonstrated the various areas where progress had been achieved, especially under the French presidency. The introduction to the updated Scoreboard also highlighted the various activities of the Commission on JHA, including several communications on crime prevention, as well as a number of communications and proposals on asylum and migration, as well as judicial cooperation on civil and commercial matters.

Overall, the Prodi Commission had received mixed reviews by fall 2000, just over one year after its installation. On the one hand, the new Commission, especially Prodi himself, had been criticized by media organizations in Brussels for a lack of vision and an inability to communicate with the public.[39] At the same time, however, there was recognition that the Commission had been successful in pushing through its economic-reform proposals at the Lisbon "dot.com summit," and that it had done most of the practical work on the coming implementation of the euro.[40] Moreover, the Commission was also credited for its contributions on JHA since the Tampere summit.[41]

The European Parliament and Concerns for Democracy

Like the Commission, the European Parliament had also displayed an unprecedented level of activity on JHA issues since the Tampere summit, and this had been noted in Vitorino's update of the Scoreboard. Under MEP

Graham Watson (European Liberal, Democratic and Reformist Party, UK), the EP's Committee of Citizens' Freedoms and Rights, Justice, and Home Affairs produced seven separate committee reports at the conclusion of its October 2000 sessions dealing with various JHA proposals before the Council during the French presidency.[42] These reports, in turn, formed the basis of EP resolutions passed at the plenary session of November 14 that were generally supportive of the initiatives agreed upon by the JHA Council. This included support for the European Police College, as well as for the extension of Europol's mandate to deal with money laundering of all kinds.

One substantive area where the EP expressed significant reservations on JHA matters dealt with the Council's proposals on the trafficking of human beings, initiated by France at the start of its presidency. Echoing the report of the EP's rapporteur on the matter, Ozan Ceyhun (Greens, Germany), some MEPs were highly critical of the French initiative, especially regarding its lack of consideration for illegal immigration for humanitarian reasons. It was argued that some refugees have no choice other than to enter the EU illegally by using criminal networks to escape their home country and find safety. For this reason, many MEPs did not want the proposed sanctions to create a "fortress Europe" that would deter or penalize the trafficking of human beings for humanitarian purposes.[43]

By the time this matter was discussed in the JHA Council at its session on December 1, 2000, the original initiative had been split into a draft directive on facilitating illegal-entry residence, and a draft framework decision defining penal sanctions for those involved in the trafficking of human beings. It was clear that many member states—though not all, such as Belgium—had serious reservations on the French proposal regarding the need for a humanitarian clause as called for by the EP. In the end, the French presidency was forced to turn the matter over to its successor, Sweden, in hopes of reaching a compromise.

Aside from the French initiative against human trafficking, the EP was, as noted, generally supportive of the Council's substantive efforts at this point. Nevertheless, the EP did use its committee reports and related resolutions to express its desires for greater democratic control over Europol, a more supranational approach to crime fighting, and the importance of protecting civil rights in the emerging AFSJ. For example, the EP supported the extension of Europol's power on money laundering, but used its resolution on this to stress its aim of gaining democratic control over Europol. With this goal in mind, the EP also called upon the director of Europol to appear if requested before EP committees for an exchange of views, as well as for the inclusion of the EP in the appointment of Europol's director.[44] The EP resolution also called for the reform of Europol's Management Board to include two seats for the EP and one for the Commission. Finally, the EP expressed its aspiration to empower the European Court of Justice to rule on disputes or conflicts regarding the Europol Convention (rather than leaving it up to the member states to permit this). As the resolution was passed under the terms of the consultation procedure, the EP's suggested amendments were not adopted by the Council in its final act on Europol's money-laundering remit.

Ignored as well were other calls from some MEPs to make Europol more responsible to the European Parliament. In the plenary debate on the matter, it was suggested that, before its mandate was expanded, funding for Europol should be brought under the Community budget. Supported by Commissioner Vitorino, such a provision would enable the EP to have some influence over the effectiveness of Europol.[45] Unwilling to share power with the EP, however, the Council predictably failed to adopt this proposal.

This outcome was largely the same for the EP's suggestions on the forerunner of Eurojust. The committee report on the matter called for the full participation of the Commission in the activities of Pro-Eurojust, a tightening of its provisions on data protection, and the eventual creation of a full-fledged European public prosecutor's office, with which the permanent Eurojust would have to be merged.[46] In the end, none of these proposals were adopted by the Council when it set up Pro-Eurojust.

The EP's opinions on other matters regarding crime and policing were similarly laced with both attempts to strengthen supranationalism and expressions of concern for democratic deficits in Council initiatives. Although supporting the creation of CEPOL, for example, the EP wanted the Council decision to stress various democratic safeguards in its instructional activities, including the protection of human rights and training on the rights of defendants. Only the latter was included in the Council's final act on CEPOL, which was formally adopted on December 22, 2000, taking effect on January 1, 2001. The EP likewise passed a resolution in support of the Council's framework decisions on money laundering. However, in the plenary debate on this, Neil MacCormick (Greens, UK) expressed his concerns about the measure's trampling on fundamental personal freedoms, arguing that they risked "Frankenstein's monster being created, while like Frankenstein there is an attempt to do good."[47]

In addition to such opinions on specific pieces of legislation, the European Parliament was critical of its own general lack of involvement in the formation the EU's overall crime-fighting strategy. This sentiment had been expressed most clearly in its resolution of September 9, 2000, which responded to the 2000 Action Plan. Substantively, this EP resolution did not object to the particulars found in the Action Plan. In this regard, the EP merely pointed out that the Action Plan's system of specifying different priorities for each prescription from one to five was not to be taken seriously.

The EP noted that only one item was given a priority of four or five and that the priority recommendations did not always reflect the urgency of an objective, but rather its practicality.

The resolution was, however, much more critical of the Action Plan in terms of its *how* it was composed. The EP's resolution argued that the spirit of the Treaty of Amsterdam was to remedy the democratic deficit regarding the EU's legal acts. Yet by passing its most recent Action Plan on crime and building these objectives into the JHA Scoreboard without consulting the EP, the Council violated this ambition. In the fourth and fifth operative clause of the resolution, the EP stated that it "opposes . . . the Council's attitude, which appears to be signaling that it regards informing Parliament of work strategic papers as a mere act of courtesy, and thus sees consultation of Parliament as unnecessary."[48] Finally, the EP expressed another fundamental concern on the issue of JHA, namely its confirmation in the resolution's first operative clause of "the need to combat organized crime at the Union level whilst ensuring that fundamental freedoms, the rights of the individual and procedural guarantees are upheld, in particular the rights of the defense and respect for privacy."

In sum, the Parliament was generally supportive of the JHA Council actions on police cooperation and crime fighting during the French presidency of 2000 (with the exception of human-being trafficking), but continued to critique what it viewed as a democratic deficit in EU JHA policy. Like the Commission, the EP supported more institutionalized cooperation and greater harmonization of criminal law. However, the EP remained concerned about the democratic deficit in EU policymaking on JHA in two ways. In one regard, the EP continued to stress that fundamental civil rights would have to be protected as international cooperation increased. In addition, having worked under the terms of the Treaty of Amsterdam for over one year by the end of 2000, the EP remained dissatisfied with its lack of influence on the formation of the EU's overall strategy on crime fighting, as well as on individual legislation.

The Treaty of Nice and JHA

By December 2000, the draft Treaty of Nice was nearing completion in the IGC, but it contained little to remedy the plight of the EP in the Third Pillar. However, it did entail a few items regarding JHA. Much of the new treaty, as well as most of the last-minute negotiating, centered around the contentious issues of reforming the Commission, Parliament, and Council in anticipation of enlargement. Following a second "conclave" session of EU ministers on December 3, as well an exchange of views with EP president Nicole Fontaine (European People's Party, France) on the following day, the French presidency distributed the draft treaty on the eve of the Nice European Council. After a good deal of last-minute logrolling and horse trading among large and small member states, the heads of state and government reached a political agreement at Nice on December 10, and the final text was formally signed on February 26, 2001.

The Treaty of Nice contains three main areas related to Justice and Home Affairs. The first of these concerns the topic of expanding QMV and co-decision to some Third Pillar issues. Although the idea of doing so for the items falling under Title VI (on "Police and Judicial Cooperation in Criminal Matters") had been abandoned early in the IGC, the question remained regarding Title IV, "Visas, Asylum, Immigration, and Other Policies Related to Free Movement of Persons."

Specifically, many delegations wanted to eliminate the five-year transitional period specified in Article 67 under Title IV of the EC Treaty (TEC) and make the shift to QMV and co-decision immediate. Article 67 stipulates that the Council shall, after 2004, "take a decision" on applying the "community" procedure of Article 251 (TEC) for policies related to visas, immigration, and free movement, giving the Commission sole right of initiative, establishing voting by QMV in the Council, and granting the EP power of co-decision. However, there was reluctance among various member states (e.g., France) across several issues to shift all aspects of Title IV (TEC) upon the ratification of the new treaty, resulting in only modest progress on changing policymaking to QMV. Under the Treaty of Nice, Article 65 (TEC) on the cross-border service of judicial documents has been shifted to QMV and co-decision, excluding family law. Article 63 (TEC) on asylum measures and the temporary protection of refugees will be similarly changed under the Treaty of Nice, provided that the Council has already agreed by unanimity to common rules and principle governing asylum (see Chapter 8). In addition, the Treaty of Nice contains a "best endeavors clause" to shift the remainder of Title IV to QMV and co-decision by May 1, 2004, or as soon as possible after that.[49]

The second way that the Treaty of Nice impinges on JHA is in the removal of the veto, or "emergency break," in the European Council for enhanced cooperation on Third Pillar items, including those falling under Title VI on "Police and Judicial Cooperation in Criminal Matters" of the Treaty on European Union (TEU). Under the new procedure specified in Article 40 of the TEU, a dissenting state will no longer be able to block enhanced cooperation by others through a veto in the European Council. Under the Treaty of Nice, the Council will be able to use enhanced cooperation for Third Pillar measures through a QMV and a dissenting state will only be able to delay this by referring the matter to the European Council for discussion before having to submit to a final vote in the Council by QMV.[50]

Finally, the French initiative to include references to Eurojust in the new treaty was also accepted. Consequently, Article 30 (TEU) on "Common Action on Police Cooperation" and Article 31 (TEU) on "Common Action on Judicial Cooperation" were amended to include reference to Eurojust and its duties.[51] With work on Pro-Eurojust already under way, the inclusion of Eurojust in the new treaty made it even more likely that the EU would reach its goals of creating the permanent Eurojust unit by the end of 2001 (see Chapter 7).

Explaining Progress After the Tampere Summit

With the conclusion of the Nice European Council, the French presidency drew to an end, having accomplished a great deal concerning many of the objectives specified in the Tampere Conclusions and 2000 Action Plan. In 2001, making progress on these goals would fall first to the Swedish presidency and then to the Belgians, with the Commission becoming increasingly active as well. Initially, the priority for 2001 would be on meeting the timetables set down in the Commission's Scoreboard. However, after the terrorist attacks on the United States on September 11, 2001, a new political will in the EU to fight organized crime and terrorism would hasten progress on completing the AFSJ. In the years following the creation of its Third Pillar, the European Union experienced relatively slow progress on many aspects of JHA, including making Europol operational. However, this began to change by mid-1999 after the entry into force of the Treaty of Amsterdam, installation of the new Commission, and creation of the DG on Justice and Home Affairs. As discussed in this chapter, the pace of progress on JHA quickened following the historic Tampere European Council and agreement on how to make the AFSJ a reality. Guided by the Tampere milestones and later the Action Plan of 2000 and Convention on Mutual Assistance in Criminal Matters, there would finally be progress on several aspects of the EU's emerging legal and institutional infrastructure of crime fighting. Although the Austrian crisis would, in general, sour relations in the EU throughout much of 2000, it would serve to highlight the significance of illegal immigration in EU politics and foreshadow the rise to prominence of this issue during the Spanish presidency of 2002 (see Chapter 8).

In a sense, the Tampere milestones and objectives contained in the 2000 Action Plan should be viewed as specific measures designed to achieve the AFSJ prescribed in the Treaty of Amsterdam. Thus, their origins can be understood in terms of the same kind of forces highlighted at the end of Chapter 4. Nevertheless, the particular salience of these internal and external factors on JHA progress should be examined from the Tampere summit through the Portuguese and French presidencies of 2000.

During this period, the development of JHA continued to be influenced by external factors. Foremost among these was the impending enlargement of the EU, which raised concerns about the crime problems that this would bring, as well as how this would exacerbate the challenge of making policy on JHA among a larger and more complex group of member states. Already having shaped several aspects of the Treaty of Amsterdam, the pressure of enlargement grew more intense following the Tampere European Council. The Helsinki summit of December 1999 cleared the way for accession negotiations with six additional candidate states, enlarging the scope and JHA-related concerns stemming from enlargement, as countries with especially weak criminal justice institutions, such a Romania and Bulgaria, were put on track to join the EU and one day participate in the Schengen free-travel area. Moreover, in May 2000, the nature and scope of the internal security challenges at hand regarding enlargement were brought into sharper focus with the start of negotiations on the JHA chapters of accession (i.e., Chapter 24) with the original six candidate states of the Luxembourg group.

In addition, external factors were also salient in the form of illegal immigration. This was evident in the increased attention paid to the trafficking of human beings during the French presidency of 2000, coming in the wake of the tragic deaths of Chinese illegal immigrants at Dover in June. In part, concern for crimes with external sources, such as illegal immigration and drug trafficking, shaped the EU's goal to deal with these problems before they reached the borders of any of its member states. The EU's new focus on the external dimensions of its internal security was evident in several regards during this period. For example, this was found in the Tampere milestones' prescriptions for stronger external action, the guidelines of the 2000 Action Plan on organized crime regarding strengthening ties with the applicant states and third countries, the international section of the new antidrug strategy for 2000–2004, and, more generally, the new strategy paper published by COREPER on external relations and JHA. In addition, the JHA Council formally authorized Europol to begin negotiating cooperation agreements with third countries and international organizations.

As before, the impact of the external pressures, such as enlargement and illegal immigration, were intensified by functional spillover from cooperation on free movement in the form of the Schengen free-travel zone. That is, it was assumed that a crime problem affecting one member state, without borders to contain it, could eventually impact others. In addition, cooperation on the Single Market's provisions for the free movement of capital spilled over into JHA, as the EU began to address the problem of money laundering that was facilitated by this. Heightened attention to financial crime was behind the decision reached during the French presidency to expand Europol's remit to any form of money laundering. These concerns also led to the first-ever joint meeting, or "jumbo session," of the JHA and ECOFIN councils during the French presidency, which established a new EU strategy for dealing with financial crime in general, and money laundering in particular.

In 1999–2000, the EU began to make progress on several aspects of the legal and institutional infrastructure of crime fighting proposed in the Tampere milestones, including the first meetings of the Chiefs of Police Task Force, and legislative activity to set up Eurojust and CEPOL. In addition, work began on harmonizing criminal law in a number of areas, entailing negotiations on framework decisions covering crime related to the counterfeiting of the euro, the trafficking of human beings, and even environmental crime (with steps regarding the latter issue representing another example of spillover from cooperation in the First Pillar). At least to some degree, the EU's willingness to pursue deeper integration in all of these areas represented a weakening salience of subsidiarity on JHA. That is, in more facets of internal security than ever before, the member states seemed prepared to pursue solutions at the EU-level, rather than dealing with many crime problems internally.

Moreover, the work on the legal and institutional infrastructure of crime fighting constituted the first steps toward the Europeanization of these aspects of JHA in the member states. For example, both the Police Chiefs Task Force and the nascent European Police College (CEPOL) were designed to promote the exchange of best practices regarding crime fighting, with the explicit intention of creating a European police culture and common approaches to fighting certain crimes. Likewise, progress on the framework decisions to harmonize definitions and sanctions for some forms of organized crimes across the member states represented the first steps toward a Europeanization of penal codes in the EU.

However, it is important not to confuse the diminishing significance of subsidiarity and first initial progress toward Europeanization on JHA with an increasing salience of federalist ideology. In fact, the continued insignificance of federalism as an internal factor driving cooperation on JHA during this period was made clear during the IGC of 2000. Although the opportunity was there to communitize what was left of the left of the original Third Pillar, this possibility was never given serious consideration during the IGC. Indeed, the member states were not even willing to advance the 2004 deadline for the planned shift of most free-movement policies (e.g., immigration, asylum, etc.) to the First Pillar. In end, the most significant change to JHA contained in the Treaty of Nice was its reference to Eurojust and elimination of the emergency break regarding closer cooperation.

Even with the continued lack of federalist ideology among the member states to propel integration on JHA, the cooperation on JHA would continue its gradual shift in the direction of supranationalism after the Tampere summit and into 2000. In one regard, the development of new common crime-fighting institutions (e.g., Eurojust) and the strengthening of Europol can be explained as a search for practical solutions to problems that seemed to be increasingly beyond the reach of unilateral solutions. The development of JHA under the Treaty of Amsterdam must also be attributed to the new role of the Commission, which, armed with a new DG, became much more active in proposing new legislation following the Tampere European Council. In addition, by developing and monitoring its JHA Scoreboard, the Commission was better able to insure that progress toward the AFSJ would be maintained.

Along the way, the European Parliament, having won the right to be consulted by the JHA, tried to increase its activity in the Third Pillar as well. In doing so, it not only used most every opportunity to call for greater democratic control over Europol and the new crime-fighting institutions, but also pushed for attention to various human and civil rights on various JHA initiatives, including the pending framework decision on the trafficking of human beings and the draft decisions aimed at setting up Eurojust and CEPOL. Although the EP's opinions would often be disregarded by the Council when reaching final decisions on specific proposals, its efforts served as a reminder that the new legal and institutional infrastructure would be at least somewhat shaped by enduring concerns for democracy in the EU.

Notes

1. Justice and Home Affairs Directorate-General (official website), "Ensuring that the European Union is an area of freedom, security and justice." http://europa.eu.int/comm/dgs/justice_home/mission/mission_en.htm.

2. Emek M. Uçarer, "From the Sidelines to Center Stage—Sidekick No More? The European Commission in Justice and Home Affairs," *European Integration online Papers (EIoP)*, vol. 5, no. 5, 2001, 12.

3. Dick Leonard, "In Pursuit of Pillar Three," *Europe*, July-August 2000.

4. Uçarer, "From the Sidelines," 13.

5. Ibid.

6. Monica den Boer and William Wallace, "Justice and Home Affairs," in *Policy-Making in the European Union*, 4th ed., ed. H. Wallace and W. Wallace (New York: Oxford University Press, 2000), 517.

7. Jörg Monar, "Justice and Home Affairs," *Journal of Common Market Studies*, September 2000, vol. 38, 138.

8. Ibid., 139.

9. *The Economist*, "Europe's Borders: A Single Market in Crime," October 16, 1999.

10. *European Report*, "Justice and Home Affairs: Agenda for October 4 Council," October 2, 1999.

11. European Council, *Presidency's Conclusions* (Tampere) (Brussels: General Secretariat of the Council October 1999).

12. *European Report,* "Justice and Home Affairs: Study into European Police College Plan," January 19, 2000.

13. JHA Council Meeting, December 2, 1999.

14. General Secretariat (Council of the European Union), "Comments by Delegations to the 'First Reflections Concerning the Tampere Conclusions as Far as They Relate to Europol' as contained in doc. 13370/99 Europol 48," Brussels, February 8, 2000.

15. *European Report,* "Justice and Home Affairs: António Vitorino Enrolls Ministers in Elaboration of AFSJ," March 8, 2000.

16. Council of the European Union, Article 36 Committee, *The Prevention and Control of Organized Crime: A European Union Strategy for the Beginning of the New Millennium,* Brussels, March 3, 2000 (Council Document 6611/00). The lower the number, the higher the priority, meaning the more quickly work should be initiated and completed.

17. JHA Council Meeting, March 27, 2000.

18. *European Report,* "Law and Order: Operational Structure for Police Forces," April 12, 2000.

19. *European Report,* "Intergovernmental Conference: IGC Group Split on Size and Shape of Commission," April 4, 2000.

20. Ibid.

21. *European Report,* "Intergovernmental Conference: Enhanced Cooperation Under the Limelight," April 19, 2000; *European Report,* "Preparatory Group on IGC Continues Work," June 7, 2000.

22. Harry Arnold, "Four Months for Each Victim Who Perished," *Daily Record* (Glasgow), April 6, 2001.

23. Roger Cohen, "Europe Tries to Turn a Tide of Migrants Chasing Dreams," *New York Times,* July 2, 2000.

24. *The Economist,* "Trafficking in Women," August 26, 2000.

25. *European Report,* "Justice and Home Affairs: Framework Decision on Anti-People-Trafficking in the Pipeline," July 21, 2000.

26. Concerning JHA, the accession "chapters" had been opened for the Luxembourg group in June. The JHA chapters of accession for the applicant states of the Helsinki group, aside from Romania, would not be opened until June 2001.

27. See, for example, Suzanne Daley, "Europe Lifts Sanctions on Austria, but Vows Vigilance," *New York Times,* September 13, 2000, and *The Economist,* "Europe: The EU 14 Give Way to Austria," September 16, 2000.

28. *European Report,* "Experts Put Final Touches to Draft Decision on European Police College," September 20, 2000.

29. *European Report,* "Justice and Home Affairs: Packed Agenda for 28 September Council," September 27, 2000.

30. *European Report,* "Europol Prepares for Co-operation Talks with Interpol," September 23, 2000.

31. See *European Report,* "European Council: Presidency Hopes to Clear the Way for the IGC in Time for Nice," October 11, 2000; *European Report,* "Intergovernmental Conference: Progress on Closer Co-operation and Article 7," October 11, 2000.

32. BBC News, "Blair Rules Our European Super-State," October 14, 2000 (www.bbc.co.uk).

33. "Eurojust and the Treaty on European Union," annex to the communication of the French delegation to the Conference of the Representatives of the Governments of the Member States to Mr. Pierre Vimont, Chairman of the Group of Personal

Representatives of the Member States to the IGC, "IGC 2000: Incorporation of a Reference to Eurojust in the Treaty," Brussels, November 19, 2000.

34. *Agence France Presse,* "EU Ministers to Tackle Money Laundering," October 17, 2000.

35. This would not apply to attorney-client privilege cases dealing with criminal matters.

36. *European Report,* "Call for Joint Schengen and Europol Secretariat on Data Protection," June 14, 2000; and *Intelligence Newsletter,* "Dovetailing European Systems," June 29, 2000.

37. *European Report,* "Justice and Home Affairs: Council Gives Green Light for Nordic States Joining Schengen," December 6, 2000.

38. *European Report,* "Justice and Home Affairs: Commission Launches Crime Prevention Strategy," December 9, 2000.

39. Stephane Barbier, "Prodi's EU Commission Fails to Impress," *Agence France Presse,* September 14, 2000.

40. Barry James, "A Year Old, EU Commission Gives Itself a Passing Grade," *International Herald Tribune,* September 18, 2000.

41. Ibid.

42. These legislative items would be decided using the consultation procedure.

43. *European Report,* "Justice and Home Affairs: MEPs Slate French Presidency's Scrappy Immigration Policy," October 14, 2000.

44. *European Report,* "Justice and Home Affairs: Parliament Wants Bigger Role in Europol and Eurojust," November 18, 2000.

45. Ibid.

46. Ibid.; *European Report,* "Justice and Home Affairs: MEPs Vote on Parents' Visiting Rights, Eurojust, and Human Trafficking," October 28, 2000.

47. *European Report,* "Justice and Home Affairs: Parliament Wants Bigger Role in Europol and Eurojust," November 18, 2000.

48. European Parliament resolution on the Council's Action Plan for "The Prevention and Control of Organized Crime: A European Union Strategy for the Beginning of the New Millennium" (B5-0506/2000), minutes of September 21, 2000.

49. David Galloway, *The Treaty of Nice and Beyond: Realities and Illusions of Power in the EU* (Sheffield, England: Sheffield Academic Press, 2001), 105–106 and 198.

50. Ibid., 133–134.

51. Ibid., 159.

6

Crime Fighting
Before September 11

SWEDEN'S PRESIDENCY OF THE EU DURING THE FIRST HALF OF 2001 differed significantly from its predecessors on JHA. The Finnish presidency had of course spawned the seminal Tampere Conclusions, while the 2000 Action Plan and several legislative initiatives had begun under the leadership of Portugal. France's presidency witnessed a variety of new proposals, as well as some progress on JHA concerning the Treaty of Nice (e.g., its reference to Eurojust).

In contrast, Sweden attempted to use its leadership term to complete work on a variety of ongoing matters rather than initiate wholly new proposals. The impetus for this approach stemmed at least partly from the implicit criticism of France's presidency by the JHA ministers at their informal session in Stockholm on February 8–9, 2001. As the Commission had explained in an earlier communication, some ministers implied that the French had concentrated on pushing through new legislation without sufficient coordination with the initiatives of other member states or adequate consultation with the Commission.[1] Some of the blame for this was also directed at the Article 36 Committee, which had become too complicated with its proliferation of various working groups. It was also overworked since activity began on creating the AFSJ.[2] The backlog of tasks facing the committee had resulted in thirty-five initiatives being put on hold at that time.[3] The outcome of this discussion at the informal JHA Council of February 2001 on progress toward the AFSJ was a new common resolve among the ministers to stick to the timetable and political will embodied in the Commission's Scoreboard.

However, efforts under the Swedish presidency to protect the euro, adopted by Greece on January 1, 2001, represented one area of activity on JHA that went beyond the goals of the Scoreboard, which only prescribed common terminology and sanctions regarding its counterfeiting. With the physical introduction of the euro into twelve countries set for a year later

(15 billion new bank notes and 52 billion coins, equivalent to 50,000 truck-loads of the new currency), Europol's director, Jürgen Storbeck, noted that there were "unprecedented criminological aspects to the introduction of the single currency."[4] As European leaders hastened their preparations for "E-Day," so too did organized-crime groups, especially potential money launderers, armored-car and safe robbers, and counterfeiters.[5]

With these concerns in mind, there was almost immediate progress on protecting the new currency during the Swedish presidency. Following a high-level meeting in Brussels of senior management representatives of the European Commission, the European Central Bank (ECB), and Europol on February 15, 2001, an interinstitutional steering group to protect the euro was established on March 7, 2001. Composed of high-level representatives from each body, this steering group published an action plan to develop a common strategy and to coordinate various kinds of efforts across the EU to protect the euro. The Commission was charged with taking the legisla-tive initiative in this area. Meanwhile, the ECB was made responsible for storing data on counterfeit notes and coins, as well as working with national central banks on an information campaign to educate the public.[6] For its part, Europol would, as with other crimes in its mandate, assist national policing agencies with information sharing, expertise, technical support, and operational and strategic analysis. In addition to its own database on the euro, Europol would also have access to the ECB's technical database on counterfeiting.[7]

Around this time, Europol noted the progress that it had made during the previous year to protect the euro. This included a threat assessment regarding euro counterfeiting and the opening of the first analysis work file on this issue with the aim of identifying and targeting the most prolific criminal groups in the European Union. The publication of this report in March 2001 coincided with increasing concerns about the introduction of the euro during the Swedish presidency.

One major worry was that counterfeiters would find it easy to pass off fake euro bank notes during the transition phase, when the public would still be unfamiliar with the new currency. Referring to the euro notes' three levels of built-in security measures, Europol's criminal division chief, Christian Jacquier, observed that "the euro is an extremely well-secured note, but it is not at all reasonable to think that it won't be counterfeited one day."[8] For example, it was feared that fake euros produced using a color photocopier might be sufficient to fool some in the general public in the first few weeks after the euro's introduction. In light of these concerns, the Swedish presidency unveiled an eleven-point plan in May 2001 to protect the euro, mainly directed at preparing the public and local authori-ties, and promoting international cooperation through the EU and the appli-cant states, as well as bilaterally.[9] Regarding a role for Europol, the plan suggested the employment of a standard form to report incidents of counterfeiting during the switchover period, with Europol receiving, analyzing, and sharing the information. Many of these plans were later incorporated into a set of conclusions on protecting the euro that was eventually passed by the May JHA Council and implemented in 2001.

Along with fears of counterfeiting, the impending introduction of the euro raised concerns about other types of crimes. There was a concern for the robbery of armored cars, company safes, and banks, as huge amounts of euros would be transported and stored prior to their introduction and in the transition phase. In addition, Storbeck warned, "because of the huge movements of money, the period of the conversion to euros will be an ideal period for money laundering."[10] This was the case, in part, because so many law-abiding European were expected to bring in cash that they had hoarded over the years, and any crime-tainted money, included counterfeited notes, would not be easily noticed.[11]

Finally, the euro itself was expected to help organized-crime groups by providing them with a new common currency of their own that would be ideal for transnational European crime and much easier to launder in Europe compared to the U.S. dollar or German deutschemark. Compounding this problem was that in eleven of the twelve euro-zone countries, the highest-value euro bank note, the €500 note, would be worth more than the most valuable domestic note, and much larger than the highest U.S. dollar in circulation, the $100 bill (worth about €110 at the time). This large denomination means that a criminal could carry about €7.4 million in a typical attaché case. According to Michael Levi, a professor of criminology at Cardiff University, "If you were to design a system to facilitate money laundering, the large euro note would be what you would design."[12] Officials at the ECB countered these fears by pointing out that the €500 note would make up only 3 percent of the new euros in circulation.[13]

Despite these concerns, the impending introduction of euro bank notes and coins was viewed by Europol as an opportunity both to fight crime and demonstrate its own institutional value. Europol Deputy Director Willy Bruggeman predicted that "no one is going to burn their money . . . all suspect money will come in. This is a good opportunity to attack various sorts of crime."[14] Storbeck also saw the potential for Europol to increase its prestige: "Until now, the first address for counterfeit currency has been a national authority. Now the first address for a counterfeit euro, wherever it is in the world, is Europol . . . It makes no sense for information about euros counterfeited in Ukraine to be addressed to the French or Portuguese police. It gives us a new dimension."[15] Among EU diplomats, there was at least some recognition that Europol had "hit the big time."[16] According to one diplomat, "In the past, the member states haven't given Europol enough information . . . the euro is so important, it will change that way of thinking."[17]

As discussed, Europol was already empowered to protect the euro, with its operational mandate having been extended for this purpose on April 29, 1999. At this point the Swedish presidency was hoping to expand Europol's remit even further, having raised the issue in the Article 36 Committee on January 18, 2001.[18] The Swedish proposal called upon the Council to allow Europol to help member states combat any form of crime, but Sweden was especially interested in empowering Europol to fight cyber-crime, fraud, and environmental crime. However, it was unclear at the time whether this could or should be done by a simple Council decision amending the Europol Convention with reference to the crimes listed in its annex or a more time-consuming revision of the convention itself. In addition to expanding Europol's remit, Sweden also expressed its desire to amend the Europol Convention to spell out Europol's relationship with Eurojust.

Progress on the Scoreboard

As work on protecting the euro and extending Europol's powers were under way, so too were preparations for the first of two formal meetings of the JHA Council under Sweden's direction, held on March 15–16, 2001. Immediately prior to the formal Council session, the Mixed Committee met and discussed illegal immigration and drug trafficking stemming from the Balkans. The Mixed Committee also confirmed the start date, March 25, 2001, for the five Nordic countries to abolish border controls and participate fully in the Schengen free-travel area. As a result, the Schengen zone would be increased to include 310 million people in fifteen countries. Only Ireland and the UK remained outside of this area by March 2001, although they maintained a free-travel area with each other and participated in some of the crime-fighting aspects of the Schengen agreements (e.g., cross-border surveillance). Also of note at the Mixed Committee meeting was the news that Switzerland had recently expressed its interest in exploring its possible accession to part of the Schengen *acquis*. In sum, the impending expansion of the Schengen zone by the end of March 2001 would increase the area of free travel not only for citizens, but also for organized-crime groups operating across national boundaries, adding to the importance of facilitating the fight against cross-border crime in the EU.

This meeting of the Mixed Committee in March 2001 also took up the two French proposals on the trafficking of human beings, which were aimed at completing the implementation of the Schengen *acquis*. Agreement was reached on the need for a clause to exclude humanitarian trafficking efforts, but discord remained on the nature of this exemption (to prevent its abuse), as well as on the level of sanctions to be applied (i.e., the lowest number of years for a maximum sentence).[19] In addition to these

French proposals, the Commission had, by this point, communicated to the Swedish presidency its own more comprehensive draft framework decision on the trafficking of human beings, but this would be discussed in the JHA Council proper in May.

Meanwhile, in the margins of the JHA Council session on March 16, the general issue of the trafficking of human beings was discussed at the first-ever joint meeting between the fifteen JHA ministers and their counterparts in the thirteen applicant countries (i.e., including Turkey). Convened on the initiative of the Swedish presidency and serving as the overall highlight of the two-day JHA Council (March 15–16), these discussions focused on strengthening practical cooperation between the two sides prior to accession, especially on the topics of drug trafficking, asylum, immigration, and the trafficking of human beings.[20]

With regard to judicial cooperation in criminal matters such as these, the Commission had hosted a conference in Brussels on March 14–16 in Brussels for some of the applicant countries (Bulgaria, the Czech Republic, Hungary, Poland, Romania, Slovakia, and Slovenia). The Commission used this event to launch its new €1.2 million project on judicial cooperation in criminal matters, financed under the €10 million PHARE Horizontal Program begun in 1999 to cover the fields of rule of law, training of judges in EC law, and management of borders, visas, and migration. The conference was also attended by the UK, which serves as the project leader, as well as eight other member states in supporting roles. Reflecting ongoing efforts in the member states, the new project was designed to help the candidate states set up an effective system of international cooperation in areas such as extradition, mutual assistance, and the confiscation of assets.

The announcement of the new PHARE project underscored the importance of Justice and Home Affairs in progress toward the eventual accession of the twelve countries of the Luxembourg and Helsinki groups into the EU (i.e., not Turkey), which the Nice European Council had affirmed should take place, at least for some states, by 2004. It should be recalled that the 1999 program had supplemented the €10 million PHARE Horizontal Program on JHA of 1996. This had been designed to help the candidate states apply the EU's asylum *acquis*, train police, and fight organized crime and corruption.[21]

As discussed in Chapter 5, the negotiations on the JHA chapters of accession for Cyprus, the Czech Republic, Estonia, Hungary, Poland, and Slovenia had been under way since May 2000. On June 1, 2001, the JHA chapters of accession for Bulgaria, Lithuania, Latvia, Malta, and Slovakia were opened as well, leaving only Romania out of such negotiations by the end of the Swedish presidency. For many of the twelve candidate states, the chapter on JHA was among the last to be opened for talks. The Nice European Council made clear that countries would be considered for accession when all of the chapters of accession were provisionally closed, regardless of whether they were among the originally projected "first wave" (the Luxembourg group) or second wave (the Helsinki group) of applicant states.

In addition to working toward the adoption of the EU's *acquis* on JHA in all areas (including the Schengen *acquis*), the candidate states were also attempting to work closely with Europol. To facilitate this, Europol was charged with concluding agreements with each of these countries, including those covering the exchange of personel. On the basis of individual reports on the status of data protection conducted by the Europol Management Board, the March JHA Council decided (without debate) to allow the director of Europol to begin to negotiate cooperation agreements with Poland and Hungary, just as similar reports and negotiations were in the works for the other candidate countries for 2001.

Similar talks with Europol were also approved for Norway and Iceland at the March 2001 JHA Council, in anticipation of their imminent participation in the Schengen free-travel area. In May 2001, Sweden proposed new rules for Europol to allow the "onward transmission" of personal data by third-party countries (e.g., Iceland, Norway, the applicant states, and the United States) or non-EU bodies (Interpol). This had not been permitted under the original rules agreed upon by the JHA Council in March 2000. The new rules would allow third-party countries and bodies to pass along data provided by Europol to other states. This would not only aid the simultaneous investigation of crimes by several actors, but would also ease the ability of Europol to share data with its partners and forge partnership agreements in the first place.[22] Ultimately, the final Council decision on the matter would have to wait for the opinion of the EP, which would not come until near the end of the Belgian presidency. By then, the matter of onward transmission, and information sharing in general, would be viewed as an important component in the fight against terrorism. That is, many would come to believe that the attacks on the United States of September 11, 2001, might have been avoided had there been more extensive sharing of information among the world's security and intelligence organizations.

As discussed in the examination of the French presidency found in Chapter 5, the March 2001 meeting of the JHA Council meeting was the occasion of the provisional agreement on setting up the European Crime Prevention Network. Following the consideration of the EP's generally favorable opinion, the network was formally established by a decision of the next JHA Council in May 2001 (without further debate). Another area of continuing concern discussed at the March 2001 JHA Council was the fight against drugs, which was the main topic of a wide-ranging debate that was televised for the press and public. Although a variety of important issues were raised by various member states during their discussions (e.g., problems with source countries, trafficking routes, permitting hot pursuit by sea, etc.), the debate mainly focused on the British proposal calling for minimum sanctions covering drug trafficking, which were supported by Greece, Belgium, and Sweden. The Netherlands and Italy cautioned against a common approach, citing differences among hard, soft, and synthetic drugs, and contending national approaches regarding this. Denmark and Austria stressed the need to distinguish between drug traffickers, to be punished, and drug addicts, who needed help.[23] Ultimately, discord among member states on the issue would endure into the Spanish and Danish presidencies in 2002.

In addition to this debate, the JHA ministers addressed two areas of harmonization of criminal law at their March meeting. First, the JHA ministers reached an agreement in principle on the goals and penal sanctions of a draft framework decision on protecting the environment through criminal law, which had been proposed by Denmark in September 2000. However, after the Commission submitted its own draft directive on the same matter in March 2001, the issue arose whether this matter was to be considered as a First or Third Pillar matter. Since penal sanctions (e.g., fines) were at issue, most member states, and eventually the Commission itself, came to recognize that the issue must be treated under the terms of the Third Pillar, requiring the need for a framework decision.[24] A second issue of criminal law discussed by the JHA ministers in March 2001 was cyber-crime, including child pornography, resulting in the Council's recognition of the need for EU legislation specifying common definitions and sanctions to combat this. As with the framework decision on drug trafficking, the proposals on the environment and cyber-crime would not be resolved in 2001, and would be taken on by the Spanish and Danish presidencies in 2002.

Finally, the March 2001 session of the JHA Council also featured a lunch meeting with the EU's high representative for CFSP, Javier Solana, regarding the state of progress on the civilian component of the EU's proposed rapid-reaction force. Based on principles established in the Treaty of Amsterdam, the Cologne European Council of 1999 had affirmed the goal of creating an EU military force that could carry out a full range of so-called Petersberg tasks related to peacekeeping and crisis management. The Helsinki summit of December 1999 had subsequently established the "Headline Goal" of assembling, on sixty days' notice, a rapid-reaction force of 50,000–60,000 troops by 2003 that could conduct such operations for up to one year, including related activities by nonmilitary personnel. The Feira European Council of June 2000 had spelled out this latter aspect of the rapid-reaction force in more detail, calling for the member states to provide up to 5,000 police officers for international missions, including the ability to deploy up to 1,000 of these personnel for such tasks on thirty days' notice.

These goals had been affirmed during the French presidency, prior to the Nice summit, and work progressed throughout 2001 toward attaining them. Thus, in addition to the building of various new crime-fighting institutions for use within member states, the EU was also busy in 2001 creating a new policing organization to serve abroad. Not only does the nonmilitary component of the proposed rapid-reaction force serve as another example of growing police cooperation within the European Union, it also provides an additional illustration of increasing cross-pillar activity with the EU, which would only intensify following September 11.

The New Institutional Infrastructure of Police Cooperation

As work continued on meeting the nonmilitary requirements of the Headline Goal, as well as on the proposals covered during the March JHA Council of 2001, the Swedish presidency was also overseeing the development of two nascent institutions in the area of crime fighting, namely the European Police College (CEPOL) and Eurojust. Activity on CEPOL's first budget and work program for 2001 had been under way since the start of the year, when Portugal's initiative took effect (see Chapter 5). On March 21 the governing board of CEPOL, then under the direction of Sweden (as it held the EU presidency), adopted a financial regulation that would keep separate the administrative costs of its secretariat from the expenses related to its training activities. Like Europol, CEPOL is funded out of the budgets of the member states, rather than out of the EU budget.

By spring 2001, no less than seven countries were vying to host CEPOL's secretariat, including France, Germany, Spain, Italy, the Netherlands, Austria, and the UK. However, by April the latter had emerged as the odds-on favorite after Britain proposed a site at its National Police Training (NPT) headquarters at Bramshill (in Hampshire) and offered to pay £150,000 annually for related expenses.[25] In keeping with the original Portuguese proposal, it was known that CEPOL's secretariat would be based in one of the member states' national police-training academies. It was therefore understood that the selection of the secretariat's site would determine the nationality of its director. Consequently, the UK also proposed the NPT's deputy director, Ian McDonald, to be the first administrative director of the CEPOL secretariat. Final agreement on CEPOL's site and director was not reached by the end of the Swedish presidency as expected. Consequently, the resolution of these matters, as well as work on CEPOL's annual programs and budgets for 2001 and 2002, was turned over to the incoming Belgian presidency.

With work continuing on CEPOL, the other new crime-fighting institution of the EU, Eurojust, moved from paper to reality on March 1, 2001, with the creation of the provisional judicial-cooperation unit, Pro-Eurojust. This was housed within the Secretariat-General of the Council in Brussels and placed under the direction of Bjorn Blomquist, who was attorney general at the Swedish court specializing in financial criminal proceedings. Meeting about twice weekly, Pro-Eurojust was composed of magistrates from each member state, with its leadership passing to Belgium when it assumed the presidency of the EU in the second half of 2001. These national representatives not only dealt with cases assigned to them by the member states, but also participated in a working group within the Council charged with drafting a decision to set up the permanent Eurojust by January 1, 2002.

Pro-Eurojust was intended to serve as test run for the operation of the full-fledged Eurojust, just as the Europol Drugs Unit (EDU) had been the forerunner of Europol. Similar to this experience, the planning stages of Eurojust were characterized by indecision and discord over many outstanding issues. The most fundamental of these was whether Eurojust should simply coordinate investigations by national authorities or be empowered to initiate these, as well as prosecutions. Related to this was the fundamental question of whether Eurojust should be built with the goal of it becoming the embryo of a future European public prosecutor's office. Answers to some of these questions were evident by late March 2001, indicating that Eurojust would not amount to a full-fledged prosecutor's office for the EU, at least not in the short run. Thus, just as Europol had fallen short of a true European FBI, it was becoming clear that Eurojust's powers would also be limited. Specifically, Eurojust was given the mandate to coordinate investigations, as well as facilitate them, for example, by encouraging better contacts among investigators, helping to simplify the execution of "letters of rogatory" (i.e., court-to-court requests for assistance or information), or advising Europol on its operations.

The latter proposal presented problems of its own, as the nature of Eurojust's relationship to Europol had yet to be specified, including the ability of the two organizations to share information. In fact, the issues of how Eurojust would store its data and who would have access to it had yet to be decided. It was also unclear whether Eurojust would have access to judicial records in the member states or data stored in the Schengen Information System (SIS). These latter matters would not be resolved until late in the Belgian presidency (see Chapter 7).

However, during the Swedish presidency of 2001, support had emerged for Eurojust to be empowered to request that member states initiate investigations. Yet, as is the case with Europol, member states would not be obliged to actually conduct these. On this point, the Swedish presidency, backed by Italy and Portugal, pushed for legislation to compel states to justify their turning down of any requests.[26] The limited institutional power of Eurojust was also reflected in the proposed ability of member states to define the nature and extent of their own representatives' powers. Furthermore, at the insistence of Sweden and Denmark, the proposed blueprint for Eurojust included a system of national correspondents who would work as liaisons between Eurojust and national judicial authorities. Although this was intended to be optional, the system of national correspondents was opposed by most other member states, as well as by the EP, due to the confusion that it could create, as well as because of its elimination of direct links between national authorities and Eurojust.

The use of national correspondents gave Eurojust an intergovernmental character, and this was evident as well in the minor role specified for the European Commission in the draft proposal. The Commission would only be associated with Eurojust through its Anti-Fraud Office (OLAF) and could only attend meetings of Eurojust if the national representatives allowed this. In addition, no plans were made for the Commission to have access to Eurojust's database. In effect, this meant that the Commission would have no greater role vis-à-vis Eurojust than would third-party countries or international organizations.[27]

Eurojust's proposed list of crimes to fight had not changed since the presentation of its original blueprint under the Portuguese presidency a year earlier. That is, Eurojust would deal with judicial matters in all of the areas under Europol's remit. At this stage this included drug trafficking, the sale of nuclear and radioactive materials, stolen cars, illegal-immigration networks, the trafficking of human beings, child pornography, terrorism, euro counterfeiting, and money laundering. However, Europol's crime-fighting duties would soon be expanded under the Belgian presidency and, with it, the remit of Eurojust when it began its formal duties in 2002 (see Chapter 8).

Finally, plans were still being drawn up during the Swedish presidency regarding the administration and financing of Eurojust. It was proposed that Eurojust should one day share its secretariat with the European Judicial Network (for criminal matters) in Brussels, and that it should have one president and two vice presidents to be appointed by the Council for a four-year term. The Eurojust president would report to the EP, but not to the Commission, and could submit proposals on improving judicial cooperation in criminal matters to the JHA Council. The operational costs of Eurojust would be supported by the EU budget, but member states would continue to pay the salaries of their national members. At the time disagreement remained on whether the permanent home of Eurojust would remain in Brussels, which Belgium favored, or housed near Europol in The Hague, as favored by the Dutch. A final decision on this, as well as regarding the site of CEPOL's secretariat, would ultimately get caught up in the embarrassing discord among the heads of state and government regarding the sites of several other new EU bodies, leading to the abrupt end of the Laeken summit in December 2001 (see Chapter 7).

In an attempt to resolve some of these and other issues surrounding the draft decision to set up the permanent Eurojust, the Council's Secretariat General had circulated a questionnaire to over one hundred of the European Judicial Network's (EJN) contact points, asking them to voice their views on their relationship with Eurojust. Collectively, the EJN saw its own role as encouraging cooperation among the member states, while it envisioned a complimentary and active role for Eurojust in fighting cross-border European crime. For example, the EJN contact points viewed Eurojust's role in coordinating and even instigating investigations to be both useful and necessary.[28]

The European Parliament also came out in favor of a strong role for Eurojust when its Committee on Citizen's Freedoms, Rights, and JHA adopted a generally favorable report on the issue on April 27, 2001. While specifying closer monitoring of the use and storage of personal data held by Eurojust, the EP report also called for Eurojust to have, among other things, powers to combat environmental crime and to launch joint investigative teams. At the ministerial level, however, there was much less agreement on these matters. In light of this discord across a variety of issues, and given the full agenda of the Swedish presidency, the final debate and decision on the nature of the permanent Eurojust unit were lifted from the plans for the next meeting of the JHA Council in May and left to the subsequent Belgian presidency (see Chapter 7).

Concluding the Swedish Presidency

The agenda was full indeed for the second and final meeting of the JHA Council of the Swedish presidency on May 28–29, 2001. Continuing progress on money laundering that had intensified under the French presidency, the Council reached a political agreement on a protocol to the 2000 Convention on Mutual Assistance in Criminal Matters, eroding secrecy in banking. The new protocol obliges EU member states, with some exemptions regarding their national fiscal laws, to respond to requests from other EU members to investigate whether a person under criminal investigation holds one or more bank accounts in their country and to disclose all details of such accounts.

The May JHA Council also followed up on combating the trafficking of human beings. Agreement was finally reached in the Council on the main elements of the draft framework decision submitted by the Commission. However, the ministers failed to reach consensus on the lowest maximum sentence to be applied. At the end of the two-day JHA Council session, the Commission's proposal on trafficking in human beings was turned over to COREPER to complete work on the outstanding sanctions issues, which it did prior to the September JHA Council under the Belgian presidency (see Chapter 7).

Technically, this decision was not final, given the outstanding question on sanctions. However, the Council's decision on the rest of the Commission's proposal came a day *before* the EP's committee report on the draft framework was even published on May 29. Although generally approving of the Commission's proposal, this report did lead to thirty-seven amendments of the text, passed by the EP after its plenary debate on June 6, 2001. Many of these amendments called for various measures designed to protect the victims of human trafficking, including a proposed fund to be raised from confiscated criminal assets. Such amendments were not only ignored by the Council, which had already reached its agreement, but most were rejected by the Commission, which found them to be in violation of the principle of subsidiarity (i.e., the Commission felt such protective measures were best left to the member states). "VOICE," a network of forty-seven NGOs, subsequently criticized the draft proposal approved by the Council for its failure to include provisions for victims to apply for asylum and, outside of legal assistance, its lack of protection for them.[29]

Meanwhile, the French proposals on the trafficking of human beings were designed as amendments to the Schengen *acquis,* which had been integrated into the framework of the EU by a protocol to the Treaty of Amsterdam. The French initiatives took the form of both a draft directive and a draft framework decision that were discussed on the second day of the May JHA Council, during a meeting of the Mixed Committee. The directive, which replaces Article 27 of the Schengen Implementation Convention, defines the facilitation of unauthorized entry, movement, and residence, including an exemption for the trafficking of human beings for humanitarian reasons. That is, the directive specifies that the nonexempted trafficking must be "committed for financial gain." The Mixed Committee also agreed on the draft of the accompanying framework decision, including a maximum sentence of not less than six years for human trafficking. Finally, the Mixed Committee reached political agreement on a separate but related draft directive supplementing Article 26 of the Schengen Convention, which calls for the harmonization of penalties for human traffickers (i.e., carriers). Initiated in July 2000 in response to the tragedy at Dover, this new directive sets up a system of fines (€3,000 per illegal passenger) aimed at airlines and shipping companies.[30]

In addition to its progress on human trafficking, the May JHA Council also reached political agreement on a draft directive establishing the terms of temporary protection of refugees in member states in the case of a mass influx of displaced persons. The Swedish minister for development cooperation, migration, and asylum policy, Maj-Inger Klingvall, described the measure as a "breakthrough in the work of creating a common European asylum policy."[31] The directive specifies temporary protection for refugees for one year, with a possible extension for a further two six-month periods, and spells out the various rights to be enjoyed by refugees in member states (e.g., housing, health care, family reunification, etc.). This measure also obliges member states to establish a solidarity mechanism, allowing refugees to be transferred from one state to another to share the burden of protection (provided that the displaced person and the welcoming member state agree to this).

The JHA Council of May 2001 also passed a set of conclusions specifying Europol's role in protecting the euro. The conclusions called upon Europol to share information and cooperate with the member states, the European Central Bank, and the Commission (i.e., OLAF) regarding counterfeiting. The conclusions on the euro also called upon Europol "on request or on its own initiative" to provide member states with assistance in carrying out their anticounterfeiting activities. In addition, agreement was reached on most aspects of a draft decision calling for information exchanges with each other and Europol, while a provision on criminal sanctions was removed from the proposal for preparation as a framework decision.

In addition, the May JHA Council adopted conclusions regarding the funding of the SIS II, the successor to the Schengen Information System. Agreement was reached to reform the SIS II in preparation for enlargement, as well as to fund the information sharing from the community budget, rather than intergovernmentally, starting in 2002. Political agreement was also reached on the signing of information-sharing agreements between Europol and Norway, Iceland, and Interpol.

The May JHA Council also provided Commissioner Vitorino with an opportunity to present the latest update of the JHA Scoreboard. This noted progress in some areas (e.g., Pro-Eurojust, crime-prevention network, etc.), but also mentioned several areas where deadlines had been missed, including the passing of a variety of legal instruments called for in the Tampere Conclusions (e.g., on asylum policy). The updated Scoreboard reminded the member states to make progress on many areas of JHA prior to the planned Laeken European Council at the end of 2001, as had been reaffirmed at the Stockholm European Council in March 2001. Continuing a trend that began with the Lisbon "dot.com summit," the Stockholm European Council had been devoted almost exclusively to economic and social matters, with no mention of JHA in its formal conclusions.

Finally, two noteworthy achievements of the May JHA Council impacted Europol directly. One was the adoption, without debate, of Europol's *Annual Report for 2000,* documenting the young police agency's accomplishments in its first full calendar year of operations. The second was Europol's budget for 2002, which had been passed unanimously by the Europol Management Board on April 18–19, raising its total expenditures from €35,391,300 for 2001 to €48,504,000. The passage of the new budget continued the pattern of steady increases in Europol spending begun years before.

New Issues for Europol

No further major activity on JHA had been planned in the Swedish presidency following the conclusion of the May JHA Council and the start of new accession negotiations on Justice and Home Affairs on June 1. However, this changed in the wake of two unexpected, but important, events that occurred in the final month of Sweden's term as EU president. Each would have significant implications for the future of Europol.

The first was the revelation in early June 2001 that a Europol staff member had been charged with the embezzlement and attempted laundering of official Europol funds. The forty-one-year-old French police officer had been working in Europol's computer data section (Technology Services). He was arrested by Dutch authorities on June 2, along with a woman working for Europol, for allegedly diverting at least €100,000 in budgetary funds intended for the Europol Computer System (TECS). The money had been diverted into a secret offshore bank account in the tax haven of Bermuda, and the discovery of the corruption was first made by Europol in May 2001 during the course of an internal audit of its own procurement budget for 1999.[32] Following an investigation by a committee chaired by a member of its Management Board, Europol suspended the staff member, lifted his diplomatic immunity, and informed Dutch authorities, who arrested him after raiding his home and office. Europol confirmed the events in a press release on June 8, the day the suspect was released from custody pending his trial.[33]

An unnamed source inside Europol commented, "It's a disaster. It is just unbelievable. The whole reputation of Europol will be damaged just when we are trying to protect the euro."[34] Europol's Management Board responded immediately to the matter by pledging to implement "several measures to reinforce the internal control functions of Europol."[35] By late July a second criminal investigation had opened, reportedly dealing with the misuse of computer software. In response to this, the internal review of both cases was widened to include its deputy director for Technology Services, the UK's David Valls-Russell, a former police superintendent in Kent, for allegedly allowing his section to degenerate into rogue operations such as those uncovered.[36]

With the Swedish presidency having been completed by this point, it was left to the Belgian interior minister, Antoine Dusquesne, to express his outrage at the breakdown of control that had allowed these incidents and the resulting blow to public confidence in Europol. Following a meeting with senior Europol staff in Brussels, he charged, "It's unacceptable and inexplicable, and I don't want even to hear an attempt at an excuse . . . we must enforce discipline with maximum severity. For unless there is public confidence [in Europol], we cannot have a decent police force."[37]

Although detected internally and taken seriously by Europol, this incident heightened concerns about the transparency and democratic control of Europol. This was especially the case given that the two matters under investigation involved Europol staff members working in the computer data section, with access to analysis files containing personal data and sensitive information on Latin American drug cartels, Islamic terrorists, and other criminal organizations and networks (although there was no evidence that these files were misused). Thus, not only was the issue of data protection, in the context of protecting civil liberties, at stake, but so too was the potential harm caused to Europol's reputation in the eyes of police and intelligence organizations both inside and outside of the EU. In general, it was feared that incidents such as these might make police organizations less inclined to share data with Europol.

The second incident impacting Europol at the close of the Swedish presidency were the events surrounding the European Council in Göteborg. This meeting provided a stage for thousands of peaceful protestors and interest groups to demonstrate, many with legitimate concerns about the EU and the negative effects of globalization. In all, the Göteborg European Council attracted 25,000 demonstrators, some protesting against various U.S. policies, given the presence at the summit of U.S. President George W. Bush, who was making his first trip to Europe since taking office.

However, as at previous summits of world leaders (e.g., the World Trade Organization in Seattle in 1999, the International Monetary Fund in Prague in 2000, and the Nice European Council), hundreds of demonstrators bent on the destruction of property and violence were mixed in with the peaceful masses at Göteborg.[38] Consequently, the Swedish police fought running battles during the European Council with "professional" anarchists from Denmark, Germany, Belgium, Italy, and other countries, as well as with other violent antiglobalization, anti-EU, and anti-U.S. protestors. Apparently overwhelmed by the scale of the protests and violence, the police at one point opened fire with live ammunition, wounding three people, including one critically. More than ninety people were hurt, and the incident caused more than €4 million damage to the city. Over five hundred violent protestors were detained by police at the summit, although less than twenty had been prosecuted by mid-July 2001. The rioting also caused the cancellation of the summit's traditional dinner, and some EU delegations had to switch hotels.[39]

Many EU leaders lashed out at the violent antiglobalization protestors. Britain's Tony Blair, for example, dubbed them "an anarchist's traveling circus," adding that authorities "should not concede an inch to them."[40] Coming on the heels of similar episodes at the Nice European Council, the EU realized that its own meetings had clearly become targets of the antiglobalization violence. This contributed to some soul searching about the perceived democratic deficit in the EU and the less than enthusiastic popular reception of some its policies and future plans. This was especially evident in light of the fact that the violence at the Göteborg summit came just a week after Irish voters had rejected the Treaty of Nice in a referendum.[41] More directly, EU leaders realized that they needed to take measures to protect future meetings from similar violence, including helping police to prepare for such events and working together to track the activities of the anarchists. Nevertheless, the presidency's conclusions for the Göteborg European Council contained only one reference to JHA, with its point number 46 calling on the member states and the Council to accelerate work toward creating the AFSJ before the upcoming Laeken European Council at the end of the Belgian presidency.

However, as a direct result of the violence at Göteborg, the Belgians began their presidency with a special session of the JHA Council on July 13, 2001, dedicated solely to the topic of security at European Council meetings and other events likely to have a comparable impact (e.g., international summits). At this meeting the Council passed a set of conclusions calling for greater EU cooperation to reduce the risk of serious disturbances of law and order resulting from high-profile international meetings. The JHA ministers identified the need for a liaison network of national police officials and intelligence officers to help identify and monitor persons or groups likely to pose a threat to public order. The Council also spelled out roles in this regard for many bodies in the EU's emerging institutional infrastructure of crime fighting.

For example, the conclusions called upon the Task Force of Police Chiefs to advise member states on the most appropriate means to provide security and public-order policing for European Councils and similar events, as well as to monitor the effectiveness of these measures on an ongoing basis. The JHA Council also prescribed the joint analysis of violent disturbances, offenses, and groups. Moreover, in the context of discussions raised by Sweden to amend the Europol Convention, the Council pledged to examine the possibility of increasing the powers of Europol to conduct such analyses. The conclusions of this Council session also called for targeted training by the European Police College in the area of public-order policing. In addition, these conclusions entailed measures for judicial cooperation, prescribing that the European Judicial Network should be used to promote greater exchanges of information on public-order policing and restrictions on travel to countries hosting events for those suspected of organizing, provoking, or participating in serious disturbances. Finally, the conclusions also called for improved dialogue with organizers of events and protests to insure that "legitimate demonstrations are not exploited by groups with a violent agenda."

Overall, the measures specified by the first JHA Council of the Belgian presidency showed a new ability of the EU to react quickly to events impinging on internal security. These initiatives also put on display the variety of means newly available to the EU for facilitating a common approach to providing law and order. The EU's ability to swiftly employ various mechanisms in its new institutional infrastructure of crime fighting in response to crises would soon be demonstrated once again in the wake of the terrorist attacks on the United States (see Chapter 7).

Despite its relatively quick reaction to the events of the Göteborg summit, the initiatives of the Special JHA Council could not be implemented soon enough to prevent a repeat of the violent disturbances less than two weeks later during the Group of Eight (G-8) Summit in Genoa on July 20–22, 2001. There, an estimated 2,500 anarchists from the UK, Germany, Greece, Spain, the United States, and other countries clashed with Italian police, who reacted very aggressively. This time, along with more than €45 million in damages, numerous arrests, and hundreds of injuries, there was also the shooting death by the police of a twenty-three-year-old protestor as he attacked a police car.[42] In addition, widespread allegations of brutality were lodged against the police, leading to the transfer of three Italian senior police officials following an investigation by a special Italian government committee of inquiry.[43]

Thus, as the Belgian presidency began, the EU appeared to have yet another chronic problem to solve before it could achieve its prized "area of freedom, security, and justice." The EU now realized that its ability (or inability) to deal with public-order disturbances such as those at Nice, Göteborg, and Genoa would be clearly and immediately evident at each subsequent meeting of the Europol Council. Similar to the public debate on the appropriate nature of antiterrorism measures that would soon follow the terrorist attacks on the United States, the conclusions of the Special JHA Council in July focused attention on the inherent tension between maintaining internal security on the one hand and preserving civil liberties on the other. In fact, the issue of dealing with the demonstrations at meetings of the European Council would later be connected to the fight against terrorism, when the Commission's definition of "terrorism" proposed soon after the terrorist attacks seemed potentially to include all antiglobalization protestors, and not just violent anarchists (see Chapter 7).

Europol on the Eve of September 11

Despite the controversy created by the corruption scandal in Europol and the violence at the Göteborg summit, the Swedish presidency was highly successful in the area of JHA. A number of important items were approved during its term, and substantial progress made on several other fronts.[44] The following items were among twenty legislative items approved during Sweden's leadership of the EU:

- The regulation listing countries for which visas are needed to enter the EU (the "blacklist") and not (the "whitelist")
- The decision to set up a European crime-prevention network
- The decision to protect the euro against counterfeiting by providing for the exchange of data between national centers
- The Protocol to the 2000 Convention on Mutual Assistance in Criminal Matters regarding personal banking information
- The framework decision on the trafficking of human beings (French initiative)
- The directives to impose fines on carriers of illegal immigrants
- The framework decision on combating fraud and the counterfeiting of noncash payments
- The directive on temporary protection for displaced persons, and
- New programs for 2001–2002 with a total budget of €18 million, including Stop II, Oisin II, and Grotius II

About fifteen outstanding initiatives, including five proposals initiated after January 1, 2001, remained deadlocked and were turned over to the incoming Belgium presidency. These included work on:

- The framework decision to impose common sanctions for trafficking in illegal drugs
- The decision to allow Europol to share personal data with non-EU countries and bodies ("onward transmission")
- The nature of the permanent Eurojust unit
- The Commission's draft decision to combat human trafficking
- The Commission's draft decision to harmonize penal law on child sexual exploitation
- The draft framework decision obliging national courts to freeze and transfer criminal assets upon request from a member state's court
- The draft framework decision on protecting the environment using criminal law (a combined initiative of Denmark and the Commission)
- The modification of the Schengen agreement to allow cross-border surveillance of family, friends, and associates of suspected criminals, and
- Sweden's proposal to extend Europol's powers to environmental and cyber-crime

The latter initiative to extend the mandate of Europol was related to Sweden's broader goals of increasing the power of Europol in general. By April 2001, Sweden had floated two related proposals in this regard. As a long-term goal, Sweden favored a protocol amending the Europol Convention that would, after its ratification and entry into force, increase Europol's powers in two ways. First, the Swedish-inspired protocol would enable Europol to fight any form of serious crime of a transnational nature (i.e., taking place in more than two member states). Second, the protocol would strengthen Europol's ability to participate in a joint investigative team set up by two or more member states, providing for direct links with the investigators and the transmission of information to and from Europol's databases.

Realizing that the ratification process for such a protocol could be quite lengthy, Sweden simultaneously presented its plan for a draft decision that would, under terms of Article 2 of the Europol Convention, extend the mandate of Europol to all of the crimes mentioned in its annex. In making this initiative, Sweden also proposed definitions of some of the crimes in the annex, notably environmental crime, computer crime, and racism and xenophobia.[45]

In June 2001, Sweden officially proposed this draft decision, with Belgium as its cosponsor. This instructs Europol to deal with all crimes listed in the annex to the Europol Convention (Article 1) and leaves it to the Council, acting unanimously on the basis of a proposal from the Europol Management Board, to determine which forms of international crime should be given priority (Article 2). With an eye toward obtaining the EP's opinion and, after that, final agreement in the Council during the Belgian presidency, the proposal was intended to enter into force on January 1, 2002. At the time, this deadline for implementation seemed rather optimistic given the apprehensions of some member states. Following the events of September 11, however, the political will to expand European police cooperation and increase Europol's powers helped insure the timely passage of the Swedish-Belgian initiative, though Europol had already been empowered to deal with terrorism.

Thus, at the close of the Swedish presidency, the European Union was poised to increase the power of Europol yet again, continuing a trend that had begun with creation of the Europol Drugs Unit (EDU) and its limited mandate in January 1994. Europol's crime-fighting mandate had already grown from combating only drug trafficking during its EDU phase, to the short-list of crimes noted in the main body of the Europol Convention. The fight against terrorism and the counterfeiting of the euro were added even before Europol became fully operational in July 1999. Then, under the French presidency in 2000, Europol's remit was expanded yet again to include the fight against money laundering of any kind, not simply that related to the crimes listed in its mandate (see Chapter 6).

In addition to this expansion of its crime-fighting concerns, Europol's *operational* powers had also been increased several times since the creation of the EDU. Even before the Europol Convention could take effect, Europol's potential investigative powers were enhanced by the entry into force of the Treaty of Amsterdam in May 1999. Based upon its provisions, the JHA Council had passed two recommendations during the French presidency (see Chapter 7). The first, in September 2000, specified how member states should respond to requests by Europol to initiate, coordinate, or conduct investigations. The second recommendation, passed by the JHA Council in November 2000, called upon member states to include Europol agents in joint investigative teams. Although these measures were not binding on member states, they indicated a further increase in Europol's powers. However, the JHA Council stopped short of granting Europol true executive policing authority, including the power to initiate and conduct investigations on its own, carry out searches, and make arrests.

Despite these limitations, efforts to further expand Europol's duties during the Swedish presidency continued to be matched by calls to strengthen democratic oversight over its activities, particularly with regard to the role of the European Parliament. As noted above, the importance of democratic control over Europol had been highlighted by the revelations of alleged wrongdoing by the Europol staff member. However, this issue had arisen during the Swedish presidency even before the outbreak of the scandal in Europol, notably in April 2001, when Europol provided the EP with a sanitized version of its *Annual Report*. Europol claimed that the missing operational details of some of its activities were too confidential to make public, but the civil-liberties group Statewatch obtained a leaked versions of the full report, and revealed that it contained nothing that could jeopardize operational security. This suggested to some that Europol was simply acquiring a troubling taste for secrecy.[46]

On June 8, 2001, Commissioner Vitorino inserted himself into the issue while delivering a speech to a joint session of the Dutch Senate and House of Representatives in The Hague, making a case for greater democratic control of Europol. While conceding that "parliaments do not normally have a direct say in the running of the police," Vitorino called for the powers of the EP to be increased regarding Europol. In particular, he proposed the creation of a joint committee of MEPs and national MPs to meet twice yearly to review the activities of Europol. This, he argued, would make the monitoring of Europol more transparent and would better institutionalize the exchange of information on JHA between the national parliaments and the EP.[47] Because Europol lacked executive policing powers, Vitorino argued that no judicial oversight was necessary, contending that Europol's national supervisory bodies and joint supervisory bodies were sufficient to monitor the use of personal data.

However, pointing to Germany's continued desire, even after establishment of Gerhard Schröder's coalition government in 1998, to transform Europol into a true European police force, Vitorino indicated that increased parliamentary and judicial oversight for Europol might some day be necessary.[48] Yet, for the near future, most other member states would not be as ready to abandon the current intergovernmental approach to controlling Europol. According to Vitorino, this sensitivity helps explain why Europol continues to be financed intergovernmentally (out of national budgets), rather than as part of the Community budget, which would give the European Parliament greater control.

The Europol *Annual Report for 2000,* with which the EP was dissatisfied, indicated how Europol had changed and grown (in terms of staff and budget) during the first full calendar year of its operations.[49] Along with this, the JHA Council, on Sweden's initiative, had passed proposals in March 2001 to improve compensation for Europol staff to meet the increased cost-of-living expenses in The Hague and facilitate recruitment. These measures included a 3.7 percent pay raise retroactive to July 1, 1999, longer-term contracts, and improved health benefits and rent allowances.

The 2000 *Annual Report* indicated that, for the third consecutive year, the number of cases initiated by member states and handled by Europol decreased, from 1,998 in 1999 to 1,922 in 2000. Of these cases, 1,757 entailed information/intelligence exchanges (investigations), 127 for sharing of special expertise, and 38 for coordination and other contacts. The majority of these cases were connected to drug-related crimes, while the others involved, in order of frequency, illegal immigration, stolen vehicles, money laundering, trafficking in human beings, terrorism, counterfeiting, and trafficking in nuclear substances.

Despite the slightly reduced number of cases, the overall workload of Europol, measured in terms of pieces of information shared via the Europol Laison Officers regarding each open "analysis work file," increased substantially. The 2000 report noted, for example, that up to 100,000 pieces of data were transmitted via the ELOs regarding just one of these files. According to the *Annual Report,* this use of the analysis work files "resulted in an enormous increase in the amount of data being exchanged."

The country-specific information contained in the 2000 report confirmed the downward trend in the total number of new cases initiated, but also indicated a significant increase in both the transmission and reception of requests for data regarding various files. Germany had initiated the most new cases (405), followed by the UK (362), and France (206). Each country highlighted the impact of Europol regarding specific cases or types of crime. The report noted, for example, that most of the cases initiated by the UK dealt with drugs, "but there was a significant rise in the number of illegal immigration cases, prompted partly by such high profile incidents as the death of 58 Chinese immigrants in the United Kingdom in June 2000." In general, there seemed to be agreement that the information transmitted via Europol's liaison network for all member states was of a higher quality and was being transmitted more quickly than in the past.

In addition to noting progress on information sharing, the 2000 report described the work of Europol in developing intelligence and specialized knowledge in several specific areas, including drugs, illegal immigration, trafficking in human beings, illicit vehicle trafficking, financial crime, counterfeiting, and terrorism. As discussed above, Europol's activities to combat the forgery of the euro intensified in 2001, as the measures initiated by the Swedish presidency and Commission were gradually implemented. In the area of illegal immigration, Europol touted its expanding and successful efforts to fight child pornography. Regarding illicit vehicle trafficking, it took credit for assisting in an operation in the Baltic region that led to the confiscation of 384 stolen vehicles and the arrest of two hundred suspects.[50]

Concerning terrorism, Europol's *Annual Report for 2000* notes its activity to support two specific investigations (unspecified in the report) and the related opening of two analysis work files. In addition, Europol highlighted its efforts to create and update a number of resources made available to the member states to facilitate their mutual cooperation and coordination of efforts to fight terrorism. These included a directory of responsibilities at the national level, a center of excellence or competencies and specialist skills, and a glossary of terrorist groups.

Europol's activity in the area of antiterrorism during the Swedish presidency in 2001 began with its role in organizing, along with the Spanish Ministry of the Interior, the first European Conference on Terrorism. The conference was held on January 29–February 2, 2001, in Madrid at Spain's national police complex in Canillas and was attended by high-level police officials from all fifteen member states. Compared with coverage of terrorist-related activities after September 11, the event drew little media coverage.

Owing to its special interest in the problem of terrorism related to the Basque separatist group ETA, Spain provided many of the most notable initiatives at the conference. One such proposal called for the creation of a European registry of terrorist groups and rewards for information leading to their capture.[51] Another Spanish initiative called for the creation of a "Euro-warrant," which would allow the immediate extradition of some "heavy" criminals, including terrorist suspects, from one EU state to another. The idea for this had grown out of Spain's ongoing bilateral efforts with several EU member states to speed up the extradition of suspected terrorists and other serious criminals. On November 28, 2000, Spain signed an agreement with Italy to create a common judicial space between the two countries to ease and hasten the extradition of suspects charged with serious offenses, including terrorism; organized crime; trafficking of drugs, arms, and human beings; and sexual abuse of children. The terrorism conference of January 2001 also served as the occasion of a Spanish-Italian agreement to set up joint investigative groups, which later proved instrumental in the capture of the right-wing Italian terrorist known as "The Black Flower," Pasquale Belsito, in Madrid on June 30, 2001.

The Euro-warrant proposed by Spain would eliminate extradition for serious crimes throughout the EU, and a feasibility study was launched at the terrorism conference to explore this idea, which, as noted in Chapter 6, had already been raised by the Commission in December 2000. In addition, at the conclusion of the terrorism conference, Spain and France signed a joint declaration envisaging the mutual recognition of court decisions and their direct execution regarding serious crimes such as terrorism, with both countries agreeing to start work on overcoming any technical or legal barriers to making this a reality.[52] In the months following the conference, Spain pursued extradition agreements not only with France, but also with Portugal, Belgium, and Germany, and signed an agreement to this effect with the United Kingdom in March 2001.

Despite its role in organizing the terrorism conference in Spain at the start of the Swedish presidency, as well as its steady engagement in this issue, Europol did *not* identify terrorism among its priority activities for the following year in its "Work Program for 2002." This program was approved by its Management Board in June 2001 and endorsed by the Council the next month. In fact, progress on developing common antiterrorism measures in the EU would be rather slow overall until after September 11. At that stage it was expected that many of the antiterrorism measures under consideration would only be formally raised in the Council late in the Belgian presidency, with Spain hoping to reach agreement on legislation during its term as president in the first half of 2002.

Instead of terrorism, Europol's Work Program for 2002 listed crime fighting related to drugs, money laundering, illegal immigration, trafficking in human beings, and counterfeiting as its highest priorities. Concerning its daily operations, Europol hoped to increase its involvement in, and support of, joint investigations and joint teams organized by two or more member states. In this regard, Europol planned to provide specific databases, coordination, analysis, as well as increased information sharing through the Europol Information System (EIS). This, it should be recalled, is one of the three databases comprising the TECS (see Chapter 4).

While the EIS had long been in the planning stages, its actual development was finally begun in February 2001 by the firm EADS Sycomore, which was awarded the €20 million contract to build, integrate, and deliver the new information system. As envisioned in the Europol Work Program for 2002, the EIS became operational on January 1, 2002. As planned, the first version of the EIS was installed at Europol and the national units, focusing on the euro and allowing for the transmission of data in English. Later in 2002, two updated versions were expected to be brought on line and cover the full range of crimes within Europol's expanding mandate, allowing officials in the member states and Europol to send and receive information in their own languages twenty-four hours a day. A similar system of information sharing and automatic translation, InfoEx, had already been in use for in-house communication at Europol.

When fully operational, the EIS will allow, for example, police in Finland to input, in Finnish, all possible information about a suspected counterfeiter there (e.g., businesses, aliases, associates, transporters, etc.) and enable a police officer working on a similar case in Portugal to download all of the information in Portuguese. In an interview published in January 2001, Jürgen Storbeck projected that 90–95 percent of the data in the EIS would eventually be input in this way by national authorities, with Europol analysts supplying the rest from its own intelligence.[53] However, if the EIS is to be used to its full potential, Storbeck argued that "member states have to commit themselves to fully participate in the work of Europol by providing it with the information and intelligence it needs," as called for by the 2002 Work Program.[54]

It would soon become clear, after September 11, that this need to exchange data more willingly was especially acute for adequate counterterrorism activities. Although not listed among the main priorities for 2001, Europol's Work Program entailed a number of activities concerning terrorism. However, much of this merely continued ongoing efforts, such as maintaining lists of terrorists groups and preparing situation reports.

Of course, Europol's attention to the problem of terrorism, along with that of the entire EU, would intensify following the attacks against the United States. These terrible events would ultimately bring more attention on Europol, at the same time that its usefulness regarding the protection of the euro was about to be tested. Moreover, the events of September 11 would rapidly elevate the importance of Justice and Home Affairs on the EU's overall policy agenda and foster new political will to expedite implementation of several projects already in the works and initiate new ones.

Explaining Progress During the Swedish Presidency

As 2001 began, the main crime challenges facing the EU were the trafficking of human beings and protection of the euro against counterfeiting. Cooperation on the latter provided further evidence of functional spillover impacting JHA, as the EU's preparations for the physical introduction of the common currency led to a much more prominent role for Europol. In addition, functional spillover from cooperation on free movement was significant once again, with the expansion of the Schengen zone to the Nordic countries. This only served to magnify the challenges of fighting transnational crime without the benefit of international borders, and also brought the EU, as well as Europol, into closer cooperation with two non-members, Iceland and Norway.

Finally, functional spillover could also be identified in the effects of activity to make the European Security and Defense Policy a reality. That is, by 2001 plans for the proposed European Rapid Reaction Force to carry out the so-called Petersberg tasks had led to cooperation among the member states to organize and prepare the civilian policing component of this force. Interestingly, this represented a case of cooperation in the Third Pillar (i.e., police cooperation) and helped the EU to meet its goals in the Second Pillar. Within a year, however, the opposite phenomenon would be evident, as the EU would be looking more and more toward using various aspects of its CFSP to help address the Third Pillar tasks of fighting terrorism and illegal immigration (see Chapters 7 and 8).

During the Swedish presidency, external factors also continued to be influential in the development of police cooperation. As noted already, Sweden had inherited the challenge of dealing with the problem of the trafficking of human beings, which seemed to be worsening when it took over leadership of the EU. In addition, there was the constant pressure of impending enlargement, with the accession negotiations for all twelve candidate states being in full swing by 2001. The member states were reminded of the JHA implications of enlargement in March 2001 when all thirteen applicant countries (including Turkey) participated for the first time in the JHA Council. Furthermore, by June, eleven of the twelve candidate states (excluding Romania) were engaged in negotiations on their JHA chapters of accession, increasing attention to the many challenges that enlargement would pose for making the AFSJ a reality in the EU.

The internal factor of subsidiary seemed to play little role during the Swedish presidency, as progress continued on the creation of the EU's emerging legal and institutional infrastructure of crime fighting. However, the Commission did explicitly use the principle of subsidiary to justify its opposition to the EP's suggested amendments to protect victims of human-being trafficking in pending legislation dealing with this crime. In addition, plans for Eurojust were drafted, which made clear that prosecutorial authority would be left to the member states and not given to the new judicial cooperation unit. This latter point also demonstrates how federalist ideology was generally insignificant during the Swedish presidency, evident in the ability of the Council to resist the aspirations of the EP, and to a lesser extent the Commission, to make CEPOL and Eurojust more supranational and less intergovernmental in nature.

As always, another area where the EP attempted to be influential was in calls for more democratic controls over Europol, which arose as plans were debated to increase the operational powers and crime-fighting responsibilities of Europol. In fact, these concerns for democracy regarding JHA were echoed by Commissioner Vitorino, who suggested a new way to insure the democratic accountability of Europol. In fact, the significance of this issue only increased in June amid the revelation of the internal financial scandal within Europol. Nevertheless, no decisions were made on fundamental reforms of democratic control over Europol. However, concerns for democracy appeared to be more influential in the debate on some legislative items in the form of attention to human rights. For example, in the development of the Schengen *acquis,* special consideration was given to the trafficking of human beings for humanitarian purposes, and several provisions on various human rights were included in the legislation on the temporary protection of refugees.

In sum, cooperation on JHA during the Swedish presidency can be explained by a mix of internal and external forces, just as in previous time periods. However, soon after Belgium assumed the EU's presidency, external forces would suddenly become even more influential. This, of course, would come in the form of the terrorist attacks on the United States and the EU's reaction to this.

Notes

1. *European Report,* "Justice and Home Affairs: EU Aims to Re-Launch Area of Justice," February 10, 2001.

2. Ibid.

3. *European Report,* "Justice and Home Affairs: Agenda for the Informal Council in Stockholm on 8–9 February," February 7, 2001.

4. *Printing World,* "Make the Money and Run," January 29, 2001.

5. See, e.g., BBC News, "Money Fakers Spy a Chance," March 23, 2001.

6. The framework decision of May 29, 2000, was provided the fundamental legislation against counterfeiting at this point, with other complimentary proposals pending.

7. Joint press release of Europol, European Commission, and the European Central Bank, The Hague, March 7, 2001.

8. Herve Clerc, "Euro Notes and Coins Set to Lure Counterfeiters," *Agence France Presse,* April 15, 2001. The first level of security is known to the public, allowing them to identify true bank notes. This includes magnetic ink, variable-optics ink, microprinting, a hologram, and a metal security strip. The two other levels of security measures are known only to banking professionals and the European Central Bank, respectively.

9. *European Report,* "Single Currency: Swedish Presidency Unveils 11-Point Plan to Beat Crime," May 16, 2001.

10. Elahe Merel, "France Struggles to Fight Money Laundering During Euro Switch," *Agence France Presse,* April 22, 2001.

11. Jimmy Burns, Francesco Guerrera, and Michael Peel, "Police Fear Big Euro Bills Have Criminal Appeal," *Financial Times* (London), May 22, 2001.

12. Francesco Guerrera and Michael Peel, "Police Fear Big Euro Bills Have Criminal Appeal," *Financial Times* (London), June 5, 2001.

13. Ibid.

14. *Het Financieel Dagblad* (Amsterdam), "Euro-Day Is the Right Time to Fight Crime, or Commit It," June 22, 2001.

15. Ian Black, "Europol Comes of Age as It Gets Ready to Battle with Euro-Forgers," *The Guardian* (Manchester), June 8, 2001.

16. Ibid.

17. Ibid.

18. David Lister, "Europol Prepares to Enter a Wider Arena," *The Times* (London), January 19, 2001; *European Report*, "Justice and Home Affairs: Council Moves to Further Boost Powers of Europol," January 27, 2001.

19. *European Report*, "Justice and Home Affairs Council: Ministers Step up Drive Against Illegal Balkans Immigration," March 17, 2000.

20. *Euro-East* (European Information Service), "EU Enlargement: Candidates' Justice and Home Affairs Ministers Meet in Brussels," March 27, 2001.

21. Ibid.

22. *European Report*, "Justice and Home Affairs: Move to Boost Europol in Transfer of Personal Data," June 9, 2001.

23. *European Report*, "Justice and Home Affairs Council: Ministers Step up Drive Against Illegal Balkans Immigration," March 17, 2001.

24. *European Report*, "New Draft Directive Seeks to Make Breaches of EU Law a Crime," March 17, 2001.

25. Ambrose Evans-Pritchard, "Britain Is Hot Favorite to Run Police College," *Daily Telegraph* (London), April 21, 2001; *European Report*, "Justice and Home Affairs: European Police College Takes Shape," May 5, 2001.

26. *European Report*, "Justice and Home Affairs: Member States Keen to Limit Powers of Eurojust," March 28, 2001.

27. *European Report*, "Justice and Home Affairs: Commission Looking Increasingly Sidelined in Eurojust Project," January 24, 2001.

28. *European Report*, "Justice and Home Affairs: Member States Keen to Limit Powers of Eurojust," March 28, 2001.

29. *European Report*, "Justice and Home Affairs: NGOs Call for More Victim Support in Human-Trafficking Laws," July 6, 2001.

30. *European Report*, "Justice and Home Affairs Council: Breakthrough on Temporary Protection Directive," May 30, 2001.

31. Ibid.

32. Ambrose Evans-Pritchard, "EU Police Investigated for Money Laundering," *Daily Telegraph* (London), June 2, 2001; *Agence France Presse*, "French Official Arrested over Fraud at EU Police Agency," June 2, 2001; *Intelligence Newsletter*, "Corrupt Cops at Europol," June 7, 2001.

33. Europol press release, The Hague, June 8, 2001.

34. Jimmy Burns and Francesco Guerrera, "Dutch Arrest Top Europol Officer," *Financial Times* (London), June 12, 2001.

35. Ibid.

36. Ambrose Evans-Pritchard, "British Police Official Faces Europol Inquiry," *Daily Telegraph* (London), July 21, 2001.

37. Ibid.

38. For a review of violence at international summits before July 2001, see BBC News (www. news.bbc.co.uk), "Flashback to Summit Flashpoints," July 13, 2001.

39. BBC News (www.news.bbc.co.uk), "Four Jailed for Gothenburg [sic] Riots," July 25, 2001.

40. BBC News (www.news.bbc.co.uk), "Iolo ap Dafydd in Gothenburg [sic],"

June 16, 2001.

41. The turnout for the referendum was alarmingly low at just 35 percent, with 54 percent opposed to the treaty. The Irish government planned to hold another referendum on the issue in 2002.

42. BBC News (www.news.bbc.co.uk), "Genoa Counts the Cost," July 22, 2001.

43. BBC News (www.news.bbc.co.uk), "Police Admit Excess in Genoa," August 8, 2001.

44. *European Report,* "Justice and Home Affairs: Swedish Presidency Takes Few Initiatives, but Makes Much Progress," June 16, 2001. Some items were passed as A-points at Council meetings other than the JHA Council.

45. *European Report,* "Justice and Home Affairs: Swedish Presidency Moves to Boost Europol's Powers," April 4, 2001.

46. Ambrose Evans-Pritchard, "Ever-Expanding Europol Refuses to Give Away Police Secrets," *Daily Telegraph* (London), April 14, 2001.

47. *European Report,* "Justice and Home Affairs: Vitorino Calls for New Parliamentary Watchdog for Europol," June 13, 2001.

48. Ibid.

49. See Chapter 8 for budget and staff figures for 1996–2003.

50. *European Report,* "Justice and Home Affairs: 2000 a Fruitful Year for Europol," May 3, 2001.

51. *Irish Times* (Dublin), "European Terror Registry Proposed," February 8, 2001.

52. BBB Monitoring Europe—Political, "Spanish, French Ministers on Mutual Recognition of Court Rulings," February 2, 2001.

53. David Lister, "Europol Prepares to Enter a Wider Arena," *The Times* (London), January 19, 2001.

54. Ibid.

7

Reacting to Terrorism

AS DISCUSSED IN CHAPTER 6, THE FIRST MONTHS OF THE BELGIAN presidency regarding JHA were consumed by the aftermath of the Europol scandal and dealing with the problem of violence at international summits. Aside from these concerns, Belgium established an ambitious agenda consisting of several broad goals, as well as agreement on a number of related specific initiatives. At least initially, fighting terrorism was not among the main priorities of the Belgian presidency of 2001.

One of Belgium's initial aims was to establish the agenda for the upcoming European Convention, which would debate EU's future during 2002 and perhaps provide the basis for the next IGC in 2004. In this regard, the Belgians intended to produce a declaration at their concluding European Council at Laeken that would begin the process of fundamental institutional reform in the EU. It was assumed that this might include the strengthening of the EU's federal character and formal incorporation of the new Charter of Fundamental Rights into a true constitution for the European Union. As it worked toward deepening European integration, Belgium was also charged with the task of overseeing the continuing negotiations with the candidate states and opening and closing chapters of accession, including the one on JHA for some countries (i.e., Chapter 24).[1]

Another original goal of the Belgian presidency was to develop a new social agenda for the EU that might entail the promotion of quality jobs and greater social protection (e.g., workers' rights and welfare). Belgium also intended to put forward several controversial taxation proposals, including a direct tax on citizens to replace national contributions and common taxes aimed at environmental protection (e.g., on energy). Lastly, the Belgian presidency was to oversee final preparations for the introduction of the euro, which was set to be distributed to banks by armored cars in the first week of September 2001. These efforts involved a number of JHA-related activities to protect the new currency, as well the task of educating the public about the euro.

With regard to continuing work on the Commission's JHA Scoreboard and realization of the "area of freedom, security, and justice," the Belgians had inherited a number of legislative initiatives in various stages of development from the Swedish presidency. Among these, Belgium initially highlighted its intention to reach a final decision in the Council on the permanent Eurojust unit to allow it to begin operations in 2002. Other initial priorities on JHA included proposals related to the trafficking of human beings, the sexual exploitation of children, racism and xenophobia, and the mutual recognition of criminal law and judgments (e.g., related to the freezing of criminal assets).[2] Finally, among its original plans for JHA, the Belgian presidency also intended to oversee work on enhancing Europol's operative powers and its role in supporting cooperation among national law enforcement authorities.

Work on all of these original objectives of the Belgian presidency would indeed continue through the remainder of 2001. However, the events of September 11 would dramatically alter Belgium's initial goals. After the attacks on the United States, the fight against terrorism would take over as the top priority in affairs of the European Union. This would lead not only to agreement on a variety of measures designed to fight terrorism, but also to an acceleration of progress on a wide variety of items already noted on the JHA Scoreboard.

The Immediate Reaction to September 11

The terrorist attacks on the United States killed just over three thousand people at the Pentagon, in the twin towers of the World Trade Center, and aboard the four hijacked airliners. The responsibility for the attacks was almost immediately attributed to the Al Qaeda terrorist network under the direction of Osama bin Laden. With many of the most horrific images of destruction captured live on television and initial reports of the deaths in New York City as high as 6,000 (instead of the actual 2,800), the impact on the world was immediate and intense. In the European Union, one of the earliest responses to the attacks came from its high representative for CFSP, Javier Solana. In a press release issued on the day of the attacks, Solana expressed the EU's support for the United States, as well as the need to devote more resources to the fight against terrorism, both within the European Union and in its external relations. In the days that followed September 11, it became clear that at least some of the individuals suspected of being involved in the attacks on the United States had recently been living or traveling in Europe, causing investigators to pursue leads in Germany, Spain, Italy, the Netherlands, Belgium, and the UK. Along with sympathetic public sentiment, this European connection increased the importance of the EU's involvement in the ensuing investigation and the broader fight against terrorism.

Europol's reaction to the terrorist attacks was swift, establishing a crisis center on September 12 that would be open around the clock to receive and distribute data concerning the attacks and possibly to coordinate efforts among national authorities. Soon after the attacks, however, Europol's director, Jürgen Storbeck, complained publicly that his agency could do more if police authorities in the member states would only be more willing to share information on terrorism, rather than keeping it to themselves.[3] In an interview with a German newspaper, Storbeck demanded that the EU member states "simply provide us with what we need for our work: information." Arguing as well for greater funding, he noted that "if Europol is to do more than simply analyze data, then it must be better equipped."[4]

In addition, Storbeck made statements in the press calling for a formal information-sharing agreement with the United States that would allow Europol and U.S. authorities to exchange data on all crimes, including terrorism.[5] Although this was already envisioned for the future and talks had been under way for months, establishing such a pact with the United States was initially "way down on the list," with other countries considered to be higher priorities for information-sharing agreements with Europol. That is, until the events of September 11 made the pressing need for this all too clear.[6] With hopes of initiating talks, Storbeck joined a delegation of the Belgian presidency in a visit to the United States in the week after the terrorist attacks.

Meanwhile, with the Justice and Home Affairs Council set to meet in emergency session on September 20, the European Commission was busy putting the final touches on a package of antiterrorism legislation to be formally proposed prior to the Council meeting. These items had actually been in the works in one form or another long before the attacks and were originally scheduled to be considered by the College of Commissioners on September 26. The Commission's antiterrorist package was at least partly inspired by the bilateral pact that Spain had reached with Italy in early 2001, as well as a more recent agreement with France in July. The latter allowed the temporary transfer of terrorist suspects for questioning.[7] Working over the weekend, officials in the Directorate-General on JHA under Adrían Fortescue rushed to prepare two proposals, and these were approved by the College of Commissioners on September 19.

The first item was a draft framework decision establishing a common definition of terrorist acts, as well as common criminal sanctions for these. This was intended to address the fact that only six member states had, at the time, any specific legislation that explicitly used the words "terrorism" or "terrorist" (Germany, Italy, France, Spain, Portugal, and Greece), and definitions of this crime varied extensively among these countries. The Commission proposed sanctions ranging from two years for less serious offenses related to terrorism to a minimum of twenty years for more serious offenses (e.g., murder).

The second measure, also a framework decision, was designed to replace the traditional extradition procedures with a system of surrendering suspects between judicial authorities on the basis of a European arrest warrant (or Euro-warrant), which would be mutually recognized throughout the EU. Once transposed into national law in all member states, this would also supercede the two EU Conventions of 1995 and 1996. These conventions had been designed to simplify and standardize extradition rules, which were governed by the Council of Europe's European Convention on Extradition of 1957.[8] However, the two newer conventions had not been ratified by all EU member states, as noted in the EU Scoreboard, and were consequently not yet fully in force by September 2001.[9]

The Commission proposal creating the Euro-warrant was intended to eliminate the principle of double criminal liability that lay at the heart of traditional extradition and replace it with automatic mutual recognition of criminal judgments. The proposed framework decision also eliminated the exception for the extradition of a country's own citizens to another EU member state, as provided for in the 1957 Convention. Commissioner Vitorino promised that "the proposed system will be faster and simpler than the existing mechanism, since the political and administrative phases of the procedure will be replaced by a judicial one."[10] Traditional extradition procedures in Europe commonly last years—often due to bureaucratic delays or domestic political concerns—whereas the proposed European warrant could be issued and potentially executed within forty-eight hours. Under the new system, suspects' civil rights would, at least in principle, continue to be protected by an appeals process that would allow them to oppose extradition, but any delays stemming from this could last no more than three months.

Collectively, the two Commission proposals on terrorism were the most notable items on the agenda of the extraordinary (emergency) JHA Council on terrorism held in Brussels on September 20, 2001. Convened a day in advance of the emergency meeting of the European Council that was called in response to the attacks on the United States, the JHA ministers discussed and reached agreements in principle on over thirty separate measures. Although all of these measures would certainly aid in the fight against terrorism, none were devised solely with the events of September 11 in mind. As with other proposals, the European arrest warrant and the common definition and sanctions regarding terrorism had been in the works since the Tampere European Council.

Among its conclusions, the JHA Council agreed to work out a final decision on the two Commission framework decisions by its regularly scheduled session set for December 6–7, 2001. Other highlights of the emergency JHA Council meetings included agreements to:

- Set up joint investigative teams on counterterrorism
- Finalize plans for Eurojust and have Pro-Eurojust oversee a meeting of antiterrorist magistrates (i.e., prosecutors)
- Instruct the Police Chiefs Task Force to oversee a first-ever meeting of the heads of the national counterterrorist units
- Instruct national police authorities and intelligence services to cooperate more intensely with each other and to share any relevant information on terrorism with Europol
- Establish a unit of antiterrorist specialists within Europol
- Expedite a variety of measures to fight financial crime related to terrorism (and other crimes), including the freezing of assets and money laundering
- Take various actions to strengthen external borders, and
- Cooperate more regularly and extensively with the United States in a variety of ways, including instructing the director of Europol to negotiate a data-sharing agreement with the United States

The commitments expressed at the extraordinary JHA Council marked a dramatic increase in tempo for the work of the Justice and Home Affairs ministers that would not have occurred in the absence of the sense of outrage and urgency and the resulting new political will created by the events of September 11. Moreover, agreements were reached on several controversial measures despite enduring worries about civil liberties, including constitutional concerns regarding the European Arrest Warrant in some member states, such as Portugal, France, Italy, and Germany.[11] Pointing to the impending difficulties in actually implementing the agreements, Belgian Interior Minister Antoine Duquesne observed, "All of us will be asking our services to think the unthinkable because the unthinkable has already happened."[12]

Despite the common resolve expressed in the agreed-upon measures, differences surfaced among member states at the emergency JHA meeting. For example, although the UK had taken the lead in backing the United States in its fight against terrorism, Britain made it clear to its fellow EU member states that it was unwilling to support the creation of an EU border police or to transform Europol into a full-fledged police organization, which Germany and France hoped to do. Meanwhile, Home Secretary David Blunkett was unable to convince all of his colleagues to agree to a British-proposed list of terrorist organizations to be outlawed.[13]

Overall, however, the "extraordinary" meeting of the JHA Council was extraordinary in the nature of the commitments made by member states to fight crime in the EU. The heightened resolve to fight terrorism in the EU was viewed by some as a political victory for Spain, which had been pushing for more common European action in this area as it continued to deal with violence perpetrated by ETA, the Basque separatist group.[14] In fact, the recent success of Spain in dealing with ETA-sponsored terrorism was attributed to improved cooperation with France, and this served as a model for wider EU collaboration against terrorism of all kinds.[15]

On the day after the JHA Council, the European Council also met, under extremely heavy security, in extraordinary session in Brussels. It was believed that the EU's initial written declaration of support and sympathy for the United States was insufficient.[16] Fresh from his meetings with U.S. President George W. Bush, British Prime Minister Tony Blair reported to his colleagues about his visit and stressed the need for the EU to back the United States as strongly as possible. The European Council did so in the first point of its conclusions, expressing itself to be "totally supportive of the American people" and pledging to cooperate with the United States. In the second point of these conclusions, the European Council outlined its "European Policy to Combat Terrorism" in the form of a seven-point plan, agreeing to:

1. Introduce the European Arrest Warrant and adopt a common definition of terrorism
2. Draw up a common list of terrorist organizations, exchange information among intelligence services, and set up joint investigations teams
3. Share all useful data with Europol and set up an antiterrorist team within Europol
4. Implement all existing international conventions on terrorism as quickly as possible (e.g., sponsored by the UN, Organization for Economic Cooperation and Development [OECD], etc.)
5. Combat the funding of terrorism by passing EU legislation on money laundering and the freezing of assets, as well as by signing and ratifying the UN Convention for the Suppression of the Financing of Terrorism and taking measures against noncooperative countries
6. Strengthen air security through actions of the Transport Council, and
7. Instruct the General Affairs Council to coordinate and provide the impetus for the EU's antiterrorism efforts, including a role for the CFSP and relations with third-party countries

The third point of the European Council's conclusions entailed a broad set of goals for the EU to become more involved in global efforts to fight terrorism through new political dialogue with countries and regions in which terrorism comes into being, as well the continued development of the CFSP and an operational European Security and Defense Policy (ESDP). The fourth and final point in the summit's conclusions addressed the potential world economic effects of the terrorists.

In sum, the European Council of September 21 endorsed the main commitments expressed at the JHA Council the previous day and placed them in the context of a broader EU fight against terrorism. For the first time since the Tampere European Council of 1999, Justice and Home Affairs was the central theme at a meeting of the heads of state and government. The ongoing work of the EU since the Tampere summit in meeting the goals of the JHA Scoreboard had put the European Union in position to act quickly on a variety of new legislative measures and programs in reaction to the events of September 11. The external event of the terrorist attacks on the United States had provided the impetus to hasten progress on these issues, helping to overcome many long-standing political logjams in the process. Initiatives that would have been branded "federalist" and unacceptable prior to September 11 were reinterpreted by EU leaders in light of the need for protection and more effective cooperation.[17] In the months to follow, it would be up to the Commission, the JHA Council, and, to a lesser extent, the EP to achieve final resolution of all of the items agreed upon by the extraordinary meetings of the JHA Council and European Council held in response to the terrorist attacks on the United States. After that, of course, the various framework decisions (or directives in some instances) would have to be transposed into national law and enforced, and the member states would have to insure that their national police and prosecutorial authorities cooperated fully with the new or enhanced EU-level crimefighting institutions that were established (e.g., Europol, Eurojust, etc.).

Making Progress on JHA and Antiterrorism

The first opportunity for the JHA Council to start work on the ambitious antiterrorist agenda was during its regularly scheduled session of September 27–28 in Brussels. During a discussion of the timetable for the various antiterrorist measures, the United Kingdom suggested creating a "roadmap" to make it more clear what was needed to be done and by whom. At first this idea was rejected, but it was eventually adopted on the second day of the Council with the intention of facilitating both progress during the Belgian presidency and the drafting of a report on this for presentation at the planned Laeken European Council set for December 14–15.[18] The resulting "Antiterrorism Roadmap" presented by the Belgian presidency originally contained forty-five items and would be updated and periodically revised at subsequent meetings of both the JHA and General Affairs Councils (GAC).

The September JHA Council avoided substantive debate of the two most noteworthy aspects of antiterrorism initiatives, namely the Commission's two draft framework decisions. However, it was clear that there was disagreement over the suggested definition of "terrorism" concerning the

one proposal, and, regarding the second, discord about the crimes to be covered by the proposed arrest warrant concerning the extradition of a nation's own citizens for foreign prosecution. Hoping to forge agreement on these and other matters related to the Antiterrorism Roadmap, the Council agreed that the Article 36 Committee should convene more frequently, and subsequently began to meet twice weekly.

Aside from establishing a course of action to expedite its fight against terrorism, the September 2001 JHA Council was the occasion of noteworthy progress on a number of key items that the Belgian presidency had inherited from its predecessor, Sweden. For example, on the basis of an initiative proposed jointly by Sweden and Belgium, political agreement was reached to extend the remit of Europol to all forms of crime listed in the annex to the Europol Convention. This measure empowers Europol to fight sixteen additional forms of serious crime, serving to continue the gradual widening of Europol's remit that began with the creation of the Europol Drugs Unit 1994 and the expansion of its crime-fighting duties the following year.

In its committee report on the matter, which was later adopted in plenary council on November 11, 2001, the EP suggested that it should be consulted before the Europol Management Board determined Europol's priorities regarding the more than twenty crimes to be included in its new remit. The EP proposed as well that the board should decide this matter using qualified majority voting. In the end, however, the JHA Council chose to retain the intergovernmental nature of Europol by rejecting these suggestions when it passed its final act on the proposal in December 2001. The decision took effect on January 1, 2002, widening Europol's remit to all of the crimes covered in its mandate. It is left to Europol's Management Board, acting unanimously, to decide its crime-fighting priorities from its expanded list of potential duties.

The initial agreement at the September JHA Council to widen Europol's remit might have been bigger news, but in the context of the rapid developments on JHA after September 11, it was hardly noticed. One reason for this was that Europol was already charged with fighting terrorism, and its potential activity in other areas was, at least at the time, not viewed as being terribly significant in comparison. In addition, the expanded remit did not come with any additional operative powers for Europol, meaning that it was still dependent on member-state governments to share information for it to fight crime effectively.

However, the September 27–28 JHA Council did discuss several topics related to Europol's authority to act, including giving it the right to participate in joint investigative teams and to ask for investigations to be started. These and other issues were raised in the context of possible amendments to the Europol Convention. Thus, as the Belgian presidency successfully oversaw the expansion of Europol's crime-fighting duties, movement was already under way to further enhance Europol's operative powers. Although Europol was still a long way from becoming a true federal police force of the EU, it continued to move in this direction, and the notion of amending the Europol Convention meant that debate on this would continue into the subsequent Spanish presidency in 2002 and beyond (see Chapter 8).

In addition to Europol, another institutional matter decided at the regular JHA Council of September 2001 was the creation of Eurojust. The Council reached political agreement on the first eight articles of the draft decision setting up the permanent Eurojust unit. These dealt with its composition, objectives, general competence, and tasks. In this regard, it was resolved that the Commission would be fully associated with the work of Eurojust. However, it would not have any authority vis-à-vis the national members, which would be represented on a "college" (executive board) that would direct Eurojust's activities. In practice this means that the Commission is able to attend the college's meetings if invited and can make legislative proposals regarding Eurojust, but it has little power. The rest of the draft decision on Eurojust, dealing mainly with issues related to data protection, was left to later meetings of the Council in the Belgian presidency.

On the topic of the trafficking of human beings, the September 2001 meeting of the JHA Council decided on the only unresolved aspect of the Commission's proposed framework decision, namely the issue of criminal sanctions. In this regard, Germany, Austria, and Denmark voiced their opposition to the general principle of establishing penal sanctions in EU framework decisions by specifying the minimum number of years for the maximum sentences for crimes (i.e., the so-called "minimum-maximum" principle for sanctions). Content to express their opposition to this in a declaration, and with the expectation of dealing with this question in the near future, these countries allowed resolution of the sanctions issue and "political" approval of the Commission's proposed framework decision. The final legislation entailed a minimum-maximum sanction of eight years. Despite this approval, the passage of the final act on this matter would be delayed beyond the Spanish presidency of 2002, by which time the JHA had agreed upon a new system of harmonizing criminal sanctions (see Chapter 8). A related Commission framework decision covering the sexual exploitation of children was also left unresolved, with discord remaining on the defined age for "children," and the issue of "virtual pornography" (where no real children are involved).

Until the terrorist attacks on the United States, attention to the problem of the trafficking of human beings in the EU had arguably become the most prominent JHA issue. Following the tragic deaths of the fifty-eight Chinese illegal immigrants discovered at Dover in June 2000, the JHA Council considered several major legislative proposals on the matter. As discussed in Chapter 6, these included three French proposals to develop the Schengen *acquis* including one directive defining the crime of facilitating illegal entry, another specifying fines for carriers, and a draft framework decision in the legislative pipeline specifying criminal sanctions (calling for an eight-year minimum-maximum sentence). In addition, EU efforts to combat the trafficking of human beings also included the Commission's recently approved framework decision defining criminal sanctions and the unresolved framework decision on the sexual exploitation of children (these are distinct from the Schengen *acquis*). Later, in February 2002, the Commission would also propose a directive calling for short-term residency permits for the victims of illegal immigration and/or human trafficking to protect them from abuse and allow them to contribute to criminal investigations and prosecutions.

The entry into force of all of these measures could not come soon enough, however, as the problem of human-being trafficking was viewed as worsening in 2001. Commenting on the passage of the Commission proposal at the September 2001 JHA Council, Willy Bruggeman, Europol's senior deputy director, admitted that "human trafficking to EU member states for sexual exploitation and illicit labor is increasing significantly." At that time, EU estimated that up to 120,000 women and children were being trafficked in Western Europe annually, with NGOs putting the number much higher.[19]

Before the end of the Belgian presidency, this enduring problem would once again grab headlines when thirteen stowaways, including eleven Turks, were found in a shipping container aboard a truck near Wexford, Ireland, on December 9, 2001. Eight of the illegal immigrants died, including three children, while another five barely survived. The container involved in this incident was owned by a Dutch firm. It had been loaded with office furniture in Italy, shipped by rail to Belgium, and crossed to Ireland by ferry from the Belgian port of Zeebrugge. Thus, the circumstances of this case highlighted the international nature of this kind of crime, as well as the difficulty in determining criminal responsibility.

At the September 2001 JHA Council, the problem of the trafficking of human beings was not only addressed in the form of the Commission's newly proposed framework decision, but also by holding an open, televised debate on the matter with candidate countries on September 28. The result of this was a common commitment among the member and candidate states to honor a twelve-point plan to combat the trafficking of human beings through greater coordination, convergence of national law, information sharing, etc. The Belgian presidency also used this meeting with the prospective EU members to inform them of the European Union's ongoing measures to fight terrorism and to stress the need for their legislative and operational cooperation with these efforts as they evolved.

With the conclusion of the regular JHA Council of September 27–28, the EU faced the difficult task of making progress on the ambitious agenda defined in the Antiterrorist Roadmap. Rather than raising any additional new proposals, Belgium attempted to bring about agreement on as many initiatives as possible before the end of its term. The schedule of activity for October 2001 included a second joint meeting of the JHA and ECOFIN Councils, a special meeting of the JHA Council on the same day, and a planned special session of the European Council in Ghent. These meetings were dominated by matters related to the fight against terrorism and, within this context, the issue of fighting financial crime acquired added significance. In fact, this form of organized crime had already been a priority for the EU, especially since the French presidency of 2000, which had presided over the first "jumbo" meeting of the JHA and ECOFIN Councils.

Fighting Financial Crime After September 11

The joint meeting of the JHA and ECOFIN Councils on October 16, 2001, featured discussion and progress on several key issues related to financial crime. Concerning new legislation, the "jumbo" Council considered three separate initiatives. First, the Council revisited a directive to prevent the use of the financial system for money laundering, amending a 1991 directive that was already in place. The new draft directive was subject to the co-decision procedure and had already moved slowly through every legislative phase since first being proposed by the Commission in July 1999. In June 2001, the Council had rejected the amendments that the European Parliament had suggested in its second reading, triggering the start of sluggish conciliation negotiations. The Council, along with the Commission, preferred the coverage of the measure to be limited to financial transactions, but wanted nonbanking professionals, including lawyers, to be subject to the new legal obligation to report suspicious activity. Meanwhile, the EP wanted to expand coverage of the legislation to casinos, auctioneers, and the purchase of expensive luxury items (e.g., jewelry), while excluding legal professionals from any obligations out of concern for lawyer-client confidentiality.

However, after the terrorist attacks of September 11 and calls by the United States for a global commitment to combat money laundering in the fight against terrorism, both the Council and the EP were suddenly more willing to reach agreement on the draft directive.[20] At the joint meeting of JHA and ECOFIN Councils, the ministers resolved to adopt the money-laundering directive "as soon as possible," signalling their new willingness to work out a deal with the EP.[21] Sensitive to accusations of being soft on money laundering, the EP was also more compliant, facilitating an agreement in the ongoing Conciliation Committee on October 20, 2001.[22] The compromise version of the directive was approved by the EP in plenary session in November, and the final act was passed in December and took effect immediately (the member states were obligated to transpose this into national law without delay). In the end the EP got its way in widening the scope of the obligation to report suspicious activity to include auctioneers, art dealers, casinos, and overseers of stock and financial markets. Professional secrecy is protected for lawyers when they are engaged in legal proceedings, unless the lawyer knows that legal advice is being sought to facilitate money laundering. The new directive also specifies stricter requirements for professionals to obtain proper client identification before engaging in financial transactions.

A second item discussed at the jumbo Council meeting of October 2001 was the draft framework decision specifying the rules by which EU member states would commit to recognize and execute rulings to freeze assets or evidence as ordered by a judge in another member state involved in a cross-border criminal investigation. Similar to the directive on money laundering, this measure had also been in the works long before September 11, having been introduced during the French presidency and formally proposed jointly by France, Sweden, and Belgium in February 2001. At the joint JHA-ECOFIN Council meeting, the ministers committed themselves to resolving their differences on the proposal as quickly as possible, but discord remained on a number of issues for several countries. This included, for example, whether requests to freeze assets would be subject to the principle of double criminality (or, alternatively, mutual recognition). Ultimately, agreement in the Council would not be reached until the first formal meeting of the JHA Council of the Spanish presidency on February 28, 2002, and was subject to the reconsultation of the EP after that (see Chapter 8).

In contrast to the slow progress on the draft framework decision covering freezing of assets in general, the pace of EU action was remarkably quick concerning action specifically directed at those thought to be involved in the terrorist attacks on the United States.[23] In response to the political will expressed by the European Council, the Commission had taken action on October 1, proposing a draft regulation (which has direct effect) to freeze the assets throughout the EU of twenty-seven suspected individuals and organizations. These had been identified by the United States on September 24 and included several persons and groups assumed to be connected, at least financially, with the attacks of September 11. Just two days later the EP endorsed the Commission proposal and its list of terrorists and terrorist-supporting individuals and groups by a wide margin, demonstrating how quickly the EU could act given sufficient political will to do so.

It should be noted that the EU had already taken steps to freeze the assets of the Taliban regime iin Afghanistan, Osama bin Laden, and members of his Al Qaeda network. This measure had followed several UN initiatives, especially its Security Council Resolution 1267 of October 1999, which called for a flight ban against the Taliban and the freezing of their assets, intended to compel them to stop supporting international terrorists, particularly those led by bin Laden. In response to this, the EU passed a common position under its CFSP in December 1999, outlining various sanctions against the Taliban, which were later implemented through specific measures contained in a regulation passed by the Council in February, entailing direct effect on the member states. By the time of the attacks on September 11, an updated version of this was in force, namely Council Regulation 467, adopted in March 2001. This included restrictions on trade with Afghanistan, a flight ban on the Taliban, and a freezing of their assets, as well as those of a long list of individuals and groups associated with them, including Osama bin Laden and Al Qaeda.

Thus, by October 2001, not only were these measures already in place, but several EU member states had taken unilateral action to freeze the assets of the additional twenty-seven groups and individuals named by the Bush administration on September 24, with more than US$90 million dollars worth of assets frozen in the UK, France, and Germany alone by that point.[24] The new regulation proposed by the Commission after September 11 was intended to require similar action throughout the EU. However, this hastily prepared measure would soon go through a series of changes over the next three months, as the EU attempted to bring this facet of its fight against terrorism in line with the recently approved United Nations Security Council Resolution 1373 of September 28, 2001. In doing so, the Council would ultimately broaden the reach of this legislation beyond those responsible for the attacks of September 11 to include several different types of terrorists (e.g., those affiliated with the Palestinian group Hamas and ETA). The end result would be a package of detailed legislation that prescribes various steps that states should take to prevent terrorism from flourishing, in keeping with the aims of the UN resolution and the broader UN Convention for the Suppression of Financing of Terrorism (1999). Progress on this package was slowed by continued disagreement on defining "terrorism" in a way that met several competing concerns, including established UN terminology, concerns for civil liberties, and the new political reality of the post–September 11 world. Hence, the legislative package covering the freezing of assets of specific terrorist individuals and groups would not be approved by the Council until just before the close of the Belgium presidency in late December 2001.

In addition to fostering continued progress on the regulation calling for the freezing of specific terrorist assets, the joint meeting of the JHA and ECOFIN Councils in October 2001 is also notable for three other achievements regarding the fight against terrorism. First, on the fringes of the Council session, the member states signed a Protocol to the 2000 Convention on Mutual Assistance in Criminal Matters that reduces banking secrecy in the fight against crime by facilitating the monitoring of financial transactions. This protocol obliges EU member states to transmit, on request from another member state, lists of bank accounts and information regarding transactions for people under investigation for an act punishable by a prison sentence of at least two years in the requesting state and four years in the requested state. The member states pledged to ratify this protocol by the end of 2002, but it was set to take effect once eight members had done so. Related to signing of the protocol, and in response to the attacks of September 11, the ministers at the jumbo Council session of October 2001 also agreed to step up cooperation and data exchange among their respective financial intelligence units, especially regarding possible activity related to the financing of terrorism.

On the international front, the JHA-ECOFIN Council resolved to take a number of steps to increase pressure on so-called "noncooperative countries and territories," which, at the time, included twenty nations as updated in September 2001. Among these were the South Pacific island nation of Nauru and the candidate state of Hungary, which had failed to change its national banking legislation on money laundering as specified by the OECD's Financial Action Task Force (FATF) on money laundering. Among other things, the Council called for the mandate of the FATF to be widened to include terrorism.

Finally, the agenda of this October 2001 Council session devoted some attention to the impending physical introduction of the euro on January 1, 2002. In autumn 2001 there was much concern that this event would be met by an influx of counterfeit euro notes, which could easily be passed off to citizens who were unfamiliar with the new currency or in banks that would be flooded with huge volumes of currency in the transition period. Fears (within Europol) of euro counterfeiting were directed at suspected operations in the southern Balkans, Bulgaria, and Italy. In fact, concern for this problem was heightened by several robberies of euros from armored trucks and banks, since the stolen notes could be used by counterfeiters to create fakes.[25] In response to these fears, Europol had opened a crisis center on September 3 with the specific task of helping police authorities in the euro states to share information and coordinate investigation on euro-related crime. In addition to this effort, the "jumbo" Council of October 2001 affirmed its intention to pass a decision calling for member states to share information on counterfeiting with Europol, as well as a new framework decision on increasing criminal sanctions against counterfeiting the euro, which amended the framework decision of May 29, 2000. Both measures were eventually agreed upon on as A-points (i.e., without debate) at the JHA Council session on December 6, 2001. The pending legislation on money laundering was also intended to fight financial crime and counterfeiting stemming from the introduction of the euro (see Chapter 6).

Fighting Terrorism

On the same day of the jumbo Council session of October 2001, the ministers of the interior and justice held a special JHA Council meeting during the evening to discuss progress on the Commission's two major antiterrorism proposals. Most of the debate on the Euro-warrant revolved around the nature of the crimes to be covered and the role of judicial authorities in the appeals process. Concerning the first issue, the question was whether to have a "negative list" of offenses to be exempt from the warrant, as the Commission preferred, or a "positive list" of crimes to be covered, which would be more limiting by restricting the application of the warrant to fewer instances. In this area there was general agreement that the principle of double incrimination would no longer be the rule, but rather the exception, for recognition of the warrant.[26] On the issue of appeals, the main question was whether national courts could refuse an extradition request through the warrant according to the actual substance of cases or just on points of law.[27]

Regarding the framework decision on terrorism, the special JHA Council of October 2001 considered several amendments to the original Commission proposal that had been worked out in the Article 36 Committee. The ministers discussed an alternative sanction structure proposed by the Belgium presidency, which called for a stiffer sentence of eight years for the lower end of terrorist-related offenses, rather than two years, as proposed by the Commission. There was also debate on the jurisdiction of the legislation drafted under the terms of the framework decision, with several member states, including Belgium, pushing for the coverage of terrorist offenses committed not only *on* a member state's territory, as proposed by the Commission, but also *by* any resident or organization of the EU. On both issues, the Belgians had yet to secure the required consensus among the member states.[28] These and other matters, including the very definition of terrorism, were ultimately referred back to the Article 36 Committee for further discussion during the remainder of the Belgian presidency.

More than a month removed from the horror of September 11, the debate in the special JHA Council of October 2001 made clear that differences had arisen among the member states regarding the best way to meet the threat of terrorism. In addition, new debate had emerged on how to support the United States, which had begun military operations in Afghanistan on October 7. Hoping to forge a united front and retain the impetus for progress, the European Council was set to hold a special session in Ghent on October 19. This was originally scheduled to deal with any final issues regarding the impending introduction of the euro, but it was used instead to follow up on the EU's plans to fight terrorism after September 11. The emergent discord in the EU on antiterrorism was evident in the run-up to the summit by the difficulty that the foreign ministers experienced in hammering out a joint statement for endorsement by European Council, requiring five hours of haggling on October 16.

The Ghent European Council itself got off to a rocky start when the UK, Germany, and France upset their fellow EU members, as well as Commission President Prodi, by holding exclusive presummit talks on the suggestion of French President Jacques Chirac. The intention was to come up with a stronger statement of support for the United Stated than the one contained in the draft composed by the Belgian presidency.[29] In the final declaration by the Ghent summit, the heads of state and government expressed their "staunchest support" for the military operation in Afghanistan and avowed their determination "to combat terrorism in every form." Noting progress on the measures specified in the Antiterrorism Roadmap, the European Council affirmed its goal of gaining final approval on the Euro-warrant and framework decision on terrorism before the Laeken European Council. The European Council also declared that while its objective was still the elimination of the Al Qaeda terrorist network, providing humanitarian aid for Afghanistan and neighboring countries was an "absolute priority." The unified front expressed at the Ghent summit could not cover up underlying differences among the member states on some of the finer points of the various proposals on JHA that were in the legislative pipeline. For example, discord remained on the two key items in the Commission's antiterrorism package, despite the fact that these had been considered twice weekly by the Article 36 Committee and weekly by COREPER.[30] These differences were revealed once again at the next meeting of the JHA Council of November 16, 2001, in Brussels, which featured a very limited agenda. Regarding the European Arrest Warrant, disagreement remained on the list of crimes to be covered, with the Commission continuing to push for a wider variety of crimes. In contrast, the consensus among the member states was for a more limiting, positive list of crimes. However, discord continued on this over the lack of a common definition of some crimes, as well as over the enduring attachment by some member states to the need for double criminality in some areas.[31] In the end, the Belgian presidency succeeded in getting thirteen member states to agree to a positive list of thirty crimes to be included in the framework decision setting up the arrest warrant.

At this point Ireland was still refusing to agree to the list, arguing that by including crimes such as swindling and xenophobia, for which there was no agreed-upon definition, the overall effectiveness of the warrant would be diminished.[32] Even stronger opposition came from Italy, which was reportedly surprised at how quickly the legislation had evolved and wanted the new arrest warrant to be limited to the fight against only the most serious crimes, such as terrorism and the trafficking of drugs and human beings.[33]

There was, however, broad consensus among all of the ministers on the time limits for the execution of the warrant and surrender of suspects to the requesting state. In cases where suspects consented to extradition, this would happen within ten days. Otherwise, decisions on refusing to recognize the warrant must be made within sixty days, with a possible thirty-day extension after that (for a total of ninety days).

Regarding the other legislative item in the Commission's antiterrorism package, the proposed framework decision on terrorism, disagreement remained on a definition of terrorism and sanctions for various kinds of terrorist-related crimes. On the first matter, there was unease among some member states about the Commission's proposed definition, which listed thirteen types of terrorist acts and defined these as offenses "which are intentionally committed by an individual or group against one or more countries, their institutions or people with the aim of intimidating them and seriously altering or destroying the political, economic or social structures of those countries." Most member states came out in favor of aligning the EU definition with that of the United Nations, which defines terrorism as "intimidating the population or forcing governments or international bodies to do, or abstain from doing, something." However, civil groups such as Amnesty International and Statewatch were worried that defining terrorism in either fashion imperiled the rights of labor strikers or political demonstrators, such as those involved in the antiglobalization movement.

There was also disagreement in the JHA Council on the nature of sanctions for various terrorist offenses. The Commission continued to press for its plan entailing different sentences for different offenses (ranging from two to twenty years) in the face of alternative proposals for the simple two-tiered system of eight/twenty years (suggested by Belgium) or five/fifteen years (suggested by Germany). The unresolved issues concerning both the framework decision on terrorism and the Euro-warrant were once again referred back to the Article 36 Committee, leaving much work to be done to meet the goal of having both items settled before the upcoming Laeken European Council.

The third and final major topic of the November 2001 JHA Council was a review of progress toward achieving the AFSJ as defined by the Tampere Conclusions of 1999. With an eye toward the presentation of a full report at the Laeken summit, the ministers examined an updated version of the Commission's JHA Scoreboard that documented promising movement toward achievement of the AFSJ in several respects. In particular, the Commission noted that there had been the creation of new crime-fighting institutions (Eurojust, CEPOL, and the Police Chiefs Task Force) and the increasing willingness of member states to harmonize national penal law through the application of the principle of mutual recognition and passage of various framework decisions defining crimes and corresponding sanctions. However, the Commission expressed its frustration concerning the lack of progress on establishing common EU policies on asylum and immigration.[34] This shortcoming was also identified in the second report considered by the JHA Council, which was prepared and presented by the Belgian presidency.

By fall 2001, however, there was finally some movement on EU asylum and immigration policy. By then, a number of asylum-related proposals were in the EU's legislative pipeline, including a draft directive submitted by the Commission in September 2000 defining minimum standards related to procedures for granting and withdrawing refugee status. On September 12, 2001, the Commission had proposed another draft directive aimed at harmonizing the criteria for the recognition of refugee status under the 1951 Geneva Convention and its 1969 Protocol. This was intended to reduce the likelihood of member states making different legal interpretations of these pacts when ruling on asylum requests.[35] Finally, on November 15, 2001, the Commission approved a communication outlining a comprehensive approach for the building of a common EU policy on illegal immigration, which the Commission viewed as a source of human tragedy and easy prey for international crime.[36] The Commission's new plan was intended to balance concern for providing an open and generous policy of legal immigration based on humanitarian principles on the one hand, with the need to control illegal immigration on the other. In the subsequent Spanish presidency of 2002, the Commission's so-called balanced approach would form the basis of a new "Global Action Plan" that was intended to guide EU policy on illegal immigration in 2002 and beyond (see Chapter 8).

Even with this new movement toward implementing the goals of the Tampere Conclusions on asylum and immigration, the Justice and Home Affairs ministers remained concerned about the overall lack of progress on this aspect of the AFSJ. In this regard, the Belgian presidency floated a plan for implementing a "standstill" agreement among member states to introduce no new national legislation on asylum or immigration until after the relevant EU measures already in the pipeline were adopted. However, at the JHA Council meeting of November 16, 2001, this plan was opposed by some member states and replaced with an agreement simply to remain "loyal" to the EU's common policies by not implementing new national laws that would conflict with EU proposals. In the discussion of this policy area, the Italians proposed the creation of a European border patrol, which would subsequently be formally studied and discussed by the Council (see Chapter 8).

Finally, in their debate on implementing the Tampere Conclusions, the ministers agreed on two ways of hastening progress on the AFSJ. While allowing for the discretion of the country holding the presidency, the November JHA Council agreed in principle on the need for their sessions to be held monthly and with shorter agendas. Second, in the conclusions of this Council session, the Belgian presidency "echoed delegations' fears about the growing number of forums dealing with JHA issues and about the need to define clearly their respective responsibilities and coordinate their activities." In fact, it would not be long before Spain would attempt to address this very concern when it took over the EU presidency in January 2002, introducing a plan for a "European Institute of Police Studies." Ultimately, however, the Spanish presidency would fail to win approval for this initiative and would eventually withdraw its proposal before the end of its leadership term (see Chapter 8).

The European Parliament After September 11

As the debate among the member states on various aspects of the proposed AFSJ was proceeding during the Belgian presidency, so too were discussions in the European Parliament on these matters. Two plenary sessions were held in November 2001, in which various reports of the EP's Committee on Citizens' Rights and Freedoms were debated. Three initiatives before the JHA Council were approved by large majorities in the EP plenary session of November 13. One of these, as already discussed, was the decision to expand the crime-fighting remit of Europol.

The second item approved by the EP was a draft decision to allow the so-called onward transmission by non-EU states or international organizations of data received by Europol. As discussed above, this had been first proposed by Sweden on May 22, 2001, but had attracted greater attention following the terrorist attacks on the United States, amid speculation that these events might have been prevented had police agencies in Europe and North America done a better job at sharing intelligence information. By autumn 2001, Europol already had data-sharing agreements with Norway, Iceland, the European Central Bank, and the European Monitoring Center for Drugs and Drug Addiction, and it was in the final stages of negotiations with several candidate states, including Hungary, Poland, Estonia, and Slovenia. In addition, Europol signed an information-sharing agreement with Interpol on November 5. The directive on "onward transmission" permits Interpol, for example, to share data that it receives from Europol with other nations or organizations, unless Europol expressly prohibits this. The final act on this draft directive would ultimately be adopted by the JHA Council without debate (i.e., as an A-point) at the first formal meeting of the JHA Council under the Spanish presidency on February 28, 2002 (see Chapter 8).

Meanwhile, the European Union was also trying to establish closer relations with the United States on fighting international crime. Although it lacked a formal data-sharing agreement with the United States, Europol had already been assisting U.S. authorities after September 11 by helping them to cross-check European telephone numbers called by the suspected hijackers. At the time Europol was doing so under the terms of a special exception in its data-protection rules, which treated the terrorist attacks as a "life-threatening situation."[37]

On December 6, 2001, Europol signed a cooperation agreement with the United States allowing the exchange of technical information, including tips on threats, crime patterns, smuggling routes, a list of criminal assets to be frozen, etc. However, this agreement did not allow the exchange of personal data, which would include, for example, names, addresses, photographs, and criminal records of suspects, as well as the names of their associates or witnesses.[38] Prohibiting this was Europol's data-protection rules, which specify that it cannot share personal information with countries or organizations that do not have a singular supervisory data-protection authority similar to its own. In the United States, there is no such institution, with each federal agency having its own body and procedures to deal with data protection and with rules governed by case law, rather than codified in directives, as in the EU.[39]

Thus, even as the agreement on sharing technical information was signed between Europol and the United States, talks were already under way to overcome the many legal and practical barriers to an agreement on the sharing of personal data that would be most useful to criminal investigators on both sides of the Atlantic. By the Spanish presidency of 2002, talks between the United States and the EU had expanded to broader judicial cooperation on criminal matters, including the issue of extradition, which was politically sensitive given the possibility of the death penalty being imposed by the United States. In the future, the onward transmission allowance, combined with an agreement on sharing personal data with the United States, would mean that information on EU citizens collected by member-state authorities could be passed to Europol, shared with United States, and then possibly transmitted to other countries or organizations. Despite the perceived need to fight terrorism, this prospect was very worrisome to civil libertarians in the European Union.

A third significant JHA matter discussed at the EP's plenary session of November 13, 2001, was a draft framework decision establishing the rules for the creation and function of a so-called joint investigative team, entailing groups of police officers from two or more member states. This proposal, which had been tabled jointly by Belgium, France, Spain, and the UK and had been under formal discussion by COREPER since October 10, 2001, essentially implemented Article 13 of the Convention on Mutual Assistance in Criminal Matters, which, at the time, had yet to be ratified by every EU member state. In approving the measure, the EP called for its scope to be widened to provide for joint investigative teams to fight all forms of organized crime, not just for terrorism and the trafficking of drugs or human beings, as provided for in the draft directive. Although the legislation mentioned a possible role for Europol agents in the joint investigative team, it was decided that the rules governing this should be developed in a protocol to Europol Convention. By the Spanish presidency, work on this was well under way, as was final activity by the Council on the original draft decision setting up the joint teams (see Chapter 8).

The European Parliament met for a second time in plenary on November 29, 2001, at which three additional key JHA items were debated. The EP gave its second endorsement of Eurojust, voting 383 to 64 with 23 abstentions, after being reconsulted by the Council since giving its first opinion on this in May 2001. The EP suggested allowing Eurojust to obtain sensitive information from the member states and the Schengen Information System (SIS), but it did not want it to have access to data that, in its view, were not fundamental to criminal investigations, including driver's licenses, bank accounts, and information revealing race, political or religious views, trade union membership, health, or sex life. Finally, the EP called for the European Court of Justice to have jurisdiction over Eurojust and its operations.[40] Having already discussed some aspects of Eurojust at its regular session in September, the JHA Council was set to discuss the remaining articles on data protection at its next session on December 6–7.

By this meeting, the Council also hoped to have an agreement on the draft framework decisions on terrorism and the Euro-warrant, which the EP also debated in its November 29 plenary session. The EP committee reports adopted on these matters expressed support for both proposals but had also suggested a number of amendments designed to protect civil liberties in various ways. These were endorsed by the EP in plenary, when it approved the terrorism framework decision by a vote of 430 to 56 with 15 abstentions and the arrest warrant by a vote of 381-75-41.

The main criticism of the EP on the pending terrorism legislation echoed the concerns of civil-rights groups, namely that the Commission's proposed definition might be employed to restrict peaceful demonstrations, especially since the Commission had explained that this legislation might be used against "urban violence."[41] Other amendments suggested by the EP were intended to bolster defendants' rights or called for additional types of terrorist offenses to be specified, such as hijacking and the release or distribution of dangerous chemical or biological substances. Regarding the framework decision creating the Euro-warrant, the EP also suggested several amendments designed to protect the rights of the person to be extradited, including provisions for free legal counsel and the translation of the Euro-warrant into a language understood by the arrested person within three days. The EP also wanted to raise the threshold for extradition to crimes with punishments of at least twelve months, which would insure that extradition would not be used for minor offenses. As a safeguard against possible changes of national legislation in the future, the EP's opinion included an amendment forbidding extradition to a country where suspects could face the death penalty.[42] Finally, the EP suggested that the ECJ should have jurisdiction concerning the arrest warrant.

Toward the Laeken European Council

Having received the opinion of the European Parliament, the JHA Council was prepared to take up these and other matters at its next official session on December 6–7, 2001, with hopes of finalizing work before the Laeken summit scheduled for the following week. The Council reached political agreement on the final aspects of the decision setting up Eurojust, settling the remaining articles concerning its data-protection rules and budget. Eurojust was granted access to the various sources of personal information that the EP had suggested excluding in its opinion, but only for persons under criminal investigation. Explicit access to data in the SIS was not granted to Eurojust, as the EP had wanted, and the ECJ was given no specified role. The task of monitoring the use of personal data was given to a "joint supervisory body" composed of one judge from each member state. Regarding finances, the salaries of the national representatives comprising Eurojust's "college" (its executive body) will be paid by the respective member states, while the Community budget will cover costs of staff and administration. After some debate at the working-group level prior to the Council session, France and Germany had persuaded Ireland and the United Kingdom to allow the European Parliament to have the authority to discharge (close the books) on the Eurojust budget. The question of the permanent home for Eurojust's secretariat was left for the Laeken Council, as part of a package of decisions on sites for several other new EU bodies.

The passage of the final elements in the decision setting up Eurojust meant that Pro-Eurojust's days were numbered. In 2001, Pro-Eurojust handled 180 cases in ten months of operation from March 1, 2001, with Italy, Belgium, and France being the lead countries requesting assistance and Germany, the UK, and the Netherlands being the most requested countries.

In its annual report for 2001, Pro-Eurojust identified a number of barriers to more efficient and fruitful cooperation among prosecutors, including the varying degrees of prosecutorial power enjoyed by its members, delays in translations, poor understanding of different legal systems, and the continued need to meet dual criminality requirements in some member states.[43]

On the latter issue, it was hoped that the proposed Euro-warrant would alleviate this problem. In fact, it was foreseen that Eurojust would be the venue through which the Euro-warrant would be issued and executed. At its first formal session under the Spanish presidency on February 28, 2002, the JHA Council passed the final act setting up Eurojust without debate (as an A-point). This allowed Eurojust to replace Pro-Eurojust on March 4, 2002, the day after the act was published in the EU's official journal.

Regarding the draft framework decision on terrorism, the December 6–7, 2001, the JHA Council reached political agreement on a compromise version of the controversial definition, balancing the contending needs to punish terrorist offenses with the protection of fundamental political rights and freedoms. This measure lists a variety of offenses that:

> may seriously damage a country or an international organization . . . where committed with the aim of . . . seriously intimidating a population, unduly compelling a government or an international organization to perform or abstain from performing any act . . . or . . . seriously destabilizing or destroying the fundamental political, constitutional, economic structures of a country or an international organization [through a variety of means specified in this article].

In the Council's conclusions, the ministers expressed their explicit intention that this definition could not be extended to prohibit legitimate political acts, including the activities of trade unions or the antiglobalization movement.

Another key issue resolved by the JHA Council was the structure of sanctions, deciding in the end for a maximum sentence of at least fifteen years for directing a terrorist group and a sentence of at least eight years for the other terrorist offenses mentioned in the framework decision. Additional terrorist crimes not specifically mentioned in the legislation are to be punished by heavier sentences than those for ordinary crimes under member states' national law. On the issue of jurisdiction, the Council decided on the wide application of the framework decision, covering crimes committed on EU territory or those perpetrated by nationals, residents, or legal entities of the member states. Ireland, which was unhappy with several aspects of the final framework decision, lodged parliamentary scrutiny reservations on the item, along with Denmark and Sweden.[44] The European Parliament reconsidered this compromise version of the draft legislation in committee and plenary session by February 2002 and once again gave its approval, but without suggesting any new amendments. Based on the assumption that the three member states would eventually lift their reservations and allow the final act on the matter to be passed by the Council as expected in 2002, the framework decision on terrorism was scheduled to be transposed into national law before January 1, 2003.

The matter of the framework decision establishing the Euro-warrant proved to be more difficult to resolve and more complex in the way it was implemented. Entering the December 2001 session of the JHA Council, the Belgian presidency had achieved agreement among thirteen member states on a positive list of crimes to be included under the warrant for which the principle of double criminality would no longer apply. As noted above, Ireland was originally concerned that the crimes of "extortion," "counterfeiting," and "swindling" were too vaguely defined to be on the list, but it announced at the Council that it had dropped its objections and would agree to the warrant.

Italy, however, was not as compliant, still preferring a much shorter list of just six crimes, namely terrorism, child sexual exploitation, pornography, and trafficking in arms, drugs, and human beings. Notably absent from its suggested list were the crimes of corruption and fraud. At the time there was speculation that the true source of Italy's unease over the longer list of crimes under the proposed Euro-warrant lay in the personal concerns of its prime minister, Silvio Berlusconi, who feared being extradited himself one day for past tax-related financial wrongdoing. Berlusconi had been investigated, though never convicted, of fraud charges in Italy stemming from his business dealings before becoming prime minister.[45] In denying these allegations, Italy claimed that its opposition to the list of thirty-two crimes was due to its concerns over civil rights, putting Prime Minister Berluscoconi into an odd alliance that included not only British Euro-skeptics, but also NGOs such as Amnesty International and Statewatch, which all opposed this proposal that went far beyond terrorism.[46]

Italy's opposition to the list of crimes notwithstanding, the December JHA Council was able to reach agreement on the other outstanding issues in the draft framework decision on terrorism. The ministers agreed that double criminality would be lifted for each of the crimes on the list, provided that they were punishable in the state issuing the warrant by a sentence of a maximum of at least three years. Double criminality would remain for crimes not mentioned, leaving open the possibility that extradition could be refused on that basis for crimes not on the list. The JHA ministers decided to push back the Commission's suggested implementation date one year to January 1, 2004, and also agreed to give the member states the option of making the Euro-warrant retroactive to crimes committed before 2004, but not earlier than 1993, when the Third Pillar was created by the Maastricht Treaty. While some member states initially did not want retroactivity to go back this far, only Italy had been completely opposed to this, prompting it to be an optional provision.[47]

The reaction to Italy's blocking of a Council decision on the Euro-warrant was immediate, public, and angry. Belgian Justice Minister Marc Verwilghen said that the Italian position was "incomprehensible" given the commitment to an arrest warrant with a wide scope that Italy had expressed at the Ghent European Council.[48] Meanwhile, German Interior Minister Otto Schily complained that "the Italian position is completely unacceptable."[49] Commissioner Vitorino declared that "we cannot be held hostage to Council unanimity," and he indicated that the Council might try to proceed despite this by using the option of enhanced cooperation to allow the fourteen to move ahead without Italy.[50] In a BBC news report on the dispute, this option was confirmed by Britain's Home Office representative Angela Eagle, while an unidentified "senior minister" warned that "we're heading for a show of force."[51]

Hoping to avoid poisoning the atmosphere of the upcoming Laeken Summit, Belgian Prime Minister Guy Verhofstadt traveled to Rome on December 11 to meet with Berlusconi. The direct personal diplomacy worked, and the two made a joint statement that day indicating Italy's intention to comply with the arrest warrant, including the list of thirty-two crimes. However, Prime Minister Berlusconi hinted that it might not be easy for Italy to amend its constitution (e.g., regarding the extradition of its own citizens) on time for it to comply with the framework decision by the end of 2003. In Italy, doing so would require either a risky popular referendum or a two-thirds majority in the lower house, for which the unlikely support of the far-right and xenophobic Northern League under Umberto Bossi would be needed. Overall, Italy's dispute with the EU over the arrest warrant, coming on the heals of its exclusion from the presummit talks at Ghent, showed its desire to be taken more seriously in the EU. Italian Justice Minister Roberto Castelli, an ally of Bossi, commented, "I am discovering that Italy counts for far too little in Brussels. We are far too supine on everything to do with Europe. We are the world's fifth largest power. We should make that strength felt."[52] Long a staunch supporter of deeper EU integration, Italy's new outspoken resistance to some of its European partners was viewed at least partly as the result of Berlusconi's desire to balance the diverging concerns of the pro- and anti-EU voices in his coalition government.[53] In fact, Berlusconi's new resolve to be more assertive in the EU would surface again just days later, when he figured prominently in the abrupt conclusion of the Laeken summit.

Nevertheless, the lifting of Italy's opposition to the Euro-warrant cleared the way for the amended version of the original Commission proposal to be approved by the Council on December 12, 2001. As with the framework decision on terrorism, the EP reconsidered and approved this legislation in committee and plenary session by early February 2002 without suggesting any new amendments.

Even before the final act could be passed by the Council, six member states announced that they had agreed to introduce the Euro-warrant as soon as possible, well ahead of the January 1, 2004, deadline. At the informal meeting of the JHA Council at Santiago de Compostela, Spain, on February 14, 2002, Belgium, France, Luxembourg, Portugal, Spain, and the United Kingdom promised to put national legislation transposing the framework decision on the fast track, aiming to have it in place sometime in 2003. Under the terms of the framework decision, this would allow them to utilize the framework decision with each other, while they waited for the remaining member states to change their legislation or constitutions. Germany also indicated that it would try to expedite its participation, but faced possible constitutional issues on the matter. Meanwhile, Italy continued to hint that it might have difficulty meeting even the later deadline (2004) for implementing the arrest warrant.

Aside from its consideration of Eurojust and the two framework decisions on terrorism, the JHA Council of December 6–7, 2001, was also notable for a few important developments related to Europol. As mentioned above, this Council was the occasion of the final act extending the crime-fighting remit of Europol to all of the crimes listed in its annex, which took effect on January 1, 2002. In addition, Jürgen Storbeck addressed the Council, briefing the ministers on Europol's new antiterrorism unit. In contrast to his remarks in the immediate wake of the terrorist attacks on the United States, Director Storbeck spoke highly of the positive changes in member states' willingness to provide information to Europol, but said that there were still some problems, particularly of a legal nature.[54]

The Council also authorized Storbeck to conclude a cooperation agreement with the United States, covering liaison exchange and the sharing of technical information, as discussed above. Parallel to the JHA Council meeting, Storbeck signed this agreement with the U.S. ambassador to the EU, Rockwell Schnabel, doing so in the presence of U.S. Secretary of State Colin Powell, which signified the importance of the pact. In light of Europol's report on data protection in the United States, the JHA Council also authorized Storbeck to initiate negotiations with the United States on the sharing of personal data. As noted above, the United States and the EU would also begin talks during the Spanish presidency of 2002 on a broader agreement covering judicial cooperation in criminal matters, including extradition.

Concerning the fight against terrorism, the JHA Council of December 2001 noted that there had been progress on thirty of the forty-five measures contained in the Antiterrorist Roadmap by that time. The Council also approved a biennial update of the list of terrorist organizations prepared by Europol, but kept this confidential as it was intended for operational use.

Finally, the JHA ministers heard a presentation by Germany outlining new ideas to be added to the Roadmap, including a database of non-EU resident aliens, as well as more secure forms of identification.[55]

In addition to outstanding items on the Antiterrorist Roadmap, the Belgian presidency would turn over several items to Spain, including a few matters discussed at the December 2001 JHA Council. One of these was the draft framework decision on child sexual exploitation, which was held up on the issue of defining the age of "children," as well as on Italy's reservations on its treatment of "virtual porn" (where no actual children are involved). The Council also continued its discussion on the harmonization of criminal law, seeking to replace the minimum-maximum system of sanction with four different levels of penalties. The intention was to ease the passage of a framework decision specifying sanctions by allowing the JHA Council to agree on the appropriate level of sanctions to be applied to the crime being considered. Discussion of this would continue into the Spanish presidency in 2002 (see Chapter 8).

One last item of note decided at the final JHA Council of the Belgian presidency was the passage, without debate, of the budget and work program for the new European Police College (CEPOL). Since being created by a Council decision in December 2000, CEPOL had gotten off to a rocky start, with no decision having been made on the site or leadership of its permanent secretariat. CEPOL's first work program was not even approved by the JHA Council until its regular session of November 2001. This allowed only a limited number of courses to be offered before the end of the year, organized by police training academies in Germany, Belgium, France, the Netherlands, and Spain and ranging in length from four days to one month. The four priority areas for the remainder of 2001 (November to December) were nonmilitary crisis management (in preparation for the possible deployment of police units as part of a European Rapid Reaction Force), the trafficking of human beings and control of external borders, cooperation with candidate countries, and community policing.[56] Additional courses were also provided in foreign languages, new training and learning methods, conflict resolution, and legal challenges related to cyber-crime.

CEPOL's budget for 2002, financed by the member states according to GNP, was pegged at €2.28 million. This was based on a full year of courses, but also on the expectation that its four-person secretariat, still yet to be determined, would likely not be operational until May 2002. Nine priority areas were established for 2002, including:

- Nonmilitary crisis management
- Trafficking in human beings and control of external borders
- Public order (including sports violence and political demonstrations, stemming from the problems faced at Göteborg and Genoa)

- Antiterrorism (added after September 11)
- Knowledge of police systems
- Leadership
- Learning and development
- Human rights (which was proposed by the EP in its opinion on the decision setting of CEPOL), entailing community policing, and
- Cooperation with candidate countries (with courses on police ethics, EU police systems, and control of immigration, including familiarity with the Schengen system)

The programs falling under the latter objective were devised at a two-day meeting of CEPOL officials from all fifteen member states and representatives of the twelve candidate countries held in Budapest on November 6–7, 2001. CEPOL's president at the time, Maurice Petit of Belgium, announced that a series of five-day courses held in member and candidate states would offer training to six thousand participants in 2002.[57] Even with all of these plans in place for 2002, the question of the site for CEPOL's secretariat was left to the Laeken summit, coming just days after the JHA Council.

The Laeken European Council and JHA

Held at the royal chateau of Laeken in the suburbs of Brussels, the concluding European Council of the Belgian presidency took place on December 14–16, 2001. Even before the terrorist attacks on the United States, the Laeken summit was intended to serve as a deadline for progress on the AFSJ, as prescribed in the Treaty of Amsterdam and the conclusions of the historic Tampere European Council of 1999. The events of September 11 had focused attention on this issue even more sharply, especially as the EU's antiterrorist measures developed after the attacks.

In this regard, the European Council considered reports from the Belgian presidency on EU actions following the attacks on the United States, as well as the evaluation of the implementation of the Tampere Conclusions and a communication from the Commission on its update of the JHA Scoreboard for the second half of 2001. On terrorism, the heads of state and government reaffirmed their "total solidarity with the American people and the international community in combating terrorism with full regard for individual rights and freedoms." The European Council also expressed its general satisfaction with the steps taken by the EU after September 11, especially the arrest warrant, and agreed that the timetable established in the Antiterrorist Roadmap was being met.[58]

Concerning the general progress of JHA matters toward the AFSJ, however, the European Council provided a much more critical evaluation.

This was especially the case for asylum and immigration policy, despite some indicators of achievement in the forms of the European Refugee Fund, progress on the Eurodac database (of asylum applicant's fingerprints), and the directive on temporary protection. The European Council called for a "new approach" to EU policy on asylum and immigration, highlighting the Commission's recent communication on illegal immigration and the smuggling of human beings and asking the Commission and the Council to expedite the measures in the legislative pipeline (e.g., the definition of the term "refugee" and minimum standards for their reception).

Concerning the related area of controlling the EU's external borders, the Belgian presidency failed to achieve consensus on the creation of a common European border police, owing to the objections of the UK and Denmark, but managed to forge agreement to study mechanisms for cooperation between border services.[59] Member states were also asked to examine ways of establishing a common identification system for visas and the possible creation of common consular offices.

With regard to police and judicial cooperation on criminal matters, the European Council noted the progress made on increasing the powers of Europol, utilizing the Police Chiefs Task Force and establishing both CEPOL, and, more recently, creating Eurojust. Pointing toward a possible deepening of cooperation, the heads of state and government asked the JHA Council to examine the Commission's green paper on the creation of a European public prosecutor. Finally, the Laeken European Council lauded the framework decisions on the trafficking of human beings, terrorism, and the arrest warrant and called for further efforts in the area of mutual recognition of judgments and the harmonization of the law, both criminal and civil. The European Council singled out the Commission's proposed framework decision on drug trafficking and called for its adoption by the end of May 2002.

Regarding the ongoing evolution of the ESDP, the presidency's conclusions contained an overly optimistic declaration that the EU was already able to carry out some crisis-management operations. In reality, the ESDP was, at the time, only in the position to contribute to disaster relief (which might entail police deployment), with agreement over access to NATO assets still standing in the way of a European Rapid Reaction Force (ERRF) of sixty thousand troops being fully operational, as targeted for 2003.[60]

However, by January 2002, the European Union was already making plans to take over the international policing of Bosnia by the time the mandate of the two-thousand-strong International Police Task Force expired at the end of that year. This would entail the preparation and deployment of at least five hundred of the police officers from the member states earmarked for use as part of the ERRF. The main aim of this force would be to help train a professional Bosnian police force and establish stronger policing structures in a country that was still beset by ethnic divisions, corruption, and the trafficking of human beings.

In addition to these specific JHA-related items, the concluding European Council was significant for its agreement on the so-called Laeken Declaration, the first draft of which had been produced by the Belgian presidency after Prime Minster Verhofstadt had toured EU capitals. The Laeken Declaration is notable not only for its vision of a newly designed European Union, but also for its prescription as to *how* this is to be achieved. In light of the EU's "new role in a globalized world," the Laeken Declaration prescribes that "the Union needs to be more democratic, more transparent and more efficient." With these goals in mind, the declaration calls for fundamental reform of the EU's decisionmaking institutions, as well as the possible drafting of a constitution for the Union that might enshrine the newly approved Charter of Fundamental Rights. Regarding Justice and Home Affairs, reform of the EU might entail a virtual elimination of the distinction between First and Third Pillar matters, including majority voting in the JHA Council, power of co-decision for the EP, and an entirely new role for the Commission in this area.

Already looking beyond the Treaty of Nice to the next IGC, the Laeken Declaration proposed the initiation of a "convention." After working for one year, this "European Convention," as it would become known, would ultimately produce a document that was intended to be a starting point for the discussions of the next IGC, which was set to begin in 2004. The Laeken Declaration specified that the convention's work would be guided by a "praesidium" (executive board) and would receive input from a broad-based "forum" composed of a variety of actors from civil society. The convention itself would be composed of 105 members, including the praesidium's president and two vice presidents, sixteen MEPs, two Commission representatives, the governmental representatives of the fifteen member and thirteen applicant states, and two members from each state's national parliament. It was known at the time that the next IGC would not necessarily be compelled to accept the convention's proposals, just as the convention itself would not be bound by the goals expressed in the Laeken Declaration.[61] However, many expected that it would be difficult for the member states to ignore the convention's recommendations if these were backed by the strong consensus of its delegates. The convention was scheduled to begin its work during the Spanish presidency (which it did on February 28, 2002) and produce its final document at some point during the Greek presidency in the first half of 2003.

The fine-tuning of the draft declaration proposed by Belgium took place on the morning of the second day of the summit, December 15, with the heads of state and government approaching the matter almost with the seriousness of an IGC. The need for significant reform seemed rather urgent indeed, given that the Laeken European Council had already endorsed the

Commission's view that the next enlargement of the EU could happen in "big bang" fashion. That is, the Commission believed that as many as ten of the twelve candidate states (not including Romania or Bulgaria) could be ready for accession to the EU before the next EP elections set for June 2004. In the end, discussions on the Laeken Declaration resulted in few substantial changes to the original draft, with many leaders expressing their support for the idea of reform and hope that this could succeed.[62] However, this optimism for a bright future of the EU was soon somewhat dimmed as the heads of state and government subsequently displayed the same kind of petty nationalism that had caused many to worry about the prospects for greater integration in the first place.

This initially arose in the discussion and debate about the leadership and membership of the convention's praesidium. Determining these positions was not easy, with each member state expressing its choices. In the end, the diplomatic efforts of Prime Minister Verhofstadt resulted in the presidency of the praesidium going to former French president Valery Giscard d'Estaing, beating out former Dutch prime minister Wim Kok. Former prime ministers Giuliano Amato of Italy and Jean-Luc Dehaene of Belgium were named vice presidents. Commission president Prodi announced that the two Commission representatives on the praesidium would be France's Michael Barnier (commissioner for regional policy and institutional reform) and António Vitorino (JHA).[63] The remaining seats on the praesidium would be filled by representatives of the state holding the presidency at that time.

The controversy over the praesidium's membership was nothing compared to the horse-trading that took place at the end of that same day over the seats for thirteen new EU policy-oriented agencies, including CEPOL and Eurojust. Compared to its successful efforts in staffing the convention's praesidium, the Belgian presidency bungled the allocation of the agencies, in part because it had included for consideration a few new bodies that had yet to be given a legal basis (e.g., the "Civil Protection Agency"). This complicated matters unnecessarily, as did proposing to locate some agencies in countries that had not even applied to host them. One of the most bitter disputes arose over the new Maritime Safety Agency, which the presidency suggested giving to Nantes, France. Portugal, however, insisted that Lisbon should be its home, and offered to move the European Drugs Observatory to Paris in exchange for this. Demonstrating how the decision on one agency's site impacted others, Portuguese Prime Minister Guterres defiantly warned about the Maritime Safety Agency, "If it's not Lisbon, Portugal will block any decision on the seats."

Of course, the most infamous dispute of all at the Laeken summit arose about the new Food Safety Authority that the Belgian presidency had proposed locating in Finland (Helsinki), which, at the time, was home to no EU agencies. Prime Minister Berlusconi argued that the city of Parma should be awarded this new agency in part because he had conceded on the arrest warrant. Thus, despite the fact that Italy was already home to three EU agencies, Berlusconi would not budge on the matter.[64] Suggesting that Finland should instead be awarded the new Civil Protection Agency or CEPOL (which Italy also coveted), Berlusconi claimed at one point, "Parma is synonymous with good cuisine . . . the Finns don't even know what good cuisine is."[65] With the debate running into the evening and with no end in site, Prime Minister Verhofstadt, in consultation with Britain's Tony Blair, brought the Laeken summit to an abrupt and embarrassing end.

As with the other agencies, the decision on the permanent sites for CEPOL and the Eurojust was handed over to Spain, which would find it tough to resolve the disputes, as it was hoping to host both the Food Safety Authority and CEPOL. The Laeken summit did manage to decide on making The Hague the temporary seat for Eurojust, so as not to inhibit its planned start of operations in 2002. This put Eurojust in the same city as Europol, but France (Paris), Luxembourg, and especially Belgium (Brussels) remained hopeful that they could permanently host this new component of the EU's emerging institutional infrastructure of crime fighting.

Meanwhile, no fewer than seven member states had expressed interest in housing the four-person secretariat of CEPOL, namely Germany (Münster), Spain (Madrid), France (Lyon), Austria, Italy (Rome), the Netherlands, and the UK. Among these, Britain's proposed site at Bramshill was the favorite going into the summit.[66] During the Laeken European Council, Finland was brought into contention when it seemed that it might not get the Food Safety Authority after all. At its first formal meeting under the Spanish presidency in Brussels on February 28, 2002, the JHA Council agreed that Denmark would temporarily host CEPOL's secretariat. However, Spanish Minister of the Interior Mariano Rajoy made clear that the Danes, who had not even applied to host any of the agencies up for consideration at the Laeken European Council, had no interest in permanently housing the new European Police College. However, final resolution of this question and those related to Eurojust and the other new agencies were dealt with neither at the Barcelona summit of March 2002 nor during the Seville European Council in June, leaving the task to the Danes in the second half of 2002, or perhaps even the Greek presidency after that.

The abrupt conclusion of the Laeken summit and its failure to reach agreement on the sites of the new agencies belied the many accomplishments of the Belgian presidency in the area of Justice and Home Affairs, especially regarding the fight against terrorism. The key JHA proposals approved during Belgium's leadership of the Council can be summarized as follows:

- Agreement on practical measures to tighten security at summits
- Agreement and progress on the multifaceted Antiterrorist Roadmap in response to the terrorist attacks of September 11

- The decision to expand the crime-fighting remit of Europol
- Agreement in principle on the framework decision on the trafficking of human beings[67]
- The regulation on freezing the assets of those suspected of being involved in the terrorist attacks of September 11
- The signing of the protocol to the Convention on Mutual Assistance in Criminal Matters reducing banking secrecy
- The directive on money laundering
- The decision to set up Eurojust
- The cooperation agreement with the United States
- Approval of CEPOL's work program and budget for 2002
- The framework decision on terrorism, and
- The framework decision creating the European Arrest Warrant

In addition to these steps, the Belgian presidency concluded with the passage of a legislative package directed at specific terrorist individuals and groups on December 27, 2001.[68] This included the passage of two common positions by the Council under the CSFP, as well as a regulation and a decision to implement specific measures. The first item, Common Position 930/CFSP, specified various initiatives to outlaw the funding of terrorism and prevent terrorist acts from occurring. The second common position, 931/CFSP, defined terrorists acts in line with the terminology contained in the recently approved framework decision on terrorism, as well as ordered the freezing of the assets of twenty-nine individuals and thirteen groups contained in its annex, including many based in the EU.[69] To implement this action, the Council finally approved the regulation first proposed by the Commission in October, which specified the details of which assets were to be frozen and how this was to be done. In addition, the Council approved a decision setting up the first list of terrorist individuals and groups covered by the new regulation, which was drawn from the list provided in the annex of the Common Position 931/CFSP. This decision contained only Middle Eastern terrorists and was needed not only to implement the aims of the common position, but also to overcome the problem that there was no treaty-basis for freezing the assets of individuals and groups in the EU. Actions against these groups was therefore limited to measures expressively permitted under Title VI of the TEU on police and judicial cooperation in criminal matters. During 2002, Common Position 931/CFSP would be revised several times, including an updating of its list of terrorists. In addition, subsequent EU presidencies would pursue some of the specific initiatives called for in Common Position 930/CFSP.

One notable feature of this process was that the two common positions, the regulation, and the decision were passed by the Council through so-called written procedure, meaning without ministerial debate. More significantly, by approving these items in this fashion, the Council effectively denied the European Parliament the right to provide its opinion on the content of both common positions, the revisions made to the regulation originally proposed by the Commission in October, and, importantly, the content of the list of terrorist individuals and groups. In addition, the final version of the asset-freezing legislation approved by the Council failed to include provisions for it to expire by the end of 2003, as the EP had proposed when initially consulted on the regulation soon after the Commission proposed it in October. Moreover, the EP had no real influence on the final definition of terrorism contained in the framework decision because the Council had reached political agreement on this, and the Euro-warrant, before the EP could formally adopt its opinion on these matters in February 2002.[70]

Along with all of its antiterrorist initiatives, the Belgian presidency had also made progress on several other proposals that it passed on to Spain:

- The package of various measures on asylum
- The publication of the Commission's "balanced approach" to illegal immigration
- The framework decision to combat child sexual exploitation and pornography
- The framework decision on drug trafficking
- The framework decision on the freezing of criminal assets
- The framework decision on protecting the environment through criminal law
- The framework decision on racism and xenophobia
- The framework decision on cyber-crime
- The decision on safety at soccer matches
- The decision allowing the "onward transmission" of Europol data
- The framework decision facilitating joint investigative teams, and
- The draft protocol to the Europol Convention facilitating Europol's participation in joint investigative teams

Overall, Belgian Minister of Justice Antoine Duquesene expressed his satisfaction with Belgium's accomplishments on Justice and Home Affairs during his remarks to the EP's committee on JHA on December 18, 2001. Pointing out that the terrorist attacks of September 11 had totally altered Belgium's agenda in this area, Duquesne spoke of the "astonishing results" in Third Pillar matters.[71] He was referring not only to the new measures passed during the Belgian presidency, but also to the various ways police cooperation had been increased on the operational level, including greater sharing of crime data and sensitive intelligence information with Europol and the unprecedented collaboration among the various antiterrorist services and intelligence agencies in the member states. At the time, the Commission's

director-general for JHA, Adrian Fortescue, observed that the Belgian presidency "had made remarkable progress under difficult circumstances."
However, in keeping with the conclusions of the Laeken summit, Fortescue
called for faster development of an EU policy on immigration and asylum
policy.[72]

The continued sluggish pace of developments on these items notwithstanding, the achievements of the Belgian presidency on JHA were all the
more impressive in light of the progress that it simultaneously made on the
accession negotiations with the twelve candidate states. Proceeding according to the schedule established by the "Accession Roadmap," Belgium had
opened detailed negotiations on JHA matters (i.e., Chapter 24) with Bulgaria, Latvia, Lithuania, Malta, and Slovakia, and took over talks with
Cyprus, the Czech Republic, Estonia, Hungary, Poland, and Slovenia,
which had begun during the Swedish presidency. In view of the new fight
against terrorism and the prospect that new EU members would soon be
charged with securing the external borders of the EU's Schengen free-travel
area, the need for the candidate states to uphold the JHA *acquis* became
increasingly important after September 11.

Before concluding accession negotiations on JHA, each candidate
country had to demonstrate that it could alter national legislation and
strengthen administrative capacity to implement the EU's *acquis* in areas
such as data protection, external border controls, visa policy, migration,
organized-crime fighting (e.g., drug trafficking and money laundering),
customs, judicial cooperation in civil and criminal matters, policy, and
fraud and corruption. On the crucial matter of implementing the Schengen
acquis, a two-step process was envisioned. To qualify for accession, a candidate state also had to achieve a high level of external border control.
However, the lifting of "internal" border controls with their fellow EU
members and participating fully in the Schengen free-travel area will be
subject to a separate decision by the JHA Council at a later date. This
expected deferred participation in the Schengen zone is similar to the way
border controls were only gradually eliminated among several existing EU
member states, such as Austria, Sweden, and Finland, even after they had
signed on to the Schengen agreement and its implementation accords.

In addition, the candidate countries are also expected to establish close
relations with Europol, which will allow them to accede fully to the
Europol Convention upon their accession into the EU. Prior to establishing
a cooperation agreement with a candidate country (as with any non-EU
country or organization), the director of Europol is charged with preparing
a report on the protection of personal data in that country. Once such a
report has been approved by the JHA Council, Europol is able to conclude
a formal cooperation agreement with that country, specifying the sharing of
personal, operational, and strategic information, the establishment of a

formal contact point in that state's police structure, and the seconding of a national police representative as liaison to Europol in The Hague. It is hoped that these agreements will not only facilitate the seamless accession of these countries into the EU regarding JHA, but also help in the fight against various kinds of international crime, for which many CEECs are important source- or transit-states. After several months of preparations and negotiations, Slovenia, Poland, Hungary, and Estonia concluded the agreements with Europol in early October 2001, followed by the Czech Republic in March 2002.

The signing of agreements with Europol by these candidate countries were indicators of their progress on accession negotiations in the area of JHA. On November 28, 2001, Hungary became the first of the candidate states to close provisionally its chapter of accession on JHA, followed by Cyprus, Slovenia, and the Czech Republic in December. Meanwhile, Romania remained the only candidate state not to have at least opened accession negotiations on JHA during the Belgian presidency, but this delay was expected. However, at its session on December 7, 2001, the JHA Council decided to remove the visa requirement for Romanians traveling into the Schengen area, starting January 1, 2002.

Explaining Progress After September 11

The development of European police cooperation and crime fighting under the Belgian presidency of 2001 can be explained by examining the same set of internal and external factors that were salient in earlier periods. However, the external event of the terrorist attacks on the United States provided, by far, the single most significant influence on JHA during this time. Indeed, the events of September 11 focused attention on Justice and Home Affairs in the EU as never before.

During its presidency, Belgium had succeeded in overseeing increased progress on the realization of the Area of Freedom, Security, and Justice in general and on a few bold antiterrorist measures in particular. Just as the external problem of terrorism with Middle Eastern origins had, along with internal sources of organized crime and terrorism, contributed to the development of the Trevi Group in 1975, the terrorist attacks on the United States hastened the pace of cooperation on JHA after September 11, 2001. It is important to emphasize that the measures proposed or agreed upon during the Belgian presidency had already been established as goals in the JHA Scoreboard or were already under discussion in the EU. This was true, for example, regarding the Euro-warrant, framework decision on terrorism, various initiatives aimed at financial crime and the funding of terrorism, and the strengthening of relations with third-party countries. Overall, the attacks on the United States generated a new sense of urgency regarding the threat of terrorism, leading to new or stronger political will to expedite progress on these measures.

The enduring pressure of impending enlargement, another external factor, only contributed to this sense of urgency. It was recognized, for example, that an effective strategy of action against terrorism would depend on the strengthening of borders and criminal justice institutions in the candidate states, which would one day form key components in the EU's external border. As noted above, the accomplishments of the Belgian presidency on counterterrorism did not detract from its ability to oversee progress on the Accession Roadmap and planning for EU expansion by as many as ten new states in 2004. This not only made preaccession preparations in these states seem more important, it also heightened awareness that expanding the EU's membership would make both decisionmaking on JHA more complex and traditional means of international collaboration on counterterrorism increasingly unworkable or ineffective. Thus, along with the attacks themselves, the prospect of the next geographic enlargement of the EU contributed to the form and timing of progress on police cooperation and crime fighting during the Belgian presidency.

In addition, the significance of the trafficking of human beings as a crime problem was highlighted by yet another prominent human tragedy when several illegal immigrants were found dead inside a shipping container near an Irish port in December. This served as a reminder that this kind of crime was still very much a problem in the EU, though the terrorist threat had grabbed most of the headlines since September 11. Despite the fact that there were no major breakthroughs in this area during the Belgian presidency, the external problem of illegal immigration continued to insure that the goal of devising common strategies on border management remained high on the EU's JHA agenda. In fact, it would not be long until these issues regained the prominence that they had enjoyed before September 11 (see Chapter 8).

As in previous periods, the external influences on JHA policy worked in tandem with functional spillover to impact progress on police cooperation and crime fighting. During the Belgian presidency, it was once again cooperation on the Schengen zone and Common Market that had contributed to collaboration on JHA. That is, the borderless travel area and free movement of capital created by these initiatives made the fight against terrorism and its sources of funding more difficult for the member states to handle unilaterally. This led them to strengthen the EU's legal and institutional infrastructure of crime fighting and augment this with unprecedented practical cooperation and information sharing among police and intelligence agencies.

In a sense, this kind of collaboration on the EU level can be interpreted as a weakening of the principle of subsidiarity concerning cooperation on counterterrorism. For example, the analysis of sensitive national security data and the defining and sanctioning of terrorist acts were no longer viewed as being best handled individually and internally by member states. In addition, when it appeared that Italy might not join in the initiative on the Euro-warrant, the possibility of utilizing the mechanism of "closer cooperation" was openly discussed.

None of this, however, should be interpreted as being driven by a surge in the salience of federalist ideology. Rather, new forms of cooperation on counterterrorism were viewed as being more practical than unilateral approaches. Had a federalist impetus been responsible for acceleration of progress on counterterrorism, then there would have likely been significant new progress on many other criminal issues. Yet this was clearly not the case in light of, for example, the continued slow progress on issues related to asylum and immigration policy and delays in approving various framework decisions covering crimes other than terrorism.

In contrast, an internal factor that was quite significant during the Belgian presidency of 2001 was concern for democracy in its various forms. Although this does not help account for the timing of various initiatives, attention to democratic values, such as human rights and civil liberties, helps explain why many collaborative measures on JHA took the form that they did during this period. For example, this was true regarding the establishment of a personal-data supervisory body for Eurojust, as well as the final definition of terrorism contained in the framework decision that was careful to avoid possible application to peaceful protestors, such as trade unions and antiglobalization demonstrators. Some attention was also paid to the rights of suspects to be extradited under the terms of the new Euro-warrant, including its many provisions on due process that specified defendants' rights to counsel, translators, hearings, appeal, etc.

In these matters, the European Parliament and NGOs hardly achieved all that they had hoped in terms of safeguards for civil rights, yet many of the same issues that they had raised figured prominently in the debates on these matters in the Council, and at least to a limited extent, in the final legislative acts themselves. Where the EP enjoyed the power of co-decision, its concerns for democracy proved to be even more influential, as evidenced by the provisions included in the directive on money laundering to protect lawyer-client secrecy when engaged in legal proceedings. Although the EP did not win concessions from the Council regarding all of its aspirations, this matter illustrates how the EP continued to be an important source of concerns about a democratic deficit regarding JHA. Its actions also provide an indication of the role that the EP might play in the future should it ever be given similar authority on other internal security matters.

In addition, the actions of the Commission further demonstrated the significance of concerns for democracy as regards the shape of JHA policy during this period. Along with its role in drafting and revising legislation on terrorism with some attention to civil liberties, the Commission's concern for human rights was evident in the publication of its so-called balanced approach to dealing with illegal immigration. Although this would later be criticized for not going far enough in this direction, the Commission's humanitarian values were quite explicit in its plans.

In sum, concerns for democracy continued to shape many aspects of JHA during the Belgian presidency, as in earlier periods. Indeed, attention to civil rights seemed to gain even more attention as the EU attempted to respond quickly to the terrorist attacks against the United States. In other words, as the timing of the EU's progress was impacted by external factors, the nature of its response was at least partly shaped by concerns for democracy. Furthermore, this tension between maintaining internal security on the one hand, and protecting basic democratic values on the other, would soon be displayed once again as the EU attempted to deal with mounting popular fears about illegal immigration during the subsequent Spanish presidency of 2002.

Notes

1. BBC News (www.news.bbc.co.uk), "Belgium's EU Agenda," June 26, 2001.

2. *European Report,* "Justice and Home Affairs: MEPs Discuss Priorities with Belgian Presidency," July 14, 2001.

3. BBC Worldwide Monitoring Service, "European Police Chief Says Only Scant Information Being Received from USA," September 15, 2001.

4. *Agence France Presse,* "EU Information Exchange a Failure on Terrorism: Europol Chief," September 15, 2001.

5. *Agence France Presse,* "European Police Tracing Arabic Suspects Linked to Terrorist Attacks," September 15, 2001; BBC Worldwide Monitoring Service, "European Police Chief Says."

6. *European Report,* "Justice and Home Affairs: Commission to Propose Common Sanctions for EU Terrorists," September 15, 2001. The low priority of the United States for Europol compared to other countries prior to September 11 was attributed to an unidentified "diplomat" in Deutsche Press-Agentur, "Europol and FBI Must Sign Cooperation Pact, E.U. Urges," September 13, 2001.

7. *European Report,* "Justice and Home Affairs: Commission to Propose Common Sanctions for EU Terrorists," September 15, 2001.

8. The 1995 Convention simplifies extradition procedures where the person to be extradited consents to both extradition and the simplified process, allowing extradition within twenty days. The 1996 Convention specifies that extradition shall be granted in cases where the punishment is one year in the requesting state and six months in the requested state. This convention also mandates that extradition cannot be refused for terrorism, drug trafficking, "political" crimes, or fiscal offenses, or because the person being extradited is a national of the requested state. *European Report,* "Justice and Home Affairs: Legal Complications Emerge over EU Arrest Warrant," October 27, 2001.

9. The UK ratified these conventions in December 2001. By March 20, 2002, Belgium, France, and Italy had yet to ratify the 1995 Convention, and France and Italy had yet to ratify the 1996 Convention. At the time France was expected to ratify both soon, as was Belgium regarding the 1995 Convention.

10. *Agence France Presse,* "EU Ministers Meet to Consider New Antiterrorist Laws," September 20, 2001.

11. Peter Norman, "Stage Set for Leaders to Show Solidarity," *Financial Times* (London), September 21, 2001; Peter Norman, "Stronger Ties Urged Between Police Forces," *Financial Times* (London), September 21, 2001.

12. Norman, "Stage Set for Leaders."

13. Charles Bremmer, "Europe Clears Way for Anti-Terror Laws," *The Times* (London), September 21, 2001.

14. Lucian Kim, "Attacks Energize Europe On A Fight Against Terror," *Christian Science Monitor* (Boston), September 26, 2001.

15. Sebastian Rotella, "EU to Move Quickly on Terrorist Plan," *Los Angeles Times,* September 21, 2001.

16. Press Association, "Heightened Security at EU Leaders Summit," September 21, 2001.

17. Paola Buonadonna, "Viewpoints: EU Finds Its Role," BBC News (www.news.bbc.co.uk), October 10, 2001.

18. *European Report,* "Justice and Home Affairs Council: Ministers Back Bigger Role for Eurojust and Europol," September 29, 2001.

19. Ralf Casert, "European Police See Big Increase in Human Trafficking Despite Increased EU Measures," Associated Press, September 28, 2001.

20. William Drozdiak and T. R. Reid, "Money Laundering Targeted in Europe, Mideast," *Washington Post,* October 2, 2001.

21. BBC News (www.news.bbc.co.uk), "EU Combats Terror Funding," October 16, 2001.

22. *European Report,* "Money-Laundering: MEPs Back Conciliaton Deal on Directive," October 20, 2001.

23. BBC News (www.news.bbc.co.uk), "EU to Freeze Terror Assets," October 4, 2001.

24. Ibid.

25. See, e.g., Rory Carroll, "Balkan Forgers Ready to Cash in on Euro," *The Guardian* (Manchester), September 22, 2000; *Agence France Presse,* "Counterfeiters also Prepare for Euro Changeover," November 8, 2001; Laurence Benhamou, "Euro Springs Leaks Ahead of E-Day," *Agence France Press,* November 25, 2001.

26. *European Report,* "Justice and Home Affairs Council: Limited Progress on Antiterrorist Package," October 20, 2001.

27. *European Report,* "Justice and Home Affairs Council: Ministers to Debate Antiterrorism and Arrest Warrant Proposals," October 13, 2001.

28. *European Report,* "Justice and Home Affairs Council: Limited Progress Antiterrorist Package," October 20, 2001.

29. BBC News (www.news.bbc.co.uk), "EU Ministers Back Terror Crackdown," October 17, 2001; BBC News (www.news.bbc.co.uk), "Blair Welcomes EU Anti-Terror Support," October 19, 2001.

30. *European Report,* "Justice and Home Affairs Council: Member States Agree to Thirty Crimes for EU Arrest Warrant," November 17, 2001.

31. Ibid.

32. Ibid.

33. *Agence France Presse,* "Italy and Ireland Block Accord on EU Arrest Warrant," November 16, 2001.

34. *European Report,* "Justice and Home Affairs Commission Pleased with Progress Made Since Tampere Summit," October 31, 2001.

35. *European Report,* "Justice/Home Affairs: Directive Harmonising Criteria for the Recognition of Refugee Status," September 15, 2001.

36. RAPID (press release of the European Commission), "Illegal Immigration: Commission Proposes A Balanced Approach," November 16, 2001.

37. Donald G. McNeil Jr., "Europe Agrees to Share Data on Terrorism with the U.S.," *New York Times,* December 6, 2001.

38. Ibid.

39. *European Report,* "EU/US: Tough Talk Ahead with Europol on Transfer of Personal Data," December 19, 2001.

40. *European Report,* "Justice and Home Affairs: Parliament Backs Eurojust," December 1, 2001.

41. *European Report,* "Justice and Home Affairs: MEPs Split over Commission Antiterrorism Package," October 10, 2001.

42. *European Report,* "Justice and Home Affairs: Parliament Backs EU Arrest Warrant And Terrorism Package," December 1, 2001.

43. *European Report,* "Justice and Home Affairs: Pro Eurojust Says It Was Impeded by Diverging Legal Systems," February 2, 2002.

44. *European Report,* "Justice and Home Affairs: Italy Blocks Deal on EU Arrest Warrant," December 8, 2001.

45. BBC News (www.news.bbc.co.uk), "Italy Heads for EU Showdown," December 8, 2001.

46. Jean Eaglesham et al., "Europe Divided As Debate over Civil Liberties Rages," *Financial Times* (London), December 10, 2001.

47. *European Report,* "Justice and Home Affairs: Italy Blocks Deal on EU Arrest Warrant," December 8, 2001.

48. Ibid.

49. BBC News (www.news.bbc.co.uk), "Italy Heads for EU Showdown," December 8, 2001.

50. *European Report,* "Justice and Home Affairs: Italy Blocks Deal on EU Arrest Warrant," December 8, 2001. Italy was not expected to block this, but it could have at the level of the European Council by applying the "emergency break" that would be in place until the Treaty of Nice took effect.

51. BBC News (www.news.bbc.co.uk), "Italy Heads for EU Showdown," December 8, 2001.

52. James Blitz, "Italy Falls into Line with EU plans for Common Arrest Warrant," *Financial Times* (London), December 11, 2001; BBC News (www.news.bbc.co.uk), "Italy U-Turn on Arrest Warrant," December 11, 2001.

53. James Blitz, "Berlusconi Toughens Italy's Stance on Europe," *Financial Times* (London), December 18, 2001.

54. Minutes of JHA Council, Brussels, December 6–7, 2001.

55. *European Report,* "Justice and Home Affairs: Italy Blocks Deal on EU Arrest Warrant," December 8, 2001.

56. The Chiefs of Police Task Force had identified community policing as a priority task at their Paris meeting of September 2000.

57. *Agence France Presse,* "EU Boosts Training for Candidate Countries' Police," November 7, 2001.

58. See, for example, BBC News (www.news.bbc.co.uk), "Laeken's Anti-Terror Agenda," December 12, 2001.

59. *European Report,* "European Council: EU Leaders Open the Door to a European Constitution," December 19, 2001.

60. Ibid.

61. BBC News (www.news.bbc.co.uk), "Big Changes Ahead for EU," December 13, 2001.

62. *European Report,* "European Council: EU Leaders Open the Door to a European Constitution," December 19, 2001.

63. The appointment of Vitorino, and, in fact, his position on the Commission itself, was briefly cast in doubt soon after the Laeken summit, when speculation arose that he would return to Portuguese politics to lead his party in elections after the resignation of fellow socialist Prime Minister Antonio Guterres. Deciding that this would be a poor career move, Vitorino decided to remain in Brussels.

64. *European Report,* "European Council: EU Leaders Open the Door to a European Constitution," December 19, 2001.

65. James Blitz, "Berlusconi Toughens Italy's Stance on Europe," *Financial Times* (London), December 18, 2001.

66. Geoff Meade, Press Association, "Euro Summit Ends in Disarray," December 15, 2001.

67. On this matter the Council had agreed to two minor amendments of the EP in November 2001, along with a few technical modifications of the text. Following the lifting of parliamentary scrutiny reservations by some member states, the final act on the framework decision was approved by the Council on July 19, 2002, including a deadline of June 30, 2004, for its transposition into national law.

68. *European Report,* "Justice and Home Affairs Council: EU Approves List of Terrorist Groups," January 5, 2002.

69. Among the European groups were several splinter groups of the IRA, but not the mainstream IRA, which had become engaged in the peace process.

70. *European Report,* "Justice and Home Affairs Council: MEPs Express Anger at Council List of Terrorist Groups," January 12, 2002.

71. *European Report,* "Justice and Home Affairs: Belgian Presidency—Good on Terrorism, Bad on Asylum," December 22, 2001.

72. Ibid.

8

Maintaining Momentum

IN 2002 THE PRESIDENCY OF THE EU WAS TURNED OVER TO SPAIN, which was certain to be an able successor to Belgium regarding JHA, as it was a longtime champion of increasing EU cooperation on internal security. This was due in large measure, of course, to its own internal terrorist problem with Basque separatists and the difficulty it had long experienced in dealing with this problem unilaterally. Even before September 11, Spain had proposed making the consolidation of the Area of Freedom, Security, and Justice a priority for its six-month leadership term. By January 1, 2002, Spain was emphasizing the specific aim of continuing the EU's new fight against terrorism as one its three main concerns. The other two priorities for the Spanish presidency were ensuring the smooth introduction of the euro and continuing progress toward EU enlargement.

Along with fighting terrorism, Spain's broader agenda for JHA included hastening progress on combating other forms of organized crime, which included continuing work on the evolving institutional and legal infrastructure of crime fighting in the EU. In doing so, Spain would oversee three official meetings of the JHA Council, as well as one informal session at the start of its presidency. In addition, the Spanish presidency would also be capped by a European Council held in Seville that would be dominated by JHA issues.

At the onset of the Spanish presidency, the fight against terrorism and the protection of the euro against counterfeiting were viewed as the most pressing JHA issues in the EU. However, by the end of Spain's term of leadership, the problem of illegal immigration had reemerged as the most prominent Third Pillar issue, recapturing the public attention that it had dominated from the time of the tragic deaths of Chinese immigrants at Dover in June 2000 until the terrorist attacks of September 11. By the concluding summit at Seville, this shift in emphasis was clear as the issue of border control topped its agenda.

Even as the problem of illegal immigration supplanted terrorism as Europe's foremost internal security agenda, a common thread had emerged linking these two issues, namely the EU's increasing use of a cross-pillar approach to fighting crime. During the Belgian presidency, the fight against terrorism was waged not only using the mechanisms of the Third Pillar, but also the First and Second, as the EU tightened banking laws regarding money laundering, examined ways of pressuring noncooperative states in the developing world, and enhanced its cooperation with the United States. In addition, at the end of the Spanish presidency, a draft declaration attached to the conclusions of the Seville European Council highlighted how the EU's emerging Common Foreign and Security Policy (CFSP) and European Security and Defense Policy (ESDP) could contribute to the fight against terrorism. The Seville summit also included a debate on dealing with illegal immigration by putting more pressure on foreign governments to improve their human-rights records and readmit their citizens who had fled, as well as linking EU aid to developing countries to their cooperation in controlling refugees, illegal immigration, and human-being trafficking.

An example of EU cooperation in its Third Pillar impacting its Second Pillar was evident early in the Spanish presidency, when the foreign ministers of the General Affairs Council (GAC) in January endorsed a plan to have the EU take over the international police mission in Bosnia and Herzegovina after its mandate expired at the end of 2002. At the European Council in Santa Maria da Feira in June 2000, the member states had agreed that by 2003 they would be able to deploy five thousand police officers for international peacekeeping missions as part of the proposed European Rapid Reaction Force (ERRF), including a thousand of these on just thirty days' notice. The EU's plan to take over the duties of the UN-led International Police Task Force (in which European police officers already participated) was made official by the GAC on February 18, 2002. This calls for 450 police officers from the EU to be deployed until 2005 to help build new policing institutions in the still-troubled Balkan state and to train a professional Bosnian police force.

The provision of a civilian policing mission for Bosnia is just one aspect of the EU's Stabilization and Association Program (SAP) for the Western Balkans, designed to assist the states in this region to make the necessary economic and political reforms on the road to possibly accession. To support the SAP financially, the EU has established the CARDS program (Community Assistance for Reconstruction, Development, and Stabilization), which provides €4.65 billion to the region for 2002–2006. In the case of Bosnia, the CARDS program funds institution building, especially in the JHA sector, focusing on the judiciary, police, and border management. The EU's plan to take over the civilian police mission in Bosnia was intended to supplement this financial support, as well as to serve as a limited first test of its ability to conduct crisis-management operations as part of the new ERRF. This also represents an additional manifestation of growing police cooperation in the EU and yet another link between the Second and Third Pillars.

Along with the decision to proceed with the new European police mission in Bosnia, another noteworthy JHA matter at the start of the Spanish presidency was overseeing the eventual introduction into circulation of 15 billion new euro bank notes and 52 million coins, which began on the first of the year. Prior to this, several robberies of euros had occurred in 2001, followed by a heist of €76,000 from a post office in Athens on January 2. However, fears of widespread counterfeiting of the EU's new currency failed to materialize, and the introduction of the euro went off relatively smoothly. Only a handful of counterfeit notes and coins had turned up by the end of January, and these were of a very crude quality. Overall, incidents of robberies or counterfeiting related to the euro were less than Europol officials had expected.

With the problem of euro counterfeiting seemingly under control, Spain turned its attention to its legislative agenda on JHA. Initially, this entailed continuing the construction of the EU's legal and institutional infrastructure of crime fighting. Concerning criminal law, the Spanish presidency had inherited several unresolved draft framework decisions covering a variety of potential areas for the harmonization of penal codes. Spain pledged to continue work on these initiatives, rather than propose new ones. One notable exception to this was Spain's goal of harmonizing laws covering the activities of private security firms, but there was not universal support for this among the member states, as many believed this was properly a First Pillar matter (i.e., related to the Common Market). In contrast, there was consensus on the need to replace the minimum-maximum sentencing principle with a new method of harmonizing criminal sanctions.

Regarding the evolving institutional infrastructure of crime fighting, Spain proposed the creation of a European institute of police studies at a meeting of the Article 36 Committee working group on police cooperation on January 8–9, 2002. Spain argued that this new body could promote consistency and cooperation among the growing number of new EU crime-fighting bodies, including Europol, Eurojust, CEPOL, and the Task Force of Police Chiefs. Similar in nature to CEPOL, the nascent European institute of police studies was to begin as a network of the national institutes. Despite the lobbying of the Spanish presidency, some member states remained unconvinced that this institution was truly needed, forcing Spain to scrap its idea near the end of its leadership term. Instead, the member states agreed to build the institute's intended coordinating functioning into the tasks of CEPOL. In addition to pursuing the doomed institute during its presidency, Spain expected to oversee the initiation of Eurojust and passage of its internal rules of operation, as well as determining where CEPOL's secretariat would be based.

Spain also hoped to strengthen the institutional infrastructure of crime fighting in the EU by increasing the effectiveness of Europol. As discussed earlier, the EU had decided during the preceding Belgian presidency to expand the powers of Europol to include all of the crimes listed in the annex of the Europol Convention. It should be recalled that, by 2001, Europol had been permitted to aid in the fight against the following types of crime:

- Drug trafficking
- Immigration networks
- Vehicle trafficking
- Trafficking in human beings and child pornography
- Forgery of money and other means of payment
- Trafficking in radioactive and nuclear substances
- Terrorism
- Money-laundering (in general)

With the extension of its remit to all forms of crime listed in its annex at the start of 2002, Europol was also empowered to assist in crime fighting in the following areas:

- Murder and grievous bodily injury
- Illicit trade in human beings and tissue
- Kidnapping, illegal restraint, and hostage-taking
- Racism and xenophobia
- Organized robbery
- Illicit trafficking in cultural goods, including antiquities and works of art
- Swindling and fraud
- Racketeering and extortion
- Counterfeiting and product piracy
- Forgery of administrative documents and trafficking therein
- Computer crime
- Corruption
- Illicit trafficking in arms, ammunition, and explosives
- Illicit trafficking in endangered animal species and plant varieties
- Environmental crime
- Illicit trafficking in hormonal substances and other growth promoters

To this new crime-fighting remit, Spain hoped to oversee the passage of proposals allowing the onward transmission of data supplied by Europol and its participation in joint investigative teams, which were themselves dependent on the passage of new legislation. Spain also wanted to give Europol access to the data stored in the Schengen Information System (SIS).

However, by February 2002, Europol was being criticized on two important fronts, namely for its worth as a crime-fighting institution and its perceived democratic deficit. On the first matter, concerns were raised by the Belgian minister of internal affairs, Antione Duquesene, at the informal JHA Council at Santiago de Compostela. With the support of Germany and other member states, Duquesene questioned the value of Europol in the fight against crime, especially in light of its increasing budget, and called for a critical review of its performance to determine whether it should continue to operate.[1]

Later that month the European Commission published a communication, on February 26, 2002, calling for greater democratic oversight of Europol through a series of amendments to its convention. This communication echoed several of the concerns raised by the EP in recent years, recounting many of its aims to increase the accountability and transparency of Europol. Nevertheless, the Commission called for a much more modest set of reforms for the short run, in keeping with the suggestions made by Antonio Vitorino in June 2001 (see Chapter 6). Foremost among these recommendations was the establishment of a committee of national parliamentarians and MEPs to meet twice annually to discuss Europol matters. The communication did propose some new powers for the EP, including the right to be given the unedited version of Europol's *Annual Report,* summon the Europol director to appear before its committees, and receive obligatory reports from the Joint Supervisory Body (on data protection). However, the Commission did not call for new judicial control over Europol or the transfer of its financing to the Community budget, as the EP has also suggested.

Ultimately, the matter of increasing democratic oversight of Europol was not resolved during the Spanish presidency. Yet this issue seems poised to intensify in the future, especially if the power and prominence of Europol continues to increase as they have since 1999. This appeared particularly probable given that democratic control over Europol was related to the broader debate on the perceived democratic deficit found in the EU's Third Pillar.

Before the end of the Spanish presidency this issue had emerged as an important topic in the European Convention. This was officially opened on February 28, 2002, under the direction of Giscard d'Estaing, with the goal of establishing the agenda for the next ICG, perhaps entailing a draft constitution for the EU. In a speech delivered in Stuttgart on May 5, Giscard identified the need to enhance the EU's ability to address the cross-border aspects of JHA as one of three priorities for the convention. On May 22, the Commission published a wide-ranging communication aimed at the convention that suggested a variety of changes to the EU's institutions and procedures, including several proposals regarding the Third Pillar. In general, these entailed greater application of the so-called Community method for JHA, which the Commission argued would hasten progress on the AFSJ.

These recommendations were echoed by Commissioner Vitorino on May 28 in a speech before the EP's Committee on JHA (i.e., Citizens' Rights and Freedoms). While presenting the Commission's plans on JHA for 2003, Vitorino criticized the member states' shared right of initiative in the Third Pillar as "demanding and disruptive."[2] He argued that most of the fifty-one legislative proposals initiated by the member states since entry into force of the Treaty of Amsterdam had not been well planned or coordinated, contributing to delayed progress on many of the goals agreed upon at the Tampere European Council. In particular, Vitorino claimed that this, combined with a lack of political will among the member states, was responsible for harming progress on asylum and immigration policy, rather than any ineptitude by the Commission. However, Vitorino also recognized that "more than any other area," the Commission's plans for JHA were "vulnerable to external events." In support of this he mentioned that the attacks of September 11 had promoted quick action on terrorism but had also contributed to the virtual standstill on immigration and asylum policy.[3]

Vitorino's remarks came just a week before the first plenary session of the European Convention on June 6–7 in Brussels, which focused exclusively on the Third Pillar during its first day. The discussion on JHA dealt with the variety of policy areas covered by the EU in this regard, as well as the possibility of expanding communitization to some of these. The wide-ranging debate revealed that a large majority of the convention's delegates supported giving fresh impetus to Europol but were concerned about the "freedom" facet of the AFSJ. That is, many representatives proposed that the Charter of Fundamental Rights could help protect civil liberties if included in the EU's next treaty (or its first constitution).

Nevertheless, no clear consensus had emerged at that stage on whether to apply the Community method to new JHA areas. On one side there were remarks such as those by Hans van Mierlo, the Dutch government's representative, who called for communitization for JHA, arguing that "citizens do not want pillars but results . . . if the structure of Treaty prevents results then it must be modified." In contrast, Hubert Haenel, representing the French senate, pointed out that rapid progress had been made on the Euro-warrant despite the intergovernmental nature of Title VI of the TEU (on police and judicial cooperation in criminal matters), while there had been little movement in Title IV of the TEC (on free-movement policies such as visas, asylum, immigration), where some communitization had already occurred.

In sum, by summer 2002 the future shape of JHA policy was unclear, as was the nature of democratic control over Europol. As made evident by the debate in the European Convention, resolution of these issues would also be shaped by enduring concerns for democracy, which would often counterbalance the desire for strengthening internal security in the EU. In addition, as indicated by Commissioner Vitorino, developments in this area would likely be impacted by the continued salience of events with sources outside of the EU, such as terrorism and illegal immigration.

Indeed, the legislative agenda at the start of the Spanish presidency had been shaped by the need to fight terrorism after September 11, but was also tempered by concerns for protecting civil liberties. It would not be long, however, before illegal immigration would reemerge as the major impetus of EU policymaking on JHA, especially when magnified by its impact on parliamentary elections in several EU states in 2002. Despite growing concerns for the EU to better manage its borders with a collective approach, the strategies adopted reflected enduring concerns for democracy in the form of attention to the human rights of prospective immigrants and refugees.

Progress on Crime Fighting
During the Spanish Presidency

The informal session of the JHA Council hosted by Spain at Santiago de Compostella demonstrated both the continued salience of terrorism and the emerging significance of illegal immigration on the minds of EU policymakers. With the aim of formulating a comprehensive strategy for dealing with illegal immigration on the basis of the "balanced approach" presented by the Commission in November 2001, the Spanish presidency presented its own plan at the start of the session. The endorsement of this plan and its many parts cleared the way for its formal adoption later that month at the first formal meeting of the JHA Council.

The approval of the plan entailed agreement to create a common visa format and establish mutual consular offices in third-party countries, starting with a pilot project in Pristina, Kosovo. The JHA ministers also asked the Commission to conduct a feasibility study on creating an EU visa database as part of the scheduled updating of the SIS. It was hoped that such a database would help prevent asylum and immigration "shopping" in the EU, where potential immigrants lodge applications in several member states. In addition, the Council gave the Commission the go-ahead to publish a green paper on the repatriation of illegal immigrants and called for the conclusion of more readmission agreements with third-party countries. At the time, the only EU-level readmission agreement with a third-party country was with Hong Kong, signed in November 2001. However, by April 2002 the green paper had been published, and accords were under negotiation with several third-party countries, including Russia, Pakistan, Sri Lanka, Morocco, and Macao.

Regarding Spain's aim to increase the power of Europol, the ministers approved the pending framework decision to create joint investigative teams, which essentially implements Article 13 of the Convention on Mutual Assistance in Criminal Matters. Building on recommendations passed during the French presidency of 2000, the Council also agreed that Europol could request that such teams be established. Related to this, a draft protocol to the Europol Convention was in the JHA Council's legislative pipeline by this time, including the rules for Europol's participation in these teams. This protocol also specified that the operational powers of Europol could be enhanced by a simple Council decision, rather than through the signing and ratification of a new protocol. At that point, however, there was not unanimous support for this measure.

Responding to the concerns of Germany, Austria, and Denmark (see Chapter 7), the informal JHA session also featured a breakthrough on the evolving legal infrastructure of crime fighting in the EU. General agreement was reached on a new system of reducing differences in criminal law by allowing ministers to select a predesignated range of sanctions for a particular crime. This represents slightly less harmonization than the minimum-maximum principle that it replaces and is intended to ease agreement on sanctions among the member states. The matter was turned over to the Article 36 Committee to work on the details of the plan, before being adopted by the JHA Council at its regular meeting in April.

In addition to this progress on the harmonization of criminal law, the EU's legal infrastructure of crime fighting was enhanced by the announcement that France, Belgium, Luxembourg, Portugal, and Spain had agreed to implement the Euro-warrant ahead of schedule. The six countries agreed to transpose the framework decision into national law and recognize the Euro-warrant among each other by the start of 2003. Germany declared its intention to join this group as soon as possible.

The final major item addressed by the informal JHA Council at Santiago de Compostella was agreement on the basic framework for the EU's negotiations with the United States on a comprehensive arrangement for judicial cooperation that would supplement the bilateral pacts the member states already had with the United States. This agreement between the EU and United States was expected to focus on fighting organized crime, especially terrorism, by enhancing mutual legal assistance, data sharing, and easing extradition. However, the JHA ministers made clear that any extradition pact with the United States would have to be tempered by proscriptions covering the death penalty, which had arisen as a significant point of contention in U.S.-European relations.

Overall, the informal ministerial meeting provided the foundation for progress during the three official JHA Councils held during the Spanish presidency. The first of these took place in Brussels on February 28, 2002, and featured a wide-ranging, televised debate on using external relations and international cooperation to fight organized crime. Although each member state used this forum to press its own priorities and proposals, there was consensus on the need to enhance cooperation with the candidate countries, including Russia, Ukraine, the Balkans, the United States, and Canada.[4] Parallel to the Council session, the JHA ministers also met with their counterparts from the candidate states and passed a declaration calling for increased preaccession support for these countries in fighting illegal drugs, especially in terms of the EU's Strategy on Drugs for 2000–2004.

This meeting of the JHA Council was also the occasion of the formal adoption of a few items that had been agreed upon informally at Santiago de Compostella, including the framework decision allowing the creation of joint investigative teams. The Council agreed, in principle, that Europol should be empowered to request that such teams be formed and to participate in their operations, yet the ministers could not finalize the protocol to this effect. They also failed to settle on the appropriate way to change the Europol Convention to facilitate its future amending. In fact, neither matter would be resolved during the Spanish presidency.

The first formal JHA Council of the Spanish presidency was also unable to reach final agreement on a variety of other matters. One was a definitive approach for launching judicial cooperation with the United States, with the member states remaining divided on whether separate agreements were needed for extradition and judicial assistance. At this same meeting the ministers reached consensus on a compromise text regarding the pending legislation on asset freezing, deciding to align it with the Euro-warrant by making it apply to the same list of thirty-two crimes. However, this matter was also left unresolved due to the parliamentary reserves of six states, especially Italy, which had serious constitutional problems with it.

The highlight of this meeting of the JHA Council was the approval of the Global Plan (action plan) for combating the fight against illegal immigration and the trafficking of human beings, which the Spanish presidency tried to cast as its own, though it was heavily based on the Commission's "balanced approach."[5] A major aim under the plan is the development of a common visa control policy for the EU, including the innovative provisions discussed earlier for common consular offices and visa identification and data-exchange systems. This plan also contains a variety of goals designed to deal with illegal immigration by increasing data exchanges, strengthening the operational role of Europol, and dealing more effectively with illegal laborers and the victims of human trafficking. In addition, the Global Plan aims to improve border control by intensifying cooperation with third-party countries, entailing agreements on liaison exchanges and repatriation agreements. In a related action, the Council also approved (as an A-point) the implementation rules for the Eurodac system for the storage and analysis of asylum applicants' fingerprints.

As the EU moved to meet growing popular concerns and tighten its borders, its new approach came under attack for being anything but balanced, with some fearing a possible "fortress Europe." The civil-liberties group Statewatch, for example, was especially critical of the evolving regime on asylum, arguing that it signaled a shift away from humanitarian values.[6] In one regard, Statewatch believed that the proposals on the table would allow member states to extradite asylum seekers before their applications could be properly considered, including cases where a death penalty might await them. Statewatch also found it "profoundly disturbing" that the new Eurodac system might, in practice, be used for crime fighting, which would contravene the EU's data-protection rules, rather than for monitoring asylum applicants, as it was intended.[7]

In addition to approving the controversial action plan on illegal immigration, the first formal JHA Council of the Spanish presidency was also the occasion for agreements regarding several of the EU's crime-fighting institutions. A supplemental budget of €3.1 million for Europol was passed for 2002 to cover the unforeseen expense of its new antiterrorism task force. As discussed above, Europol's budget had been increased substantially since it began its formal operations in 1999, continuing a pattern of budgetary growth since the inception of the EDU (Table 8.1).

These budget increases came not only in response to the expanding crime-fighting remit of Europol, but also the increasing size of its staff, which was projected to grow to over 350 by 2003 (not including its ELOs or Europol Liaison Officers) (Table 8.2).

In addition to the budget increase, the JHA Council of February 2002 passed the final act on legislation allowing the onward transmission by third parties of data supplied by Europol. The JHA ministers also formally approved Ireland's request to participate in some aspects of the Schengen *acquis* on police and judicial cooperation, including the use of the SIS, but excluding provisions on border controls and cross-border surveillance.

As discussed in Chapter 7, this meeting of the Council also featured passage of the final act setting up Eurojust, allowing it to become operational at its provisional home in The Hague. However, at this same session the ministers decided that the time was not right for the radical move of setting up a true European public prosecutor, even for the limited task of protecting the financial interests of the Community through criminal law. Thus, barring some kind of dramatic shift in political will among the member states, Eurojust can be expected to remain simply a liaison network of national prosecutors for the foreseeable future. Finally, the matter of a host site for CEPOL was temporarily resolved with Denmark's consent to house its secretariat in Copenhagen, pending agreement on a permanent address

Table 8.1 EDU/Europol Budget 1996–2003 (rounded in millions of ECU/euros)

	1996	1997	1998	1999	2000	2001	2002	2003
Operational	5	5.6	6.7	12.3	19.1	23.7	34.6	38.7
TECS	1.4	2.2	3.3	3.4	6.7	9.5	17.1	16.8
Total	6.4	7.8	10.0	15.7	25.8	33.2	51.7[a]	55.5[b]

Notes: a. The figures indicate funds allotted to EDU/Europol. Starting in 1999, budget figures are in euros. In some cases (e.g., in 1996 for TECS), less money was actually spent than was allocated. Europol is funded from contributions by the member states (intergovernmentally and not from the Community budget) according to their GNP. Budget allotments for 2002–2003 are based on projections available in June 2002.

b. The operational budgets for Europol in 2002 and 2003 do not reflect its obligation to pay for TECS-related personnel. These costs are reflected in the amounts given for TECS for those years.

Table 8.2 EDU/Europol Personnel 1996–2003

	1996	1997	1998	1999	2000	2001	2002	2003
ELOs	37	42	42	43	47	73	66	68
Staff	79	93	118	169	198	242	302	356
Total	116	135	160	212	245	315	368	424

Source: Data obtained as of January 2003 from the official Europol website, Europol annual reports, and the Europol budget for 2003. "Staff" figures represent all other personnel working at Europol (e.g., Europol officers, local staff, security personnel). Data reflects personnel numbers at the end of the specified calendar year.

Note: The original budget for 2002 was €48.5 million, but this was increased at the February 28–March 1, 2002, JHA Council to fund new efforts in the fight against terrorism.

for the EU's virtual police academy. However, this issue was not addressed at the subsequent European Councils in Barcelona or Seville, leaving it, along with the open question of Eurojust's definitive home, to be decided in the future.

As had become the norm, the focus of the EU's mid-presidency meeting of the European Council was economic reform. At this session, held in Barcelona on March 15–16, the heads of state and government liberalized the electricity and natural-gas markets by allowing industries and businesses to shop around for different suppliers in the EU starting in 2004. Agreements were also reached to raise the retirement age to sixty-five and to increase worker mobility by instituting an EU-wide health insurance card. In addition to increasing funding on research and development, EU leaders also approved the creation of the Galileo satellite program for global positioning, which, among its many possible applications, might someday be useful in border management.

This meeting was not without its more direct JHA overtones, as over 8,500 police officers were called up to protect the summit, buttressed by helicopters, air force jets, navy ships, and hundreds of soldiers. Spain even temporarily suspended its Schengen obligations during the summit, preventing twenty buses of protestors from entering the country from France at one point, which touched off clashes with police. The largest demonstration of the European Council came on its final day, drawing over 300,000 marchers. Despite this massive number of protestors, precautions on both sides kept violence and arrests down compared to the pre–September 11 incidents at Göteborg and Genoa. By the end of the summit, less than 100 people had been detained or were arrested, only twenty were injured, and relatively limited property damage had occurred, with most of the trouble stemming from the actions of a small group after dark on the last day.

The Barcelona European Council is also noteworthy for featuring the first-ever full participation of the heads of state and government from the thirteen applicant states, underscoring the importance of the next EU enlargement. Based on the Commission's regular reports of November 2001 and the conclusions of the Laeken European Council, ten states were projected to join the EU in 2004, just before the next EP elections. With EU assistance (under the PHARE program), preaccession preparations were proceeding in the candidate states, as were negotiations according to the Accession Roadmap. The so-called twinning projects under the PHARE program continued in 2002, with over two hundred civil servants from the member states working with their counterparts in the candidate states, including many engaged in institution building on JHA. In addition, the Czech Republic signed a cooperation agreement with Europol on March 5, 2002, joining Hungary, Poland, Slovenia, and Estonia. Plans were in the works for the other candidate states to do so as well, which would also allow them to develop liaison contact points with Europol and share information with it.

During Spain's presidency the accession negotiations on JHA issues (i.e., on Chapter 24) proceeded relatively smoothly. On March 21–22, these talks resulted in the provisional closing of this chapter for Malta and Estonia. Romania became the last of the candidate states to open its chapter of accession on JHA at the next round of negotiations on April 19 and 22. This was also the occasion for Lithuania to close this chapter provisionally, which entailed a commitment for it to harmonize its visa policy with the EU by July 1, 2003. Lithuania also pledged to issue visas for the citizens of the Kaliningrad region from this date, although the EU and Russia had yet to agree on arrangements to handle travel to and from this region through the future Schengen zone.

Subsequently, Latvia and Slovakia closed Chapter 24 (provisionally) at the next negotiating session on June 10–11, leaving only Poland among the first-wave countries not to have done so.[8] However, after coming up with an early revision of plans in the area of border management (related to the

Schengen *acquis*), including new financial commitments, Poland was able to close its accession chapter on JHA on July 31, under the direction of the Danish presidency. Consequently, this left only Bulgaria and Romania to continue discussions on this chapter during the remainder of 2002, and the Danes were eager to wind up talks on all accession chapters before the Copenhagen European Council of December 2002. No "transitional measures" were planned for any of the ten countries that had, by end of July 2002, provisionally closed negotiations on Chapter 24. With the formal talks on JHA concluded, attention turned to insuring that these countries would actually meet the commitments that they had made during their accession negotiations.

As preparations for the next EU enlargement continued, the midpoint in the Spanish presidency of 2002 saw the clear reemergence of illegal immigration as the primary JHA concern in the EU, recapturing the spotlight from the issue of terrorism for the first time since September 11. Soon after the Barcelona European Council in March, this topic came to dominate the headlines in several member states, creating new political will throughout the EU to implement many of the measures suggested in the Tampere milestones and the recently approved Global Plan. For example, Italy's long coastline had long been a favorite point of entry for illegal immigrants, but this problem reached a crisis point on March 18 when the merchant ship *Monica,* containing 828 would-be Kurdish immigrants from Iraq, was intentionally disabled and then towed into a Sicilian port.

A month later, Europe was stunned by the second-place finish of the far-right politician Jean-Marie LePen in the first round of France's presidential elections on April 21. Although LePen would ultimately suffer a crushing loss in the second round, as would his xenophobic National Front Party in the national assembly elections that followed, the initial success of LePen sent shock waves throughout the EU and put the problem of illegal immigration atop the political agenda in many European capitals. On May 6, the urgency of this issue was further intensified following the assassination of the Dutch anti-immigrant politician Pim Fortyn, and the success of his namesake party list in the subsequent parliamentary elections. Meanwhile, as these political events were unfolding, Europe was also experiencing an increased number of violent incidents regarding racism, xenophobia, and anti-Semitism, which were at least partly related to the increasing violence in the Israeli-Palestinian conflict.

Elsewhere in the EU, many political leaders had grown concerned about the potential impact of growing popular concerns over illegal immigration in their own countries. For example, by May 2002 the parliaments in Denmark and Italy were considering tighter laws on immigration and refugees, with strong support from the anti-immigrant parties in those countries. This increased the salience of illegal immigration in the domestic politics of the member states and elevated the importance of dealing with this problem at the EU level. In fact, the remainder of the Spanish presidency came to be defined by this issue, just as Belgium's leadership term had been shaped by the fight against terrorism after September 11. Thus it is worthwhile to note that for the first time in the history of the EU, issues pertaining to JHA rose to the top of the political agendas for two consecutive Council presidencies. This is even more impressive given that this overshadowed simultaneously mounting concerns for the next enlargement and increasing attention to institutional reform.

Illegal Immigration and Police Cooperation

The significance of JHA issues in the Spanish presidency was evidenced by their consideration by the General Affairs Council of April 15, which considered the problem of illegal immigration and took stock of progress on the Antiterrorism Roadmap. Both issues would not only figure prominently at the two remaining JHA Councils, but also at the concluding European Council in Seville. Although Spain would ultimately not be as successful as it had hoped in winning support for many of its new initiatives, it would oversee the resolution of several holdover proposals regarding the EU's evolving institutional and legal infrastructure of crime fighting, as well as foster a long-awaited movement on issues related to illegal immigration, border control, and asylum policy.

Progress in these areas was evident at the next formal meeting of the JHA Council held in Luxembourg on April 25–26, 2002. At this session, several agreements were reached regarding the multifaceted issue of better controlling the EU's external borders using an interlinked set of common policies, many of which fell under the broad framework of the new Global Plan. One important achievement was consensus on the directive establishing the minimum standards for the reception of asylum applicants in the member states. Designed to insure that such refugees can enjoy a dignified standard of living no matter where they enter the EU, this measure contains specific provisions on freedom of movement, education, employment, family unity, etc.

Reacting to growing concerns in several member states, the JHA Council also passed a detailed set of conclusions on illegal immigration and human trafficking by sea. Among other things, these conclusions established the goal of cooperating more closely with third-party countries to help combat these problems, including taking measures against states that refuse to assist the EU in this matter. However, the EU stopped short of naming and shaming the particular countries that many of the ministers had in mind, which included Syria, Lebanon, Morocco, Egypt, Albania, and Turkey.[9]

Along with this progress toward a common EU asylum policy, the April JHA Council is notable for two accomplishments dealing with border control. First, it approved the new Argo program, which provides funding for training, personnel exchanges, and research projects that promote international administrative cooperation in the fields of external borders, visas, asylum, and immigration. Replacing the Odysseus program and its smaller budget of €12 million for 1998–2001, Argo offers up to 80 percent in cofinancing for projects, totaling €25 million over the period of 2002–2006.[10] While supporting this initiative, the EP warned at the time that a much more extensive program would be needed once the EU expanded.

At this Council session, the Spanish presidency was able to report on the successful outcome of the Risk Immigration Operation (RIO) that it had initiated, which was conducted April 2–4 at sixteen airports in the EU. Aside from the resulting arrests, this endeavor collected valuable information on the nationalities and planned itineraries of illegal immigrants, revealing that a large proportion of illegal immigration from Latin America enters the EU through Spain and Portugal, while a high number of Chinese immigrants enter through the UK, often via Paris.

In addition to these efforts in the area of border control, the April JHA Council of 2002 is also noteworthy for several other achievements. Regarding police cooperation, the Council reaffirmed its consensus on the protocol to the Europol Convention to enable Europol to request the creation of joint investigative teams and to participate in these. On the insistence of Denmark, the Council president, the ministers clarified that Europol would only play a supporting role and would not have any operative powers, particularly the ability to use coercive measures. Europol would have the right to ask member states to initiate investigations in specific cases. The April 2002 JHA Council did not deal with the more sweeping proposal of Spain and Belgium to allow the Europol Convention to be amended by a simple decision of the Council, rather than via a protocol, which takes much longer.

In May 2002 the European Parliament adopted a report approved by its Committee on Citizens' Rights and Freedoms, which rejected the protocol on joint investigative teams. The EP's opposition stemmed its contention that Europol continued to lack sufficient parliamentary oversight and that this needed to be addressed before its powers were further enhanced. Despite the views of the European Parliament, the JHA Council formally adopted the protocol at its session on November 28, 2002, starting the process of its ratification by the member states in 2003.

However, this would turn out to be only the first of two protocols approved during the Danish Presidency. In July 2002 Denmark introduced another protocol to the Europol Convention, aiming to address some of the EP's concerns by requiring Europol to keep the European Parliament better informed of its activities and allow the director of Europol to appear before it to answer questions. This wide-ranging proposal was also intended to eliminate any ambiguities regarding Europol's crime-fighting mandate, permit direct links with national police agencies (rather than just via the national units), and give it greater flexibility regarding the use and exchange of data. In record time the member states were able to work out their differences on the new protocol, allowing the JHA Council of December 2002 to reach a general agreement on the text and submit it to the EP for its opinion.

Returning to the events of JHA Council of April 2002, the ministers approved a recommendation for establishing multi-national *ad hoc* teams for gathering and exchanging information on terrorism. In fact, this was one of the few successful new initiatives of the Spanish presidency of 2002. In addition, the Council also enhanced police cooperation by approving a Belgian initiative to improve security at international soccer matches by establishing a network of contact points of police authorities for strategic and operation information sharing, as well data on high-risk fans.

The April JHA Council is also noteworthy for its work on the legal infrastructure of crime fighting in the EU. The most important achievement in this regard was the passage of a set of conclusions specifying the new method for the approximation of penal sanctions. This entailed a system based on four ascending levels of penalties for imprisonment, providing for sanctions of at least one–three years, two–five years, five–ten years, and ten years respectively. For the approximation of criminal law, these levels are intended to serve as the minimum levels at which member states must set sanctions in their national legislation for the crime at hand. A range of sanctions represents less harmonization than the more precise specification of a minimum-maximum term of imprisonment. Thus it was hoped that the new system would help ease the construction of the EU's legal infrastructure of crime fighting, but only where the issue of contending penal structures among the member states is more significant than different definitions of criminal acts.

Indeed, the approval of this system did not bring immediate results. This was particularly evident at the April JHA Council regarding the delays in approving the draft framework decision on the sexual exploitation of children and child pornography, which remained deadlocked not on sanctions but on issues related to the age of consent and "virtual" pornographic images. The pending framework decision on combating racism and xenophobia also remained unresolved at that stage, though the JHA ministers adopted a set of conclusions condemning these crimes, as well as anti-Semitism. This came in response to a number of violent attacks aimed at Muslims and Jews in Europe that had been sparked by the war on terrorism and the ongoing conflict in the Middle East.

The final significant developments at the April 2002 JHA Council came in the area of the EU's increasing efforts to strengthen relations with third-party countries to deal with its internal security problems. The Council considered two matters pertaining to the United States and were briefed on the results of the results of the Euro-Med conference held earlier that week. In addition, the JHA ministers also met with their Russian counterparts to discuss a variety of pressing issues.

The first item regarding the United States dealt with the EU's efforts to increase its cooperation with the United States on border control, including coordinating security measures aimed at transit passengers at boarding gates, detecting false documents, and information sharing. Second, the Council gave its final authorization to the Spanish presidency to negotiate a formal agreement with the United States on judicial cooperation, covering mutual legal assistance, data exchange, creating single contact points and joint investigative teams, and extradition. As already noted, the latter matter entailed provisions guaranteeing the nonimposition of capital punishment. Negotiations on the judicial agreement with United States were formally launched during the EU-U.S. summit held on May 5, 2002, in Washington, D.C.

The JHA Council was also briefed on the Euro-Med conference held on April 22–23 in Valencia, which brought together the foreign ministers from the fifteen member states and twelve Mediterranean countries. Among these were several Arab nations and Israel. This meeting was intended to reinvigorate cooperation between the EU and these states that had begun at Barcelona in 1995 with the aim of achieving a free-travel area in the region by 2010. However, progress at the conference was inhibited by the escalating violence in the Palestinian-Israeli conflict, which dominated much of the discussion.

Nevertheless, the ministers were able to reach agreement on an action plan covering a wide range of economic, political, and social issues. One aspect of this was the endorsement of a framework document spelling out various forms of regional cooperation on several JHA matters, including organized crime, drug trafficking, terrorism, migration, and the social integration of immigrants. In addition, the so-called Valencia Action Plan also contains a number of goals related to trade, economic development, and human rights, which, if achieved, could help mitigate several JHA-related problems in the EU stemming from the Mediterranean region. In keeping with many of these goals, the Euro-Med conference signed an association agreement with Algeria, as it had already done with several other states in the region. By July 2002 the incoming Danish presidency expressed its desire to intensify the Euro-Med partnership, including the development of a common code of conduct for dealing with terrorism. Beyond this, a number of ministerial meetings were in the works, as well as the next conference of foreign ministers planned for the Italian presidency in the second half of 2003.

The JHA ministers also met with their Russian counterparts in the margins of the April 2002 Council session to discuss the fight against organized crime. This resulted in the passage of a joint declaration establishing a liaison network with law enforcement authorities in Russia, the member states, and Europol. Similar to their evolving ties with the United States, this agreement with Russia demonstrated the member states' new resolve to fight organized crime by enhancing the EU's ties to third-party countries in the area of criminal justice. Despite this achievement, the meeting with Russia was generally deemed to be a failure because it did not resolve the issue of border control regarding the Kaliningrad region, separated from Russia by the two future Schengen countries of Poland and Lithuania.

Nevertheless, the EU's relationship with Russia, as with the United States, highlighted its new commitment to enhancing the external dimension of internal security. This was highly visible during the remainder of the Spanish presidency, especially regarding the issues of border control and illegal immigration, which figured prominently on the agendas of both the June JHA Council and the concluding European Council at Seville. As already noted, European political leaders had, by this point, become concerned about their constituents' growing sense of insecurity regarding these issues, as reflected in the electoral successes of Jean-Marie LePen in France and the Pim Fortyn list in the Netherlands. Moreover, these concerns were echoed by Valery Giscard d'Estaing in his Stuttgart speech in May, in which he indicated how the delegates of the European Convention "felt that the Union should be able to take more effective action, notably against terrorism, large-scale organized crime, illegal immigration, drug-trafficking and trafficking in human beings—women and children."[11]

After years of only very slow progress, even by JHA standards, toward the milestones established in the Tampere Conclusions, there was suddenly major impetus in the EU toward greater cooperation on matters related to border control and illegal immigration. The new momentum on these issues continued in the final months of the Spanish presidency with the publication on May 7 of a much-awaited Commission communication containing a long-term approach to managing the borders of the EU. The centerpiece of this plan was the creation of a European border guard corps that would supplement, but not replace, national authorities by carrying out surveillance missions with mixed-nationality teams, checking identity documents, interrogating foreigners, and boarding civilian sea vessels. Along with this ultimate objective, the plan also contained a number of short- and medium-term proposals designed to insure not only greater efficiency in border management, but also more uniform application of EU legislation and the Schengen *acquis*. This would be achieved by a redrafting of the EU handbook on border control, the creation of an "External Border Practitioners Unit" (of experts) to carry out inspections and make policy, and the eventual establishment of a border patrol college for training. In addition to these measures, the Commission also suggested more equitable financial-burden sharing among member states on border management and closer cooperation with non-EU countries, including the posting of police liaison officers abroad.[12]

The response to the Commission's plans was mixed. For example, Amnesty International and other NGOs complained that the new proposals constituted the creation of a "fortress Europe" that would ignore the legitimate human rights of potential immigrants and refugees.[13] Meanwhile, Germany and France, despite their desire to control immigration, were not sold on relinquishing any sovereignty on border control to an EU agency, as suggested by the Commission. Attempting to counter this, Antonio Vitorino and Romano Prodi argued that the Commission's plan came in response to the clear message from public opinion that any enlargement of member states must also entail raising or at least preserving internal security.[14] Responding to this kind of justification for tighter borders, Amnesty International pointed out that asylum applications in the EU were down considerably since the early 1990s, and the rate for the first quarter of 2002 was lower than the same period in 2001.[15]

Soon after the Commission announced its proposals, the impetus for addressing the problem of illegal immigration in the EU was given a further boost when the Spanish presidency came out in favor of British Prime Minister Tony Blair's plans for a tighter EU asylum policy. "We should not be afraid to use whatever economic and financial levels we have," said Blair, as he called for making the EU's aid to developing countries conditional on their cooperation in readmitting asylum seekers who had unsuccessfully attempted to enter one of the member states.[16] Hoping to deflect criticism that doing so would have a negative impact on human rights, Blair believed that the electoral success of the far right in the recent French and Dutch elections indicated that Europeans were demanding that the problem of illegal immigration be addressed.[17] After meeting with Blair in London on May 20, 2002, Spanish Prime Minister José-Maríe Aznar not only came out in support of the British initiative, as well as the Commission's plans, but he also announced that illegal immigration would top the agenda of the upcoming Seville summit, where he would push for bold solutions. On the same day, during a speech at Oxford University, Aznar admitted that Europe needs immigration for its economic development, but "if immigration is not legal, it results in suffering, the undermining of people's dignity, and insecurity."[18] As with the Commission's proposals, the suggestion of linking the issue of border control to development aid was not universally supported.

In spite of this the drive to jump-start progress toward more effective border management in the EU was bolstered by the encouraging findings of a feasibility study on border management presented by Italy at a seminar held on May 30 in Rome and attended by interior ministers of the member states and the thirteen applicant countries. Since October 2001, Italy, Spain, Belgium, Germany, and France had carried out this study, which was funded 80 percent by the Odysseus program. The plan approved by the ministers in Rome called for common training, rapid-response units to react to immigration crises, and a pilot program of liaison officers to be instituted at airports. As under the Commission's plan, the feasibility study envisioned the eventual creation of a European border patrol that would not replace national authorities. In light of the similarities with its own proposals, the Commission was, in general, supportive of the findings and goals contained in the feasibility study.

In addition to endorsing the initiatives presented in the study, the ministers at the Rome seminar also received reports on two international operations coordinated by Europol that were aimed at stopping illegal immigration. Based on the success of the first Risk Immigration Operation (RIO), and on the initiation of Italy with the support of Spain, Europol had subsequently coordinated a larger sting, RIO II, from April 25 to May 31. With the cooperation of law enforcement authorities in all of the member states, as well as in Norway, Bulgaria, Hungary, Latvia, and Poland, this operation focused on twenty-five airports and resulted in the identification of 4,589 illegal immigrants, nearly a thousand false documents, and the arrest of thirty-four facilitators of illegal immigration belonging to criminal networks. In addition, five hundred penalties were imposed on airlines for allowing passengers to board flights without proper documentation. Along with this operation, Europol simultaneously helped coordinate another sting, Pegasus, which involved the checking of nearly 30,000 shipping containers being transported by road, rail, and seaports. Although lasting only three days at the end of May 2002, Pegasus resulted in the interception of two hundred illegal immigrants and the arrest of ten human traffickers.

Concluding the Spanish Presidency

On the heels of the high-profile sting operations came the final JHA Council of the Spanish presidency, held on June 13 in Luxembourg. This was the occasion of the formal adoption of the final acts on the framework decisions on terrorism, the European Arrest Warrant, and the creation of joint investigative teams. As discussed earlier, the real work on these had been conducted much earlier. A large portion of the one-day Council session was devoted to the topic of illegal immigration, but there were also a few noteworthy developments regarding other aspects of the EU's institutional and legal infrastructure of crime fighting.

The discussion on illegal immigration included reports by the presidency on the comprehensive action plan (the Global Plan) that had been approved in February, as well as one on external borders. The latter entailed proposals that drew heavily on those presented by the Commission in May, with the addition of various deadlines of one to five years for various actions. The JHA ministers also passed yet another extensive set of conclusions covering illegal immigration via the trafficking of human beings by sea.

Along with the long-range planning embodied in the formal conclusions, the JHA ministers also accepted a less extensive set of concrete measures proposed by the UK for the short run. These included plans for joint border control operations by autumn 2002 in "weak spots" such as Turkey, Lebanon, Poland, and the Balkans, as well as setting target dates for signing readmission agreements with several third-party countries, especially Afghanistan. In addition, the June 2002 JHA Council instructed the Commission to launch negotiations to this effect with Ukraine.

Concerning the so-called Dublin II legislation, this session of the JHA Council also discussed but could not agree on criteria for determining which member state is responsible for an asylum applicant. The dispute centered on whether this should be the country of entry or the intended final destination of the refugee. This issue pitted Greece and Italy, where many asylum seekers first arrive, against Germany and the UK, where many hope to end up.[19]

Ultimately, further consideration of these matters would have to wait until the upcoming European Council in Seville. The same was true for the definitive endorsement of the two reports accepted by the Council regarding longer-range proposals for action, which contained several sensitive items. Greece, for example, was concerned about suggestions for financial-burden sharing, while France and Sweden remained unconvinced about the European corps of border guards.[20] In addition, at the General Affairs Council held on June 17, Sweden, France, Finland, and Portugal expressed their opposition to the Spanish/British proposals to link development aid and trade concessions to third-party countries' cooperation on controlling illegal immigration and facilitating readmission. Along with concerns for human rights, these member states worried that the plan would not work, arguing that many poor countries might not have the infrastructure necessary to carry out commitments made under pressure from the EU.[21]

In addition to its extensive work on illegal immigration and border control, the JHA Council of June 2002 also accepted Europol's annual report of its operations in 2001 and endorsed its work program for 2003. Unlike its agendas for the previous two years, Europol not surprisingly placed the fight against terrorism at the top of its list of priority crimes, followed by illegal immigration and the trafficking of human beings, drug trafficking, crimes against the euro, and financial crime. Europol predicted extensive involvement in the newly approved joint investigative teams and noted that, by the end of 2002, it would be hosting liaison officers from twenty different third-party countries and international organizations, while stationing one of its own representatives with most of these as well. As part of its effort to extend information gathering beyond the EU, the JHA Council authorized Europol to negotiate a cooperation agreement with the World Customs Organization and pacts with Albania, Bosnia, Croatia, the (new) Federal Republic of Yugoslavia, and Macedonia covering euro counterfeiting. In July 2002, the Council formally agreed to increase Europol's budget over 7 percent for 2003 to €55 million, in part to help pay for an increase in staff members in 2003, not including over sixty ELOs seconded by national authorities.

The final JHA Council of the Spanish presidency also reached agreement on other measures aimed at strengthening police cooperation. One was Spain's proposal to set up a network of police and judicial contact points in the member states to exchange information specifically on terrorism. Originally criticized by the Commission for not adding any extra value and possibly detracting from the perceived urgency of sharing information on other types of crimes, Spain's proposal was ultimately endorsed by Commissioner Vitorino at the June JHA Council.[22] The creation of contact points followed some of the prescriptions made in Common Position 930/CSSP of December 2001, but was most closely linked to Article 4 of the other common position passed at the end of the Belgian presidency, namely 931/CFSP. This called upon the member states to "afford each the widest possible assistance in preventing and combating terrorist acts" (see Chapter 7).

Along with approving the antiterrorism contact points, the JHA ministers reviewed the latest version of the list of terrorist individuals and groups that had been created under Common Position 931/CFSP in December 2001. Once again approved by "written procedure," the new list had been adopted on May 2, along with a revised implementing decision identifying seven additional individuals and ten new groups for a total of thirty-six individuals and twenty-three groups.[23] Although the provisions for freezing assets still pertained only to the twenty non–EU-based individuals and groups included on the list, the antiterrorism contact points, once formally created, would be encouraged to share information on the terrorists and organizations mentioned on the updated list.

Related to this, the June JHA Council also examined the most recent assessment of the terrorist threat to the EU and heard from Jürgen Storbeck on Europol's antiterrorist activities since September 11. Additional legislative items related to police cooperation were passed by the Mixed Committee and included a decision to widen the possibilities for cross-border police surveillance under the Schengen *acquis*, new requirements for the SIS, and rules to allow the UK and Ireland to participate in the SIS in the near future. Norway and Iceland, as full members of the Schengen zone, also affirmed their cooperation with the EU's new plans to manage its external borders.

The JHA Council also approved regulations for the internal functioning of Eurojust. On July 12, the Council of Ministers used these procedures to elect a new president for this body, the UK's Michael Kennedy, as well as two vice presidents. In addition to endorsing the new rules for Eurojust, the June JHA Council also reached political agreement on a Dutch proposal to create a network of judicial contact points to share information on the war crimes covered by the newly established International Criminal Court (ICC), which would begin operations on July 1, 2002. During the subsequent Danish presidency, the EU made progress on additional legislation designed to strengthen its support of the ICC.

Compared to progress on the EU's various crime-fighting institutions, the June JHA Council made much less new progress on the legal infrastructure of crime fighting. Receiving support from neither the Commission nor other member states, Spain abandoned its proposals to develop common rules for the regulation of private security firms in the member states. Instead, it oversaw the passage of a nonbinding recommendation to increase information sharing among national monitoring authorities for this industry, which many still believed should be handled as a First Pillar issue. Furthermore, despite the new system for assigning penal sanctions for harmonized crimes, a final agreement on the framework decision covering drug trafficking continued to allude the Council. This was mainly due to the Netherlands' dispute with the other member states on how to punish traffickers of only small amounts of drugs, with the Dutch supporting lighter penalties. Holding little optimism for agreement on other outstanding legislative proposals, including the outstanding framework decisions on racism and xenophobia and human trafficking and child sexual exploitation, the Spanish presidency wrapped up the JHA Council after just one day. However, as already noted, issues related to JHA remained very much on the EU's political radar, with the Seville European Council set to take up several controversial items regarding illegal immigration and border control.

In fact, when the heads of state and government met in Seville on June 21–22, immigration topped the agenda, marking the second time in less than a year that a JHA issue had dominated the debate at a European Council session. The prominence of illegal immigration was all the more impressive in light of the other two main issues to be covered by the European Council, namely institutional reform and enlargement. Regarding the latter, the European Council affirmed that it intended to admit the ten candidate states identified at the Laeken summit by 2004. However, the sensitive negotiations on the financial terms of accession were left to the incoming Danish presidency and were due to be hammered out in November 2002, before the Copenhagen European Council. As the largest contributor to the

EU's budget, Germany warned that November was a goal, not a deadline, indicating that it might delay enlargement beyond 2004 unless the candidate states scaled back their financial aspirations in terms of the EU's structural funds and Common Agricultural Policy.

To prepare for eventual enlargement, the Seville European Council also discussed the reform of its own working procedures, as well as those of the Council of Ministers. For example, the heads of state and government decided to reduce the size of their delegations at summits and to allow portions of their debates to be televised, including voting, for which they would be permitted to explain their decisions. However, France blocked the implementation of any qualified majority in the European Council. The number of versions of the Council of Ministers was reduced from sixteen to ten, but no agreement was reached on dividing the work of the General Affairs Council between two bodies. Other related issues, including lengthening the term of the presidency, were left for the European Convention and, ultimately, the next IGC.

Despite the importance of the these issues in EU politics, the highlight of the Seville summit was the debate and progress on the fight against illegal immigration. The official conclusions contained endorsements of a variety of ongoing projects related to this, including the initiatives discussed at the last JHA Council. For example, the European Council called for the creation of a unit composed of the heads of national border control agencies to help coordinate efforts aimed at achieving many of the goals outlined in the Commission's new plan on managing external borders. To facilitate this, the Seville summit also endorsed the creation of the liaison network of national immigration officers and the deployment of joint operations at external borders before the end of 2002.

However, the heads of state and government were unable to resolve differences on the proposed European corps of border guards, preventing its creation. In its place there was agreement to implement a common training curriculum, as well as harmonized practices, all by June 2003. The European Council also set that deadline for the results of a study to be conducted by the Commission on financial-burden sharing regarding the managing of the EU's external borders.

As with the discord on the EU border patrol, divisions remained on the controversial proposal to tie EU developmental assistance to third-party countries' cooperation on fighting illegal immigration. In the face of continued opposition from France and Sweden, the best Spain and the UK could achieve on this front were warnings that inadequate cooperation could hamper the establishment of closer cooperation with the European Union and that the EU could adopt measures against noncooperative states. In fact, the conclusions of the Seville summit made clear that such relations would not entail the breaking of agreements or the jeopardizing of developmental assistance. The European Council did agree to expedite policies and bilateral agreements on repatriation, especially with Afghanistan, and to strengthen cooperation on migration flows and illegal immigration in the EU's relations with third-party countries (e.g., trade expansion). Thus, despite the mounting political pressure in many member states (from right-wing populist movements), the EU leaders decided not to pursue more punitive measures against noncooperative third-party countries. The European Council instead reaffirmed its intention to fight the root causes of illegal immigration, namely economic underdevelopment. Nevertheless, this aspect of the EU's JHA policy had now acquired a much more prominent external dimension, similar to terrorism. Concerning this latter issue, the Seville European Council also affirmed that the EU would fight illegal immigration by using its CFSP and (soon to be operational) ESDP.

The Seville European Council made noteworthy progress on several other items regarding the control of the EU's external borders. For example, the heads of state and government called for a review of the list of third-party countries whose nationals require a visa to enter the EU. They also called for the formal adoption of the pending EU legislation on the trafficking of human beings at the next JHA Council session, including the long-delayed framework decision that harmonizes penal sanctions for this crime.

Significant movement was also achieved on the development of an integrated, common asylum policy for the EU, mainly by setting deadlines for the formal adoption of various initiatives already in the legislative pipeline at that time. For example, the European Council called on the JHA Council to finalize work on the Dublin II regulation specifying which member state is responsible for an asylum seeker by the end of 2002 (specifying whether this should be the state of entry or final destination). June 2003 was set as the deadline for the adoption of the directives on the minimum standards for qualification and status as a refugee and on family reunification for long-term legal resident foreigners (e.g., successful asylum seekers). In addition, the European Council called for the passage of the directive on defining the common standards for processing the applications of asylum seekers by the end of 2003.

Together with the measures that had already been adopted, including, for example, legislation setting up the European Refugee Fund, Eurodac, and the minimum standards on reception conditions, these legislative initiatives were expected to form the basis of a true common EU policy on asylum by the end of 2003. However, as with the related issue of illegal immigration and dealing with third-party countries, the EU's work on a common asylum policy was impacted by differing concerns by member states over human rights, which have slowed negotiations and resulted in watered-down, compromise legislation. For example, while Sweden continued to press for a relatively permissive approach for dealing with refugees, countries such as Denmark, Italy, and the UK were tightening their asylum laws in 2002.[24] Of course, the whole point of a common EU asylum policy is to harmonize member states' handling of refugees to prevent "asylum shopping." It should be recalled that the Treaty of Amsterdam specifies that a common EU asylum policy must be in place by May 1, 2004.

Summary of the Spanish Presidency

The decisions reached at the Seville European Council provided a fitting end to Spain's leadership of the EU in the first half of 2002, which, like the Belgian presidency, was dominated by progress on JHA. To be sure, there was notable movement on other fronts as well. For example, Spain oversaw the very successful circulation of euro notes and coins, which was relatively free of major technical problems or widespread counterfeiting, as had been feared. In addition, progress was made under Spain's direction in several economic areas at the Barcelona European Council. Moreover, the European Convention began its work during the Spanish presidency, holding the potential for major changes in the handling of Third Pillar matters. Finally, the EU continued to move forward in 2002 toward enlarging its membership, as negotiations with the candidate states proceeded on schedule, including good progress on the JHA chapters of the accession treaties.

Nevertheless, Spain's presidency will be remembered most for its progress on JHA, but not as one might have expected at the start of 2002. At the beginning of Spain's term, with the events of September 11 still close at hand, the EU's internal-security focus was initially on terrorism. However, with the success of far-right parties in several member states, issues related to asylum policy, border management, and illegal immigration had risen to prominence on the European Union's political agenda by spring 2002.

As discussed above, there was at last significant movement toward a common asylum policy during the first of half of 2002. Legislation was adopted setting up the Eurodac database of fingerprints, and a directive was passed defining the minimum conditions for the reception of asylum seekers. In addition, the Seville European Council set deadlines calling for the rest of the asylum package of legislation to be adopted by the end of 2003.

During the first half of 2002 the fight against illegal immigration and the trafficking of human beings once again became a hot topic in the Third Pillar, recapturing the prominence it had been gaining prior to September 11. In this context, the Spanish presidency oversaw progress toward a review of visa requirements for third-party countries and the possible creation of an information exchange system for visa information. Activity also intensified on readmission negotiations with several states, with target dates set for the conclusion of particular agreements.

Concerning border management, there was less dramatic progress than had been hoped, with the rejection of the proposal to create an EU border patrol and continued disagreement over financial-burden sharing. However, the member states did endorse the sweeping action plan presented by the Commission, and the European Council agreed to launch a unit (contact group) of the heads of national agencies, a new liaison network in this policy area, common training, and joint operations at border trouble spots. Furthermore, the potential of international cooperation, as well as the promising contribution of Europol, was made evident by the success of the RIO and Pegasus operations, which were coordinated by Europol. In addition, the new Argo program was approved to provide cofinancing for administrative cooperation on border management through the end of 2006.

With regard to problems related to asylum, illegal immigration, and border management, the European Union showed an increased interest in addressing these issues through new forms of engagement with third-party countries, including the countries of origin or transit of those trying to enter the EU. In this regard, however, the Spanish presidency was not as successful as it had hoped. Although enjoying the backing of the UK and Germany for taking a harder line in dealing with third-party countries, Spain was unable to win over other member states, notably France and Sweden, which opposed linking EU developmental aid to third-party countries' cooperation on immigration issues.

Nevertheless, during the first half of 2002 the EU was once again addressing the external dimensions of its internal security in a variety of ways. Negotiations were launched with the United States on a judicial cooperation agreement, and talks were held on JHA matters with Canada and Russia. Combined with the intensified cross-pillar approach to dealing with internal security, there was also the contribution of the Third Pillar to the Second, as efforts in the area of police cooperation helped facilitate the EU's decision to take over the civilian policing mission in Bosnia in 2003.

During the Spanish presidency significant progress was also made on building the legal infrastructure of crime fighting in the EU. Eurojust was officially launched and the framework decisions on terrorism and for setting up the Euro-warrant were formally adopted. The JHA Council also reached agreement on the framework decision regarding the freezing of assets and evidence, but several countries continued to hold out parliamentary scrutiny reservations on this, preventing its final adoption. With hopes of easing progress on the approximation of criminal law in the future, the JHA ministers agreed on a new system of ranges for the specification of penal sanctions. However, by the end of the Spanish presidency this had failed to promote the passage of the outstanding framework decisions that were already in the legislative pipeline, notably the measures covering drug trafficking, the trafficking of human beings, and child sexual exploitation.

The incoming Danish presidency also inherited the task of overseeing the passage of several other pending framework decisions aimed at harmonizing criminal law, including money laundering, fraud and noncash payments, environmental crime, racism and xenophobia, and cyber-crime.

Throughout its leadership term Spain also helped direct noteworthy progress concerning the construction of the EU's evolving institutional infrastructure of crime fighting. The administrative secretariat of the European Police College, CEPOL, was finally given a home, albeit temporary, in Copenhagen, allowing the virtual police academy to carry out its growing agenda of training programs. Related to this, with the rejection of Spain's proposal for a European institute of police studies, CEPOL was also charged with helping to analyze and coordinate the efforts of the expanding number of new JHA bodies and liaison networks.

Europol's budget was increased yet again in the context of its increased list of responsibilities, covering all of the crimes listed in the annex of the Europol Convention. Not surprisingly, the fight against terrorism was made a top priority. By spring 2002, however, Europol was also helping to coordinate successful police operations in the area of illegal immigration and the trafficking of human beings, indicating the reemergent prominence of these problems. Another important step taken during the Spanish presidency of 2002 was the adoption of the decision allowing the creation of a multinational, joint investigative team of police officers, as well as agreement on the need to modify the Europol Convention to allow Europol to request that such teams be formed, coordinate them, and even participate in their operation.

In addition, new liaison networks were established to gather information on terrorism and war crimes, and to provide security at international soccer matches to prevent hooliganism. Along with this, some of the provisions in the Schengen *acquis* on cross-border police surveillance were strengthened, and new methods of information sharing and cooperation were successfully tested in the area of maintaining public order and security during international summits. Although the proposed European corps of border guards was rejected, plans for a new unit of high-ranking officials, a liaison network, a common training curriculum, and joint operations were launched in the area of border management. Finally, with regard to the fight against illegal immigration, the EU's institutional infrastructure was enhanced by the passage of legislation setting up the Eurodac database containing the fingerprints of asylum seekers, and plans were made for the storage and sharing of information on visa applications in the future.

In addition to all of this, the Article 36 Committee's working group on police cooperation finalized its amendments on the Commission's proposal of November 2001 to establish a successor to the various EU cofinancing programs that have promoted partnerships, sharing of best practices, training, etc., in the area of crime fighting. These programs, which were due to expire at the end of 2002, included:

- Grotius II, for judicial personnel on criminal matters
- STOP II, on trafficking of human beings and sexual exploitation of children
- Oisin II, for law enforcement officials (police and customs)
- Falcone, for organized crime, and
- Hippokrates, for crime prevention[25]

To replace these, the Commission had proposed the new framework program known as "AGIS," providing €65 million in funding from January 1, 2003, until the end of 2007. In most cases, this program provides cofinancing of up 70 percent for projects involving at least three member states or two EU members and at least one other country (candidate states, applicant states, or Schengen countries). In exceptional circumstances, AGIS resources may be used to fund the entire cost of a project. By April 2002 the EP had given its positive opinion on this new framework program, and it was formally adopted on July 23, 2002, as an A-point by the Agriculture and Fisheries Council.

In sum, Spain did indeed prove to be an able successor to Belgium, maintaining the momentum on JHA matters that had been sparked by the events of September 11. The new political will spawned by the attacks on the United States remained sufficiently strong during the presidency of Spain, which had its own domestic reasons to promote stronger cooperation on terrorism. However, by spring 2002 problems related to border control reemerged as the most pressing JHA issue in the EU, exacerbated by the continued influx of illegal immigrants into the EU and the popularity of far-right political parties in several member states. In fact, the prominence of border issues at the concluding Seville European Council seemed to indicate that the EU was finally prepared to make significant progress on this aspect of the Third Pillar. Doing so would only compliment the ongoing construction of the EU's new legal and institutional infrastructure of crime fighting, highlighted by the growing role of Europol.

Explaining Progress During the Spanish Presidency

Progress on JHA during the first half of 2002 continued to be influenced most prominently by external forces, just as had been the case under the preceding Belgian presidency. Whereas the terrorist attacks on the United States had contributed to an acceleration of several initiatives after September 11, so too had the flow of illegal immigrants into the EU sparked progress on a host of issues related to border management. However, it was not solely the endurance of this problem or the occasional "crisis" involving stowaways found dead or boatloads of refugees arriving into a port that pushed events along. It was also the fact that illegal immigration became a hot electoral issue in Europe during 2002 and, fearing the advance of far-right political parties, many member states wanted to deal swiftly with the issue.

Moreover, the problem of illegal immigration, like terrorism, was perceived as being particularly difficult for member states to deal with unilaterally given the Schengen free-travel zone throughout much of the EU. The countries of destination for many immigrants (e.g., Germany) were particularly aware of how the porous external borders of one member state— without physical checkpoints to restrict the flows of illegal immigrants or asylum shoppers who had managed to enter the EU—could eventually lead to problems for them. Thus, as during the Belgian presidency, functional spillover from cooperation on free movement combined with external forces to promote cooperation on JHA during the Spanish presidency.

Although nothing compares to the impact of illegal immigration as an influence on internal-security cooperation during the Spanish presidency, the impact of the continued progress toward enlargement is at least noteworthy. The opening of accession negotiations on JHA with Romania, beset with relatively weak criminal-justice institutions and troubling problems with organized crime, served as a reminder that the coming enlargement would bring many challenges for the EU's Area of Freedom, Security, and Justice. Along with the perceived crisis of illegal immigration at the time, this continued to provide an impetus for the EU to meet the various goals noted on the JHA Scoreboard before the addition of new member states complicated decision-making and possibly exacerbated internal-security problems.

As well as combining with the external factor of illegal immigration, functional spillover was also evident during this period in the form of cooperation on the Second Pillar impacting collaboration on JHA. After a lull of several years as a major influential force of EU JHA policy, events in Bosnia once again became significant. This time, however, it was not refugees fleeing ethnic conflict but this fledgling country's continuing need to receive international assistance to build and reform its new police force. As discussed at the beginning of this chapter, the EU decided in January 2002 to take over this task once the United Nations mandate for doing so expired at year's end. This decision set in motion a new form of police cooperation among the member states that would offer a limited test of the civilian policing component of the planned rapid-reaction force.

Thus, internal factors continued to combine with functionalism to influence developments on JHA during the first half of 2002. It would be a mistake to attribute progress during this time to any kind of federalist impetus.

Rather, decisions to enhance cooperation in various regards should properly be viewed as practical responses to pressures stemming from both external factors and functional spillover, as noted above. Although not a driving force on JHA, federalist ideology was indeed evident during this time in the discussions and debate of the European Convention, which had begun in February and would continue throughout 2002. In fact, the federalist notion of eliminating the intergovernmental nature of policymaking on police and judicial cooperation, as well as doing away with the whole pillar structure of the EU, was seriously considered. By the end of the Spanish presidency, however, it was not clear what the final recommendation of the convention would be on JHA. It was also not certain whether or how its suggestions would be handled by the next IGC.

In addition to its expressions of federalist ideology, the European Convention is also notable for continuing to pose questions about the democratic deficit in the Third Pillar. In fact, concerns for democracy in this regard were raised more prominently by the Commission in its communication of February 2002. This called for a greater role of MEPs and national MPs in the oversight of Europol, as well as various proposals to strengthen the democratic control of EU police cooperation by strengthening the role of the European Parliament in several regards.

Although these initiatives of the Commission did not have much of an immediate impact on JHA during the Spanish presidency of 2002, other instances during this time indicated the salience of concerns for democracy in shaping progress on internal security. These were clearly influential, for example, in the EU's negotiations with the United States on a new agreement covering judicial cooperation. That is, the EU's positions on civil and human rights concerning, respectively, data protection and the death penalty, inhibited the conclusions of a new cooperation pact with the United States during the Spanish presidency.

Concerns for human rights emerged once again in the debate over illegal immigration. While the UK and Spain pushed for tightening external border controls and linking developmental aid to third-party countries to their cooperation with the EU in controlling illegal immigration, other member states, including France and Sweden, joined in expressing fears of creating a fortress Europe. These member states were especially concerned about making economic and social conditions in developing countries even worse by cutting off EU assistance. In the end these EU members, motivated by concerns for democracy expressed in the form of respect for human rights, prevented the EU from taking a more hard-line approach to the problem of illegal immigration when this issues topped the agenda of the Seville European Council of June 2002.

Nevertheless, the Seville summit did manage to reach agreement on several new forms of EU-level cooperation on border control, including several initiatives that were designed to promote more Europeanization in this area through, for example, agreement on harmonized practices for border police and a common training curriculum. To some degree this progress indicates a weakening of member states' attachment to subsidiarity on JHA, as they were clearly more willing than in the past to deal with the problem of border control at the EU-level, rather than on their own. Nevertheless, the salience of continued subsidiarity in this policy for some member states was evident as well in the failure of the proposal to create a common EU border patrol.

In sum, the development of police cooperation and crime fighting in the EU during the first half of 2002 was influenced by the same mix of internal and external factors that had helped propel progress in earlier periods. External factors, combined with functional spillover, continued to provide the main impetus, while enduring attachment to subsidiary served to limit what some member states were prepared to do in terms of EU policy. Likewise, concerns for democracy, in terms of attention to civil and human rights, remained important in shaping the nature of this EU cooperation.

Notes

1. *Financial Times,* "Belgian Interior Minister Urges Critical Evaluation of Europol," February 16, 2002.
2. *European Report,* "European Convention: Call for Bigger Role in Justice and Home Affairs," June 8, 2002.
3. Ibid.
4. *European Report,* "Justice and Home Affairs Council: Italy Drags Its Heels on Asset-Freezing," March 2, 2002.
5. *European Report,* "Justice and Home Affairs Council: Deal on Freezing Of Assets Initiative Hangs In Balance," February 27, 2002.
6. *European Report,* "Justice and Home Affairs Council: Human Rights Group Slams Commission Asylum Paper," March 2, 2002.
7. Ibid.
8. *European Report,* "Polish Land Deal Highlight of Major Negotiating Round on March 21," March 23, 2001.
9. *European Report,* "Justice and Home Affairs Council: Deal on Reception Conditions for Asylum-Seekers," April 27, 2002.
10. This was formally approved as an A-point at the June JHA Council.
11. Stephen Castle, "Far Right Spurs EU Focus on Crime," *The Independent* (London), May 14, 2002.
12. *European Report,* "Justice and Home Affairs: Commission Calls for EU Border Control Guards," May 9, 2002.
13. *Deutsche Presse-Agentur,* "EU's Anti-Immigration Drive Endangering Rights, Warns Amnesty," June 12, 2002.
14. *Agence Presse France,* "EU Commission Proposes Beefed-Up External Borders," May 7, 2002.
15. *Deutsche Presse-Agentur,* "EU's Anti-Immigration Drive Endangering Rights, Warns Amnesty," June 12, 2002; *European Report,* "Justice and Home

Affairs: Human Rights Under Threat From Fortress Europe, Says Amnesty," June 15, 2002.

16. Brian Groom, "Blair Urges Firm Line on Asylum," *Financial Times* (London), May 20, 2002.

17. James Mackintosh and George Parker, "EU Leaders Try to Reduce Illegal Immigration," *Financial Times* (London), May 20, 2002.

18. Text of speech by Aznar at St. Anthony's College in the University of Oxford.

19. Ibid.

20. *European Report,* "Justice and Home Affairs Council: Ministers Agree Deadlines For Measures To Tackle Illegal Immigration," June 15, 2002.

21. Judy Dempsey, "EU Ministers Defer Anti-Immigration Decision," *Financial Times* (London), June 17, 2002.

22. *European Report,* "Justice and Home Affairs Council: Commission Slams Spanish Anti-Terrorism Initiative," May 1, 2002; *European Report,* "Justice and Home Affairs Council: Deal on Anti-Drug Trafficking Law Falters on Sanctions," June 15, 2002.

23. The list would continue to be revised and updated after this as well.

24. See, for example, Michael Mann, "EU Rhetoric on Asylum to Be Put to the Test," *Financial Times* (London), June 13, 2002; Sarah Lyall, "When Asylum Seekers Knock, Europe Is Deaf," *New York Times,* June 20, 2002.

25. In addition to these, the EU has also funded several other cofinancing programs in the field of JHA. These have included the Daphné program for preventing violence against children, youth, and women; the Robert Schuman Project on Community law for judges, prosecutors, and lawyers; the Grotius-Civil program for judicial personnel on civil matters; and the Odysseus program for asylum and immigration. As discussed, the latter has been replaced by the new Argo program.

9

The Lessons of
EU Police Cooperation

THIS BOOK HAS TRACED THE EVOLUTION OF JUSTICE AND HOME Affairs in the European Union from the 1970s to 2002, emphasizing progress on police cooperation and crime fighting. As discussed in Chapter 3, a major early development in this regard was the creation of the Trevi Group in 1975, which would prove to be the first step in a deepening pattern of European cooperation on Justice and Home Affairs. However, cooperation under the Trevi Group lay outside of the treaty structure of the European Community and promoted only limited and largely ad hoc forms of international collaboration on internal security.

By 1993, this would change with the creation of the so-called Third Pillar on Justice and Home Affairs, replacing the Trevi Group as the EC became the European Union. Although cooperation on JHA was intended to be intergovernmental, the new Third Pillar brought police cooperation and other forms of collaboration on crime fighting formally into the EU. Moreover, the Maastricht Treaty specified new permanent structures for doing so and set the EU on the road to a much more supranational approach to dealing with internal security compared to the era of the Trevi Group and before.

With respect to crime fighting, the centerpiece of the Third Pillar was Europol, but, as discussed in Chapter 4, its actual creation proved to be complicated and difficult. Indeed, cooperation on most aspects of the JHA, especially on immigration and asylum policy, was quite slow in coming. In fact, in the time that it took the EU to bring Europol to life, the Treaty of Amsterdam had been negotiated, signed, ratified, and entered into force.

In recognition of this slow progress and with the goal of creating the Area of Freedom, Security, and Justice (AFSJ) prescribed in the new treaty, EU leaders convened a special session of the European Council in Tampere, Finland, in October 1999. Since then the nature and variety of EU progress on JHA has been remarkable. In particular, the building of the EU's legal and institutional infrastructure for crime fighting since the Tampere summit

223

has been especially impressive, as detailed in Chapters 5–8. This has contributed to both increased Europeanization on JHA, as well as broader and deeper collaborative efforts in many regards, particularly in the areas of crime fighting and police cooperation.

Between the Tampere summit of 1999 and the end of the Spanish presidency of 2002 the JHA Council has made use of the framework decision instrument to begin the process of harmonizing criminal law throughout the EU in a number of key areas. By the end of 2002 framework decisions had been adopted or seemed likely to be approved in the near future for the following crimes:

- Counterfeiting (of the euro)
- Money laundering
- Trafficking of human beings
- Child sexual exploitation
- Fraud and counterfeiting of noncash payments
- Environmental crime
- Corruption in the private sector
- Cyber-crime (attacks on information systems)
- Terrorism
- Racism and xenophobia
- Trafficking of illegal drugs[1]

Once all of these measures are formally approved and transposed into national law they will entail an unprecedented level of Europeanization in the area of crime fighting in the EU, specifying common definitions for offenses and similar criminal sanctions for these.

Along with its evolving legal infrastructure for fighting crime, the EU has provided funding (i.e., cofinancing) for a variety of training activities and personnel exchanges concerning JHA, many of which now fall under the two broad framework programs known as Argo (border management) and AGIS (crime fighting). These programs contribute to the exchange of best practices, tactics, strategies, and information throughout the EU, furthering Europeanization on JHA. In addition, it is hoped that the Crime Prevention Network, Operational Task Force of Police Chiefs, and European Police College (CEPOL) will eventually contribute to this kind of Europeanization of crime fighting as well.

Combined with Europeanization, the EU has also experienced broader and deeper cooperation in this area. This has entailed the building of an institutional infrastructure of crime fighting centered around Europol. For example, in response to the provisions of the Tampere Conclusions, the EU has created Eurojust to facilitate cooperation on criminal matters among judicial authorities. In the future, cooperation in this area will also be facilitated by the implementation of the Euro-warrant, which expedites searches and hastens extradition proceedings. Regarding policing, the coordination provided by Europol has been supplemented by the Operational Task Force of Police Chiefs, which has met regularly since the Portuguese presidency in the first half of 2000. Training for top-level police officers has been added through the new CEPOL, which began operations in 2002. As well as contributing to Europeanization, the task force and CEPOL have also strengthened police cooperation in the EU by increasing awareness among national authorities regarding news ways to collaborate with each other and showing how these can be used effectively (e.g., information exchanges and coordination via Europol). Combined with all of this, the Convention on Mutual Assistance in Criminal Matters and its protocols, once ratified, will further broaden and deepen police cooperation. By the Spanish presidency of 2002, new planning units, contact points, and liaison networks had been created in the fields of counterterrorism and border management. Within Europol, new specialized units were created to fight counterfeiting and terrorism and to increase its ability to assist member states in crime fighting in these areas.

Finally, Europol itself has been strengthened in several regards since 1999. In addition to increases in staffing and funding, Europol was given a variety of new duties. By the end of the Belgian presidency of 2001, long-running efforts to broaden the scope of Europol's mandate resulted in the decision to widen its remit to all forms of crime noted in the annex to the Europol Convention.

Europol's operational powers have also been enhanced since 1999. For example, during the French presidency of 2000, the JHA Council passed recommendations intended to promote Europol's ability to initiate, coordinate, and conduct investigations, as well as take part in joint investigative teams established among member states. Although not binding, these recommendations were intended to remind member states of Europol's value and encourage them to make greater use of its services.

Acceptance of this kind of a role for Europol was enhanced a year later, following the terrorist attacks against the United States. This contributed to renewed resolve among member states to strengthen the capabilities of Europol and make better use of its potential services. In particular, member states committed themselves to be more willing to share sensitive intelligence information with Europol, allowing it to perform its analysis duties and data pooling more effectively. This helped foster the agreement reached under the Spanish presidency of 2002 for Europol to participate in joint investigative teams and request that such teams be created. In the future, all of this should help Europol to coordinate the policing activities of the member states more effectively, thus enhancing their crime-fighting efforts. In sum, police cooperation in the EU developed rapidly following the Tampere European Council of October 1999. This entailed both increased areas of Europeanization and new means of cooperation through the creation of new or strengthened crime-fighting institutions.

Explaining EU Police Cooperation

Conceptualizing and explaining the development of police cooperation and crime fighting in the EU since the 1970s can be accomplished by identifying the impact of various internal and external factors on four main junctures of this development. Noted atop the columns of Table 9.1, these are the formation of the Trevi Group, creation of the Third Pillar, drafting of the Europol Convention and Treaty of Amsterdam, and progress made after the Tampere European Council. The internal factors considered in each row of Table 9.1 are functional spillover, federalism, concern for democracy, and subsidiarity. External factors, sources of change that originate outside of the European Union but affect the member states, are also included. The evidence provided in this book has demonstrated how these internal and external factors have collectively helped shape the timing, nature, and form of EU police cooperation over the years.

As discussed in Chapter 3, the idea of increasing collaboration on internal security in Europe had been around for over a century, starting with attempts to deal with anarchism at the end of the nineteenth century and eventually becoming based on the exchange of criminal information through Interpol. With the creation of the European Coal and Steel Community in 1952 and the entry into force of the Treaties of Rome in 1958, the European Community (EC) came into being. However, matters of internal security remained totally outside of the realm of common policymaking as the member states carefully guarded their sovereignty in this area.

As in North America, the use of illicit drugs had increased in Europe by the mid-1970s, such that the problem of international drug trafficking, often with source countries lying outside of Europe, was recognized as a pressing public-policy issue. But, the worsening problem of drug trafficking was, by itself, not sufficient to prompt the creation of a new form of cooperation on internal security among the EC member states. The most direct impetus to do so was the terrorist killings at the 1972 Olympic Games in Munich, which brought the problem of international terrorism to Europe and served to highlight the threat posed by it. This new threat only exacerbated growing concerns over Europe's "home-group" terrorist organizations that were quite active at this time. Thus, in response to both drug trafficking and terrorism, and owing to a renewed optimism concerning European integration that was produced by the 1974 Paris summit, the Trevi Group was created.

The activity of the Trevi Group lay outside of the formal treaty structure of the EC and consisted largely of periodic meetings at the ministerial level. Its work was facilitated by a network of ad hoc working groups that handled various types of international crime and policing issues. As noted in Table 9.2, the Trevi Group contained no permanent, central authorities for planning and operations. Its activities were largely limited to the building of secure communication links among the policing agencies of the member states, as well as the sharing of some tactical information and data on a very limited number of international crimes.

The European Parliament, Commission, and Court of Justice played no role in the work of the Trevi Group, as it lay outside the Treaty of Rome. Furthermore, where the Trevi Group was active, its work was directed by the ministers of the interior and justice from the member states, who met informally and acted by consensus. Although the nature and number of its working groups would evolve somewhat, this is essentially how the Trevi Group operated throughout the 1970s and into the 1980s.

By the late 1980s, however, a number of factors would lead to the creation of the so-called Third Pillar of the new European Union, replacing the Trevi Group and setting the EU on the road to a much more supranational approach to dealing with internal security (see Table 9.1). Functional spillover played a significant role in this development, as member states realized that their efforts to create a single market and free-travel area, based on the Single European Act (SEA) and the Schengen agreement respectively, would lead to free movement for criminal activity, and not just for legal people, goods, services, and capital. Unlike criminals, however, law enforcement authorities in the member states would continue to be restricted by legal and physical boundaries within the EU. Thus, increased cooperation on free movement promised to exacerbate enduring crime problems, including terrorism and drug trafficking.

This contributed to the need for cooperation on crime fighting and the prescription to create Europol in the Maastricht Treaty. In addition, by 1990 it was also evident that the end of the Cold War would bring additional problems in the area of internal security, as flows of legal and illegal immigrants and refugees from Central and Eastern Europe, as well as criminals, began moving into the EU. In sum, functional spillover, along with the external factors of drug trafficking, terrorism, and the end of the Cold War, contributed to the need for greater cooperation on internal security. This in turn prompted the creation of the new Third Pillar on Justice and Home Affairs, as well as Europol.

Additional factors also help to explain this development, but to a lesser degree. For example, federalist ideology was salient during this time. That is, some member states, notably Germany, hoped to move beyond the intergovernmental limits of the existing community and, concerning JHA, aspired to

Table 9.1 Internal and External Sources of EU Police Cooperation

	Formation of the Trevi Group	Creation of the Third Pillar	Drafting the Europol Convention and Treaty of Amsterdam	Developments Since the Tampere European Council
Functional Spillover	Not significant	Impending impact of SEA and the Schengen agreement on free movement	Impact of Schengen free-travel area	• Expansion of free-travel area • Impact of SEA on money laundering • Introduction of the euro • Civilian component of EERF
Federalism	Optimism from Paris summit of 1974	Aspirations of Kohl	Not significant	Not significant, but increasing acceptance of "closer cooperation" for some member states
Concerns for Democracy	Not significant	Criticisms of secrecy in the Trevi Group	Attention to the "democratic deficit": • Increased legitimacy of EP • Concern for civil liberties	• Concern for civil liberties • Concern for human rights • Pressure for more oversight
Subsidiarity	Not expressed but weakening significance on internal security	Significant: Expressed in SEA	Significant: Expressed in new Article K.5 (Article 34)	Weakening significance: More JHA matters subject to action at EU level
External Factors	• Terrorism • Drug trafficking	• Terrorism • Drug trafficking • End of Cold War	• Balkans crisis and refugees • Organized crime and migration from former Soviet Union and CEECs • Impending enlargement	• Organized crime and migration from the former Soviet Union and CEECs • Impending enlargement • Terrorist attacks on the U.S. • Illegal immigration

create a true federal police force for the EU. Although this would not come to be, it was from this combination of factors that the idea for Europol arose.

At this time there was also some political will to correct the democratic deficit on internal security, namely the secrecy under which the Trevi Group had normally operated. Thus, there was pressure to insure that the new Third Pillar in general, and Europol in particular, would be more transparent than collaboration under the Trevi Group. In the eventual creation of Europol, issues related to accountability and the protection of civil liberties also became salient.

While these forces helped to cause and shape the development of the Third Pillar, another factor served to limit its progress, namely subsidiarity, which had been openly expressed in the SEA. As the Maastricht Treaty was being negotiated in 1991, the member states' attachment to the concept of subsidiary seemed to limit what the new Third Pillar would be designed to do. Concerning crime fighting, this would mean the creation of a European Police Office (i.e., Europol) with neither executive police powers nor an extensive institutional or legal infrastructure to facilitate or supplement its work.

Despite these shortcomings, the nature of police cooperation under the Treaty on European Union (TEU) was significantly more supranational than under the Trevi Group (see Table 9.2). The new Third Pillar possessed permanent, central bodies for planning and operations, which the Trevi Group had lacked. The EU ministers of justice and the interior could meet within the bounds of the new Treaty as the JHA Council, and their work was planned by a permanent body known as the K.4 Committee. To this institutional permanency, a task force on JHA was created within the General Secretariat of the Council, and JHA was added to the portfolio of a commissioner. Beyond this, a liaison network for information sharing on illegal drugs was created—the Europol Drugs Unit (EDU)—which would serve as the embryonic European Police Office.

The EDU was a far cry from a European FBI. Its operative powers were limited to information pooling and analysis on a limited number of crimes under various restrictions, and its crime-fighting remit was confined to drug trafficking until 1995, when a few other crimes were added by joint action of the JHA Council. The European Parliament had won the right to be kept informed of the activities of the JHA Council, but little more. The Commission was to be "fully associated" with the Third Pillar but was only given the power to initiate legislative proposals on some aspects of JHA, sharing this right with individual member states on the Council, which acted by unanimity for all matters. The Commission had no right of initiative at all concerning police or judicial cooperation on criminal matters. Even with these limits, the development of permanent bodies for police cooperation and the creation of new roles for the EP and the Commission, though weak, represented a shift in the direction of supranationalism.

After the entry into force of the TEU in 1993, the further development of police cooperation in the EU was initially quite slow. As discussed in Chapter 4, the most important activity during this time was the negotiation of the Europol Convention and its protocols, as well as changes to the Third

Table 9.2 The Changing Nature of EU Police Cooperation, by Era

	Trevi Group 1975–1993	Treaty on European Union 1993–1999	Treaty of Amsterdam and Europol Convention 1999–Present	Additions/Changes Needed for Supranational Cooperation Future (Potentially)
Permanent, central authorities for planning and operations	• None	• JHA Council • K.4 Committee • JHA Task Force • Commission • Europol Drugs Unit (EDU)	• Article 36 Committee • Europol • Europol Management Board • Commission • Directorate General • Eurojust, CEPOL, Task Force of Police Chiefs, Crime Prevention Network, etc.	• Greater role for COREPER • Stronger role for Commission on Europol's Management Board • QMV voting on Europol's Management Board • Office of EU Public Prosecutor • Common Border Patrol
Powers of central authorities	• Communication links • Limited sharing of tactics and information	• Limited pooling of information • Analysis • Coordination	• Build and maintain TECS • Share information with third parties • Analysis • Coordination • Immunity for staff • Potential to request investigations and participate in joint teams	• Initiate independent investigations • Conduct independent field operations (e.g., searches) • Make arrests • Europol branch offices in the member states • Larger staff and budget
Actual and potential crime fighting remit	• Very limited	• Initially limited to drugs but expanded somewhat by joint actions after 1995	• Initially as limited by Europol Convention, but expanded in 2002 to include all crimes in its annex	• All serious forms of crime, particularly those specified by framework decisions or common EU penal code
Role and powers of:				
• *Council of Ministers*	• Ministerial group acting by consensus	• JHA Council acting by unanimity	• JHA Council acting by unanimity, but implementation measures, possibly by QMV	• JHA Council acting by QMV

(continues)

Table 9.2 Cont.

	Trevi Group 1975–1993	Treaty on European Union 1993–1999	Treaty of Amsterdam and Europol Convention 1999–Present	Additions/Changes Needed for Supranational Cooperation Future (Potentially)
• *European Parliament*	• No role	• Must be kept informed	• Consultation procedure	• Co-decision procedure • Authority over Europol budget • Greater oversight of Europol
• *European Commission*	• No role	• "Fully associated" • Shared right of initiative only in some JHA areas but not police cooperation	• Shares right of initiative for all JHA areas	• Exclusive right of legislative initiative
• *European Court of Justice*	• No role	• No role	• Possible role	• Full power to make preliminary rulings

Pillar under the Treaty of Amsterdam. These negotiations were affected by a variety of internal and external factors, as noted in Table 9.2. Regarding the latter, the full impact of the end of the Cold War was being felt in the area of JHA by the mid-1990s, with a marked increase in the activity of criminal organizations based in the former Soviet Union and CEECs. Compounding this new source of crime, the EU also had to contend with dramatic flows of refugees who were fleeing the conflict in the Balkans.

Finally, the Europol Convention and Treaty of Amsterdam were drafted under the optimistic expectation, at the time, that at least a small group of new states among the CEECs would be joining the EU by 2002, bringing with them many of their existing problems and shortcomings regarding JHA. With the Schengen free-travel area having progressed from the planning stages to implementation by 1995, it was assumed that organized crime and weak criminal-justice institutions in the applicant states would surely prove to be problems for the existing member states. Thus, as in early periods, functional spillover combined with external factors to influence deeper cooperation in the field of JHA.

Although federalism was not a significant factor during this stage of European police cooperation, other internal factors continued to be relevant. By the mid-1990s, there was rising concern about the overall democratic deficit in the EU. There was also criticism of the shortcomings of the Third Pillar. Among other things, concerns for democracy contributed to the strengthened role for the EP in JHA matters and highlighted the need to protect civil liberties and human rights as EU police cooperation was strengthened. In fact, the debate on civil liberties was a factor in the creation of supervisory bodies for Europol, as well as delays in the ratification of the Europol Conventions and some of its protocols in a few member states. Meanwhile, attachment to subsidiarity, as expressed in Article K.5 of the Treaty of Amsterdam, continued to limit the perceived need and desirability of deeper integration on JHA in general, and police cooperation in particular.

Only after several years of negotiation and debate were the Treaty of Amsterdam, the Europol Convention, and its protocols finally ratified by the member states and entered into force, taking effect by summer 1999. Recognizing the need to jump-start progress on JHA and work toward the creation of the Area of Freedom, Security, and Justice as prescribed in the Treaty of Amsterdam, the EU held a special meeting of the European Council in Tampere, Finland, in October 1999. In its aftermath, progress on JHA was made in the EU as never before.

As described in Chapter 5, the rapid development of JHA policymaking after the Tampere summit was, on a practical level, due to the increased activity of the European Commission. By this time the Commission was being directed by António Vitorino, who had at his disposal a new Directorate-General (DG) on JHA. Following the example of the EU's successful progress on creating its single market according to the "Europe 1992" timetable, the Council charged the Commission with monitoring progress on the AFSJ, which it did by using its new JHA "Scoreboard." By bringing together the goals and deadlines expressed in the Tampere Conclusions and 2000 Action Plan on organized crime, as well as updating progress on these, the Commission helped to oversee steady progress on JHA after 1999, especially in the area of police cooperation.

In addition to the new role of the Commission, internal and external factors also contributed to progress on crime fighting during this time (see Table 9.1). As discussed in Chapters 5 and 6, the physical introduction of the euro, impact of the SEA on money laundering, expansion of the Schengen free-travel area to new states, and development of the European Rapid Reaction Force had spillover effects in JHA, particularly in the area of police cooperation. As before, these effects were made worse by external factors.

These initially included the enduring problems of organized crime and migration stemming from outside of the EU, as well as the mounting attention paid to preparations for enlargement. Later, the terrorist attacks on the United States on September 11, 2001, provided an additional external impetus for increased cooperation on crime fighting. As explained in Chapter 7, this led to rapid progress on police cooperation during the Belgian presidency of 2001, most notably including decisions to exhance the crime-fighting capabilities of Europol and agreement on the Euro-warrant and framework decision harmonizing member states' criminal codes on terrorism.

As described in Chapter 8, this new momentum to implement the goals established at the Tampere European Council continued during the Spanish presidency of 2002, propelled by yet another external factor, namely the continued flow of illegal immigration. This contributed to movement on a number of border control issues, after many years of stagnation and delay. In fact, external sources of terrorism and illegal immigration were highlighted by the EU's increasing efforts during this time to address its internal security issues through new forms of cooperation with third-party countries, including the United States, Russia, and developing countries in Africa, Asia, and Latin America.

Adding to these factors, attachment to subsidiarity seemed to weaken after 1999. That is, member states appeared more willing to address an increasing variety of JHA matters at the EU level. Although federalism remained largely insignificant during this period, there was new recognition that "closer cooperation" on some JHA matters among some member states might be desirable, even when the entire EU membership was not ready for this commitment. However, the increased willingness to utilize closer cooperation, though never realized, stemmed more out of a desire to find practical ways to make progress than from an attachment to federalist aspirations. Finally, concerns for democracy continued to be expressed after the Tampere summit, with references to various democratic principles evident in virtually every JHA debate and legislative proposal. For example, concerns over civil liberties proved influential in the drafting of the Euro-warrant and framework decision on terrorism, while concerns for human rights prevented the EU's developmental assistance from being made conditional on cooperation in the fight against illegal immigration, as some member states had hoped.

All of these factors have contributed to a new form of police cooperation in the EU that contrasts sharply with past models (see Table 9.2). Changing the name of the preparatory body of the JHA Council to the "Article 36 Committee" has been only a superficial development, but other changes have strengthened the institutional infrastructure of police cooperation in the EU. The focal point has been the creation of Europol, which began full operations in 1999 under the direction of its Management Board. In addition, as noted above, the new Commission that entered office in 1999 had at its disposal a new DG dedicated to JHA. Finally, since the Tampere summit, rapid progress has been made to supplement the work of Europol, with a host of new permanent EU institutions, including Eurojust, CEPOL, the Operational Task Force of Police Chiefs, the new Crime

Prevention Network, and new liaison networks linking high-ranking officials dealing with terrorism and border control.

This new institutional infrastructure was intended to supplement the work of Europol in two regards. First, these institutions should promote the sharing of best practices and common approaches to certain types of crime, representing a form of Europeanization of JHA regarding crime fighting. This Europeanization was also facilitated after 1999 by the increasing use of the framework decision, aimed at harmonizing criminal law for transnational crimes such as counterfeiting, money laundering, trafficking of human beings, and terrorism. Thus, by 2002 the process of Europeanization in the area of EU crime fighting had begun, brought about by the new institutional and legal infrastructure that was being gradually established since the Tampere European Council. In sum, since 1999 the EU has experienced both intensified police cooperation and gradual Europeanization in the area of internal security.

Along with both of these phenomena, Europol itself represented a vast improvement over its forerunner, the EDU. By the end of 2001, work on the Europol Computer System (TECS) and its databases was nearly complete, allowing Europol to carry out its tasks of pooling and analyzing criminal data, which helped it to coordinate police cooperation among the member states. Unlike the EDU, Europol can also obtain information from third parties, and it has won the right to ask member states to initiate investigations, as well to request that its staff participate in joint teams of investigators. Finally, the day-to-day autonomy of Europol was enhanced by the immunity of its staff from legal prosecution. Concerning the breadth of its crime-fighting duties, Europol was initially restricted to a relatively small number of crimes, but by the start of 2002 these had been expanded to include the long list of criminal offenses noted in the annex of the Europol Convention.

The increasing operational powers, autonomy, and crime-fighting remit of Europol after 1999 have not been the only signs of a shift in the direction of supranationalism concerning the Third Pillar since 1999. This can also be identified in the changing nature of policymaking on JHA after the entry into force of the Treaty of Amsterdam (see Table 9.2). The JHA Council still acts according to unanimity, but the use of qualified majority voting (QMV) for decisions on implementing measures is no longer optional. Meanwhile, the EP has won the right of consultation, providing it with the power to at least delay, if not occasionally influence, the final passage of legislation by the JHA Council. In addition, the European Court of Justice has acquired a new potential role, as the Treaty of Amsterdam specifies that it may have jurisdiction to make preliminary rulings on matters of police and judicial cooperation in criminal matters, provided that individual member states agree to its authority. Finally, the Commission has won the right to initiate legislation in all areas of the Third Pillar, including police and judicial cooperation in criminal matters. Although the Commission's right of initiative in the new Third Pillar is only shared with the Council, unlike in the First Pillar, it has become increasingly active in this area since 1999, contributing to the building of the institutional and legal infrastructure of crime fighting in the EU. This was especially evident in the passage of new antiterrorism legislation after September 11, 2001, much of which had been proposed by the Commission.

The changes experienced by each of these institutions may not be dramatic when compared with their nature under the Maastricht Treaty, but they represent further evidence of a shift in the direction of supranationalism concerning crime fighting in the EU. In fact, relative to the state of European police cooperation during the era of the Trevi Group, the development of the EU in this area is very striking indeed. From this perspective, the new institutional and legal infrastructure on JHA is also quite noteworthy, representing an increase in breadth and depth concerning police cooperation at the EU level that further indicates a shift in the direction of supranationalism.

Of course, these developments constitute only a shift in this direction, not the achievement of a truly supranational approach to crime fighting in the EU. A better understanding of what that might look like requires consideration of the additions and changes that would need to be made to EU police cooperation in the future (see Table 9.2). This implies the creation of new institutions and new roles for existing ones, as well as transforming the nature of the Third Pillar so that policymaking more closely resembles the process found in the First Pillar, which is usually considered to be more supranational than intergovernmental.

Concerning permanent, central authorities for planning and operations, several changes and additions would be needed before police cooperation could be characterized as being more supranationalism than not. One example of this would be a greater role for COREPER in the Third Pillar, and a decreased role for the Article 36 Committee. Although this would cause policymaking on JHA to resemble the processes found in the First Pillar, the impact on supranationalism would only be slight, as national officials constitute both institutions. In addition, the increased activity of the Article 36 Committee in recent years means its officials are now spending nearly as much time working in Brussels as their diplomatic colleagues in COREPER.

With regard to police cooperation, a more significant change would be a stronger role for the Commission on Europol's Management Board, including its right to vote at meetings or even control the general activities of this body. Alternatively, bringing Europol under the direction of the commissioner for JHA, rather than the Management Board, would constitute an even larger step in the direction of supranationalism. Although few of these potential changes seemed very likely in 2002, many related issues were being discussed during the ongoing European Convention, and a fundamental change in the nature of the Third Pillar remained a possibility for the next IGC in 2004.

In fact, by 2002 a number of new institutions in the area of crime fighting were being considered, including a European public prosecutor's office, common border patrol, and a European institute of police studies. Of these, the public prosecutor's office was the most bold suggestion, but with gradual harmonization of criminal law and the passage of the Euro-warrant by the end of 2001, such a body is not entirely unthinkable in the future of the EU. Nevertheless, this deepening of judicial cooperation, which would go far beyond the role of Eurojust, would be akin to granting Europol executive policing power, and this does not appear to be likely in the near term. Indeed, the proposals for the common police studies institute and border patrol were also rejected by the end of the Spanish presidency of 2002. Nevertheless, the EU's institutional infrastructure of crime fighting seems very likely to be enhanced in the future, especially as internal security will become more difficult to maintain following the next enlargement and eventual expansion of the Schengen free-travel area.

Granting executive policing powers to Europol would make police cooperation in the European Union supranational, similar to the FBI, at least conceptually, though certainly not in terms of size or budget. Such new powers would include the right to conduct independent activities, including field investigations, surveillance operations, and searches. It would also entail granting Europol officers the power to make arrests. Just as the FBI focuses on federal criminal offenses in the United States, so too could Europol one day handle investigations and make arrests based on harmonized criminal law in the EU. However, as with the idea of a European public prospector's office, there did not seem to be sufficient political will in the EU to grant these powers to Europol in 2002. Moreover, enabling Europol to exercise such powers would also require the creation of Europol branch offices throughout the EU, as well as a massive increase in Europol's staff and budget.

As Europol gains responsibility and prominence, it is likely that its development will be impacted by enduring desires to correct any remaining democratic deficits in the EU. This, in turn, will surely result in pressure to expand the powers of the European Parliament on JHA, including authority on police and judicial cooperation in criminal matters. This could take a number of forms beyond simply granting the EP the power of codecision on JHA. For example, the EP will likely continue to call for budgetary authority over the various crime-fighting institutions in the Third Pillar, just as it already possesses some authority over the Community budget in the First Pillar. The EP may also want the power to confirm the JHA

Council's choice of Europol's director, including the ability to question a nominee in committee hearings. Finally, the European Parliament could also play a greater role in examining cases of corruption and protecting citizens from the potential abuse of Europol power by the establishment of an oversight committee that could act parallel to the joint supervisory body. Alternatively, the EP could establish a special Europol ombudsman in each member state to provide citizens with a direct avenue for their complaints and concerns regarding Europol. In sum, the more powerful Europol becomes, the more pressure there will likely be to increase the role of the European Parliament in its affairs. Consequently, as parliamentary influence increases, EU police cooperation will necessarily become more supranational.

In addition, a supranational Third Pillar might feature a commission that would have the sole right to initiate legislation on JHA, as well as a council that would decide on these proposals using QMV. In fact, the use of qualified majority voting could, for example, be extended to the Europol Management Board. The alternative would be to risk inhibiting future decisionmaking by allowing the need for unanimity to continue even after the EU has grown to more than twenty-five member states. By preventing any one member state from dominating policymaking, the use of QMV on the JHA Council or in the Europol Management Board would make EU police cooperation more supranational. In addition to these changes in roles for the EP, Commission, and Council of Ministers, making the Third Pillar more supranational would entail granting the European Court of Justice the authority to make preliminary rulings on all aspects of the Third Pillar, including its various conventions and protocols, without member states needing to declare their willingness to accept its rulings.

In essence, creating a supranational Third Pillar would entail bringing the entire JHA *acquis* into the First Pillar, which would make the distinction between these two pillars irrelevant. However, given the modest changes to the Third Pillar in the Treaty of Nice, these kinds of sweeping changes should not be expected any time soon. At the earliest, they might come about after the entry into force of the next treaty, which will not be until 2005 at the earliest.

Nevertheless, the continued evolution of the Third Pillar should be expected, pushed especially by the eventual expansion of the Schengen free-travel area to the future members of the EU, as well as driven by the enduring problems of drug trafficking, terrorism, and illegal immigration of all kinds. There seems to be little doubt that organized crime will continue to be a problem in the member states, and much of this will continue to originate outside the EU, in places as far away as China and Columbia, or as close as Russia and the Balkans. Likewise, terrorism will continue to threaten the member states, both from within and from sources external to the EU. Moreover, as new members are added to the Schengen zone, cooperation in fighting organized crime, illegal immigration, and terrorism across the increasingly irrelevant national boundaries will continue to be propelled by functional spillover, or at least the perception of it.

With the past movement of European integration into the areas of CFSP and JHA and the achievement of the common currency, federalist ideology may have exhausted its impact as a highly significant force for driving European integration. That is, a federalist impetus on the part of some European leaders may not be sufficient to convince policymakers and their constituents to transform the intergovernmental nature of policymaking of the Third Pillar. However, the member states may eventually find supranational forms of decisionmaking simply to be more practical, recognizing the difficulties of consensual decisionmaking in an expanded European Union.

For now, police cooperation in the European Union remains more intergovernmental than not, and, to a large extent, continues to be controlled by the member states. However, recent developments indicate that the nature of collaboration on policing in the EU has become more supranational since the days of the Trevi Group. The likelihood that the internal and external factors described above will endure leads to the expectation that the future will bring a further shift in this direction. In the process, the EU will move even closer to having a supranational approach to police cooperation, including a role for Europol that increasingly resembles that of the U.S. FBI.

Note

1. Following the JHA Council of December 19, 2002, the Netherlands' unique treatment of soft drugs continued to inhibit agreement of the framework decision on drug trafficking. Meanwhile, the proposed framework decision covering racism and xenophobia continued be held up on the issues of defining criminal liability and whether discrimination based on religion should be covered.

Chronology of European Police Cooperation, 1898–2005

1898	International Police Conference on anarchy held secretly in Rome
1914–1918	World War I
1923	Vienna, International Criminal Police Commission (ICPC) formed
1939	World War II begins
1945	World War II ends and Cold War begins
1946	ICPC re-forms in Paris as International Criminal Police Organization (ICPO), a.k.a., "Interpol"
1950	Schuman Declaration calls for European Coal and Steel Community (ECSC), marking the start of European integration, 5/9
1958	Treaties of Rome take effect, leading to the eventual creation of the European Community with six member states
1970s	Repeated incidents of domestic terrorism occur in several European countries
1971	"Pompidou Group" is formed in the Council of Europe
1972	Hostage-taking and killing of Israeli athletes at Munich Summer Olympics
1973	
January	UK, Ireland, and Denmark join the EC
	Oil crisis in Middle East leads to economic recession in Europe
1974	Idea of European Police Office discussed in meetings of the German Trade Union for Criminal Detectives
1975	(Irish presidency)
March	First meeting of the European Council held in Dublin
	(Italian presidency)
December	**Rome European Council**

	Trevi Group is formed among EU ministers
1976	(Luxembourg presidency)
June	**Trevi Group** meets for first time in Luxembourg
	(Dutch presidency)
July	**Brussels European Council** discusses terrorism
1977	(British presidency)
	(Belgian presidency)
	Trevi Working Group I established on internal security intelligence links
1978	(Danish and German presidencies)
	Discussion and launch of European Monetary System (EMS)
	Trevi Working Group II established on information exchange on training, equipment, tactics, etc.
1979	(French presidency)
	Rising oil prices once again lead to economic recession in Europe
	(Irish presidency)
1980	(Italian and Luxembourg presidencies)
1981	(Dutch presidency)
January	Greece joins EC
	(British presidency)
1982	(Belgian and Danish presidencies)
1983	(German and Greek presidencies)
1984	(French presidency)
June	**Fontainebleau European Council** leads to momentum for deepening integration
	France and Germany agree to eliminate controls at their mutual border
	(Irish presidency)
1985	(Italian presidency)
March	**Brussels European Council**
	Publication of Dooge Report calling for greater powers for Commission and European Parliament (EP)
	Agreement reached on single market by December 1992
June	Soccer hooliganism leads to 39 deaths at Heysel stadium in Brussels
	Soccer hooliganism added to Trevi Working Group II
	Trevi Working Group III established on serious forms of international organized crime

Schengen, Schengen agreement signed

(Luxembourg presidency)

1986 (Dutch presidency)

January Spain and Portugal join EC

February Single European Act (SEA) signed, establishes free movement of people as a basic principle of a perfected common market

(British presidency)

December **London European Council** discusses terrorism, internal security, and drugs

1987 (Belgian presidency)

(Danish presidency)

July SEA enters into force, with goal of perfecting common market by the end of 1992. EP gains power with "cooperation procedure" for some policies

December **Trevi Group** meets in Copenhagen and approves guidelines for establishing drug-liaison offices

1988 (Germany presidency)

(Greek presidency)

December **Trevi Group** meets in Athens and creates "Trevi '92" Working Group

1989 (Spanish presidency)

Interpol relocated to Lyons, France

(French presidency)

November Berlin Wall is opened

1990 (Irish presidency)

June Signing of Schengen Implementation Agreement, including plans for Schengen Information System (SIS)

Trevi Group meets in Dublin and publishes Program of Action on police cooperation and plans approved for network of National Drug Intelligence Units and a central European Drugs Intelligence Unit (EDIU)

(Italian presidency)

October German unification

December **Dublin European Council** approves EDIU network

Intergovernmental Conferences (IGCs) on political union and monetary union begin

Slobodan Milosevic comes to power in Yugoslavia. Slovenia declares its independence

1991 (Luxembourg presidency)

Partly stemming from the economic costs of German unity, most of Europe enters period of recession

Crisis in Balkans unfolds

June   **Luxembourg European Council**
              • Kohl makes bold proposal for a Europol with executive policing powers

              Croatia declares its independence, prompting large-scale attacks by the Yugoslavian army. Refugees begin to flee northward

              (Dutch presidency)

August   Trevi Group establishes "Ad Hoc Working Group on Europol" (AHWGE)

December   **Maastricht European Council** unveils Treaty on European Union (TEU), calling for Europol in its Title VI (Articles K.1–K.9)

1992   (Portuguese presidency)

February   TEU is formally signed

April   Bosnian independence is recognized by the United States and EC. Serbian paramilitary units, soon joined by the Yugoslavian army, attack Bosnia. "Ethnic cleansing" begins, and refugees flee northward

June   **Lisbon European Council** agrees on need to draft Convention for Europol, leading to work on this by the Trevi Group's AHWGE

              Trevi ministers agree to establish Europol Project Group (EPG)

July   EPG staff is appointed, including its director, Jürgen Storbeck

              Refugee crisis in Europe reaches its peak

              (British presidency)

September   EPG begins to meet in Strasbourg

1993   (Danish presidency)

June   **Copenhagen European Council** agrees on enlargement to Eastern Europe and establishes basic accession criteria

              Trevi Group Ministerial Agreement establishes Europol Drugs Unit (EDU)

              (Belgian presidency)

October   Trevi Group agrees to base EDU in The Hague

              Brussels Special European Council
              • discusses guidelines for implementing the TEU and Europe
              • endorses decision to base Europol in The Hague in context of discussion regarding sites of other new EU institutions

November   **Treaty on European Union (TEU or "Maastricht Treaty")** enters into force
              • EP gains power of co-decision for some policies

- creates the "European Union." TEU's Title IV replaces Trevi Group with its intergovernmental Pillar Three on Justice and Home Affairs (JHA), including JHA Council and K.4 Committee with Steering Groups I–III
- Steering Group II continues work of defunct AHWGE on Europol Convention

1994 (Greek presidency)

European economies begin to show signs of improvement, but high unemployment persists

February EDU begins official operations in The Hague with its remit limited to drug trafficking

JHA Council decides not to include fight against terrorism in Europol Convention, but agrees to take up the matter again at later date

(German presidency)

December **Essen European Council** reaches agreement on organization, powers, and expanded remit of EDU

1995 (French presidency)

January Austria, Sweden, and Finland join EU

Anita Gradin of Sweden becomes new Commissioner for JHA

March **JHA Council** passes joint action on the organization, powers, and expanded remit of EDU, including the smuggling of nuclear materials, illegal immigration, and trafficking of stolen vehicles

Agreement reached to include terrorism in Europol's remit two years after it begins operations

Schengen Implementation Agreement takes effect
- free-travel zone created among Germany, France, Belgium, Spain, Netherlands, Luxembourg, and Portugal

June **Cannes European Council**
- UK opposes role for European Court of Justice (ECJ) in settling disputes regarding Europol. Issue of ECJ's role for Europol postponed

(Spanish presidency)

July Europol Convention is signed

1996 (Italian presidency)

March JHA Council passes joint action on racism and xenophobia

June **Florence European Council**
- IGC begins on TEU revisions

Agreement reached on opt-out for UK on role for ECJ regarding Europol

(Irish presidency)

July	Protocol to Europol Convention on role of ECJ is signed
December	**Dublin II European Council,** 12/13–14

• calls on ongoing IGC on political union to include operative powers for Europol

• endorses creation of High Level Group (HLG) to develop action plan on organized crime

1997	(Dutch presidency)
February	**JHA Council** passes joint action expanding the EDU's remit to include trafficking in human beings
April	HLG adopts "Action Plan to Combat Organized Crime" and communicates it to the ongoing IGC. Council endorses Action Plan
May	Tony Blair becomes prime minister after Labour Party victory in UK parliamentary elections, 5/1
June	**JHA Council** adopts Protocol to Europol Convention on the Privileges and Immunities of Europol Personnel

Amsterdam European Council

• Treaty of Amsterdam unveiled, including transfer of free-movement policy areas of pillar III to pillar I, incorporation of Schengen *acquis* into EU, and granting of some operative powers for Europol

• HLG's Action Group approved

Multidisciplinary Group (MDG) on Organized Crime established to oversee progress on Action Plan, with implementation ending on July 31, 1999

(Luxembourg presidency)

October	Italy implements Schengen agreement for air travel

Treaty of Amsterdam is signed

December	**Luxembourg European Council** approves applications for EU membership of Estonia, Poland, the Czech Public, Hungary, Slovenia, and Cyprus ("Luxembourg group"). Under the terms of the Treaty of Amsterdam, all new members must fully adopt EU *acquis,* including JHA and Schengen
1998	(British presidency)
January	EU fails to meet goal of Europol's entry into force

Discord within EU on how to handle recent influx of Kurdish refugees from Turkey and Iraq

February	Agreement reached in K.4 Committee to include terrorism in Europol's remit by January 1999 (rather than later as originally planned)
March	**JHA Council** approves idea of expanding Europol's remit to include terrorism by January 1999

Negotiations on accession begin with the six applicant states of the Luxembourg group, 3/31

April	Austria implements Schengen agreement, removes border controls. Italy removes border controls for travel by land and sea. At this point, "Schengenland" (free-travel zone) consists of Germany, France, Netherlands, Belgium, Luxembourg, Spain, Portugal, Italy, and Austria

May **JHA Council**
• CEECs and Cyprus sign Pre-Accession Pact on organized crime with the EU

June Belgium becomes last member state to ratify the Europol Convention

Cardiff European Council recognizes "excellent progress" made by the MDG on implementing the "Action Plan to Combat Organized Crime," (6/15–16)

(Austrian presidency)

September Inauguration of European Judicial Network (EJN)

Social Democratic–Green coalition government formed in Germany after Helmut Kohl's CDU is defeated in elections of September 27

October **Europol Convention** enters into force, but Europol is not yet fully operational due to lack of agreement on the nature of its Joint Supervisory Body and failure of eight member states to ratify the Protocol on Privileges and Immunities

Informal Meeting of the European Council at Pörtschach am Wörthersee
• brainstorming session on the future of the EU results in decision to hold Special European Council on JHA at Tampere, Finland, in October 1999

December **JHA Council**
• passes "Action Plan on Establishing an Area of Freedom, Security and Justice (AFSJ)," setting two- and five-year deadlines for implementation of various measures specified in the Treaty of Amsterdam
• political agreement reached on composition of Europol's Directorate General (under Storbeck) and on most aspects of rules of procedure for Europol's Joint Supervisory Body
• political agreement reached to expand Europol's role to include fight against counterfeiting of the euro

Vienna European Council
• endorses progress report on the 1997 Action Plan
• approves the new Action Plan on the AFSJ submitted by the JHA Council

1999 (German presidency)

January Monetary Union (euro-zone) takes effect among eleven member states

France, Italy, Luxembourg, and Portugal have yet to ratify the Protocol on Privileges and Immunities of Europol Personnel

Greece, Belgium, and France have yet to ratify the Treaty of Amsterdam

February   Informal Meeting of the JHA Council in Berlin, 2/11.

March   **JHA Council,** 3/12
• discusses preparations for changes to the Third Pillar after entry into force of the Treaty of Amsterdam
• considers Dutch proposal to extend Europol's mandate to combat forgery of money and means of payment

Collective resignation of the Commission in wake of report regarding fraud, mismanagement, and nepotism in the Commission, 3/15

Berlin Special European Council, 3/24–25
• Romano Prodi nominated to be new president of the Commission
• agreement reached on Agenda 2000

France deposits the instruments of ratification of the Treaty of Amsterdam, becoming the last member state to do so

April   **Special JHA Council,** (4/7) discusses Kosovo and related refugee crisis

Rules of Procedure agreed upon for Joint Supervisory Body

Europol's mandate formally extended to combat counterfeiting of the euro

May   **Treaty of Amsterdam** enters into force
• establishes goal of creating an "Area of Freedom Security and Justice" (AFSJ) in the EU
• includes new provisions for decisionmaking in the JHA Council and some new operative powers for Europol
• under the terminology of the post-Amsterdam consolidated version of the treaties, the K.4 Committee becomes the Article 36 Committee
• the Schengen *acquis* is integrated into the *acquis* of the EU

EP approves Romano Prodi's nomination as Commission president

First meeting of the Mixed Committee, composed of representatives of the Commission, the member states, and Norway and Iceland in association with the implementation and development of the Schengen *acquis*

JHA Council, 5/27
• passes resolution calling for new guidelines to protect the euro when it is introduced in 2002, including possible role for Europol
• UK and Ireland express interest in participating in the provision of the Schengen *acquis* on law enforcement and criminal judicial cooperation

By end of May, Italy and France have ratified the Protocol on Privileges and Immunities and deposited the instruments of ratification, becoming the last two states to do so and allowing Europol to become fully operational on July 1, 1999

June	**Cologne European Council,** 6/3–4

                   • Javier Solana named name high representative for CFSP and secretary-general of the Council
                   • plans established for next IGC and work on Charter of Fundamental Rights

                   NATO bombings in Kosovo and Serbia come to an end

                   European Parliament elections held, 6/10–13

                   (Finnish presidency)

July   Europol becomes fully operation following entry into force of the protocols under the Europol Convention, 7/1

                   In accord with conclusion of Vienna European Council, the General Affairs Council meets, along with representatives of the applicant states on transnational crime and the Balkans

August   Hearings held in EP for Commission nominees

September   New Commission installed. António Vitorino of Portugal becomes commissioner for Justice and Home Affairs

October   **JHA Council,** 10/4
                   • first debate on Commission's new action plan to combat drugs
                   • final report and action plans of High-Level Group on Asylum and Immigration

                   Tampere Special Meeting of European Council on Justice and Home Affairs, 10/16
                   • establishes ten "milestones" toward the building of an AFSJ
                   • plans made for the Commission to devise and maintain a "Scoreboard" to monitor progress on these milestones

                   Javier Solana sworn in as EU secretary-general and high representative for CFSP, 10/18

                   JHA Council, 10/29
                   • follow-up talks held on the Tampere Conclusions

December   **JHA Council,** 12/2
                   • notes state of progress made on some of the Tampere milestones, including the receipt of operational data and the initiation of investigations by Europol, creation of the Task Force of European Police Chiefs, and the establishment Eurojust
                   • notes preparation of report on the finalization and evaluation of the 1997 Action Plan

                   Helsinki European Council, 12/10–11
                   • agreement reached to open accession negotiations additional new applicant states of Romania, Slovakia, Latvia, Lithuania, Bulgaria, and Malta (the "Helsinki group"). Turkey is accepted as a candidate for EU accession
                   • final agreement to open new IGC in February on institutional reform
                   • agreement to assemble, by 2003, military and civilian personnel capable of the full range of "Petersberg" tasks, including policing,

as part of a strengthened Common European Security and Defense Policy (CESDP)
- takes note of JHA Council report on the finalization and evaluation of the 1997 Action Plan

2000   (Portuguese presidency)

February   "Political quarantine" of Austria in the EU begins in response to inclusion of the Freedom Party in its new coalition government, 2/5

IGC on institutional reform opens in Brussels, 2/14

Accession negotiations open with the six applicant states of the Helsinki group, 2/15

March   **Informal Meeting of the JHA Council,** 3/2–3
- Commission presents provisional version of the JHA Scoreboard

Lisbon Special European Council ("dot.com summit")
- deals with strengthening economic and social cohesion as part of a knowledge-based economy

Greece abolishes its last travel restriction on implementation of Schengen agreement, joining the nine EU members that had already done so, 3/26

JHA Council, 3/27
- adopts new (2000) Action Plan on organized crime to follow up on the 1997 Action Plan
- formally authorizes the director of Europol to begin negotiating with third parties (i.e., nonmember states, Interpol, etc.)
- reaches political agreement on framework decision to improve criminal-law protection of the euro

April   First meeting of Chiefs of Police Task Force held in Lisbon, 4/7–8

May   High-Level Conference on crime prevention held in Portugal, 5/4–5

Conference on Adriatic cooperation in fight against organized crime held at Ancona, 5/19–20

Applicant states of the Luxembourg group open negotiations on their JHA chapters of accession, 5/26

JHA Council, 5/29
- takes note of presentation by Commissioner Vitorino, who officially unveils consolidated version of the JHA Scoreboard, with regard to conclusions of the European Councils of Vienna and Tampere and the newly passed Action Plan 2000
- notes progress on European police college
- considers two different initiatives to create Eurojust
- signing of Convention on Mutual Legal Assistance in Criminal Matters

United Kingdom signs on to Schengen *acquis* provisions for police and judicial cooperation (but not cross-border surveillance and hot pursuit), 5/30

June   Fifty-eight Chinese illegal immigrants discovered dead in Dover in
              tragic people-trafficking incident, 6/19

              Santa Maria da Feira European Council, 6/19–20
              • agrees to add enhanced cooperation as formal agenda item in the
                ongoing IGC
              • endorses comprehensive antidrug Action Plan for 2000–2004
              • endorses strategy for the external dimension of JHA

              (French presidency)

July   **Informal JHA Council** in Marseilles, 7/28–29
              • discussion held on mutual recognition, immigration, and cyber-
                crime

September   Unofficial EU sanctions against Austria are lifted after its human-
              rights record gets a clean bill of health, 9/13

              Task Force of Police Chiefs meets in Paris, along with participation
              of the Commission, General Secretariat, and Europol. Community
              policing identified as priority area, 9/14–15

              JHA Council, 9/28
              • political agreement reached on protocol to the Europol Convention
                to extend the competence of Europol to money laundering related
                to any crime
              • political agreement reached on setting up a provisional Eurojust unit
              • reaches agreement in principle that, before enlargement, the EU
                needs some approximation of laws concerning criminal sanctions
                for crimes against the environment
              • adopts recommendation regarding how member states should deal
                with requests by Europol to initiate, coordinate, or conduct
                investigations

October   **Biarritz Informal European Council,** 10/13
              • notes progress on Charter of Fundamental Rights
              • considers outstanding issues in ongoing IGC

              JHA Council, 10/17
              • adopts decision establishing secretariat for joint supervisory
                data-protection body for Europol, customs, and the Schengen
                agreement
              • political agreement reached on framework decision to combat
                money laundering

              Joint Meeting of ECOFIN and JHA Council, 10/17
              • notes progress on and establishes plans for fight against money
                laundering

November   Commission publishes its regular country reports on enlargement

              Plan for Eurojust is agreed upon in the ongoing IGC and included in
              the draft treaty

December   **JHA Council,** 11/30–12/1
              • makes final decision to extend Schengen area to Nordic states in
                March 2001

- political agreement reached on regulation listing which third-party country nationals need a visa ("blacklist") to enter the Schengen area, and which do not ("white list")
- debates French initiatives to set up judicial training network
- considers French initiative to set up unit within Europol to protect euro, as well as mutual-assistance measures
- debates French and Swedish initiative to create a European crime-prevention network
- takes note of the Commission's first formal updating of JHA Scoreboard
- reaches political agreement on establishing the European Police College (CEPOL)
- is notified, in the context of its debate on terrorism, of the Commission's intention to make proposals on accelerating and simplifying extradition and creating a European arrest warrant
- passes recommendation to allow Europol agents to take part in joint investigative team set up by member states

Formal adoption by Council of proposal to create CEPOL

Nice European Council, 12/8–9
- political agreement reached on Treaty of Nice, entailing some changes for JHA, including:
- partial and deferred switch to QMV on parts of Title IV of the TEC on refugees and asylum
- removal of potential veto regarding enhanced cooperation in the Third Pillar, and
- supplementing of Articles 30 and 31 of the TEU, specifying role of Eurojust

2001   (Swedish presidency)

January   Greece becomes twelfth member of the euro-zone

Work on creating CEPOL begins

Spain hosts conference on terrorism for leaders of national police organizations and Europol in Madrid. The creation of a European arrest warrant for terrorists is discussed, 1/29–2/2

February   **Informal Meeting of the JHA Council in Stockholm,** 2/8–9

Interinstitutional steering group set up by high-level meeting of representatives of the Commission, Europol, and European Central Bank (ECB) to protect the euro against counterfeiting, 2/15

Treaty of Nice is formally signed, 2/26

March   "Pro-Eurojust" begins operating, as work continues on developing plan for a permanent Eurojust unit, 3/1

Police Chiefs Task Force meets in Stockholm, 3/8–9

Commission launches new PHARE project on judicial cooperation to fight crime in candidate countries, 3/14–16

JHA Council, 3/15–16

- political agreement reached on comprehensive crime-prevention policy, including:
- European Crime Prevention Network
- financing of Hippocrates Program
- future reporting by Europol and the Commission on organized crime and prevention
- televised debate on drug trafficking
- political agreement on a framework decision to protect the environment using criminal law and criminal sanctions
- agreement to fight cyber-crime with criminal law
- first joint meeting with JHA ministers from the thirteen applicant states
- acceptance of country reports on data protection, clearing the way for Europol to negotiate agreements with Norway, Iceland, Poland, and Hungary

Stockholm Special European Council on Economic and Social Matters, 3/23–24

Entry into force of Schengen Convention in the five Nordic states (including Norway and Iceland). This enlarges the free-travel zone in Europe to about 310 million people in fifteen countries, including all EU member states except Ireland and the UK, which have their own free-travel zone with each other, 3/25

May   Swedish proposal to allow "onward transmission" of personal data provided by Europol to third-party countries and organizations

JHA Council, 5/28–29
- adoption of Europol budget for 2002 (€48,504.00, compared to €35,391.300 for 2001)
- formal adoption of European Crime Prevention Network
- agreement reached on protocol to Convention on Mutual Assistance in Criminal Matters (2000) regarding investigations and sharing of information on bank accounts
- adoption of conclusions on Europol's role to protect the euro
- final agreement reached on signing of agreement between Europol and Norway, Iceland, and Interpol
- second formal update by the Commission on the JHA Scoreboard

June   Accession chapters on JHA opened with Bulgaria, Lithuania, Latvia, Malta, and Slovakia. Romania is the only state of the twelve candidate countries not to have opened its accession chapter on JHA, 6/1

Europol reveals that, after its own internal investigation, one of its staff members has been arrested for allegedly diverting Europol funds to a secret bank account in Bermuda, 6/8

Irish voters reject Treaty of Nice in referendum

Göteborg European Council, 6/15–16
- notes excellent progress on accession negotiations with all candidate countries and sets goal of concluding 2002 to close all chapters for those states that are ready

- affirms need to accelerate progress toward Tampere Conclusions before Laeken European Council
- this meeting was disrupted by antiglobalization demonstrators, resulting in violent clashes between police and protestors

Europol signs cooperation agreements with Iceland and Norway, 6/28

(Belgian presidency)

July   JHA chapters of accession for candidate countries processed according to the "Accession Roadmap"

Special JHA Meeting on security at European Council meetings and at other events likely to have comparable impact, 7/13
- political agreement reached that Europol should have a role in analyzing violent disturbances at EU summits

G-8 summit in Genoa is disrupted by antiglobalization protestors. One person shot dead by police in violent clashes, 7/20–22

Council of Ministers approves Europol Work Program for 2002, 7/23

September   Europol establishes crisis center, staffed twenty hours daily, to facilitate the sharing of information and coordination of investigations for euro-related crimes, 9/3

Terrorist attacks on the World Trade Center and Pentagon in the United States kill over 3,000 people. Initial reports claim over 6,000 deaths, 9/11

Europol establishes crisis center to facilitate the investigation of the attacks, staffed twenty-hours daily, 9/12

The European Commission proposes two framework decisions regarding a common definition and sanctions for terrorism, as well as a European arrest warrant, 9/19

Extraordinary JHA Council on Terrorism
- general agreement reached on over thirty internal and external measures related to the fight against terrorism, including agreement in principle on the two framework decisions just proposed by the Commission, 9/20

Extraordinary Meeting of the European Council in Brussels regarding terrorist attacks on the United States, 9/21
- declares total solidarity with the United States in its fight against terrorism
- endorses antiterrorist measures agreed upon in JHA Councils, as part of its seven-point antiterrorist plan, including creation of an antiterrorist unit in Europol
- calls upon member states to share any relevant intelligence on terrorism with Europol

Publication of 2001 Work Program for CEPOL by its governing board

JHA Council, 9/27–28
- decision reached on extending Europol's remit to *all* forms of crime mentioned in the annex of the Europol Convention

- political agreement reached on framework decision on human trafficking
- agreement reached on first eight articles of draft framework decision on Eurojust, regarding its establishment, composition, objectives, and mission, including giving the Commission permanent representation in Eurojust
- approves "roadmap" to hasten progress on antiterrorism before the Laeken European Council, containing forty-five items

Article 36 Committee begins to meet twice weekly to accelerate adoption of antiterrorism package

October   Commission proposes regulation to freeze assets of twenty-seven persons or organizations suspected of being involved in the terrorist attacks on the United States, 10/2

Europol signs cooperation agreements with Slovenia, Poland, Hungary, and Estonia, 10/1–10

COREPER begins discussion of a draft framework decision to allow and facilitate joint investigative teams from two or more member states to combat terrorism and trafficking of drugs or human beings, 10/10

Heads of antiterrorist units of EU member states meet for first time at EU level in Brussels as called for by September meeting of European Council, 10/15

Commission proposes to establish Argo program for 2002–2006 as successor to the Odysseus program, entailing €25 million for projects dealing with external border controls, visas, asylum, and immigration, 10/16

Joint Meeting of ECOFIN and JHA Councils (in Luxembourg), 10/16 (day)
- agreement reached on compromise version of directive to prevent money laundering, allowing conciliation deal with the EP
- discord remains on draft framework decisions on freezing of criminal assets
- agreement reached to intensify pressure on noncooperative third-party countries regarding financial crime
- protocol to Convention on Mutual Assistance in Criminal Matters to reduce restrictions of banking secrecy in the fight against financial crime signed

Special Meeting of the JHA Council (in Luxembourg), 10/16 (evening)
- discusses issues and possible amendments to Commission proposal for the European arrest warrant and framework decision on terrorism

Ghent Informal European Council, 10/19. Originally intended to discuss the euro, meeting focused on the fight against terrorism
- reaffirms its intent to abolish principle of "double criminality" to allow direct surrender under the proposed European arrest warrant
- reaffirms desire to achieve final legislation on freezing of assets

- reaffirms desire to promote increased cooperation on terrorism among Europol, Eurojust, and national authorities (i.e., intelligence services, police forces, and judicial agencies)
- reaffirms desire to achieve common definition on terrorism and list of terrorist organizations

Task Force of Police Chiefs meets in Belgium, along with counterparts from the candidate countries, Norway, and Iceland, 10/29–31

November   Europol signs cooperation agreement with Interpol, 11/5

Publication of regular Commission reports updating progress toward accession by each applicant state. Ten of twelve candidate countries on course for possible accession by 2004, 11/13

Commission proposes new framework program for €65 million in funding for projects on police, customs, and judicial cooperation in criminal matters for 2003–2007, which consolidates and succeeds existing programs due to expire, 11/9

Commission publishes communication calling for "balanced approach" to problem of illegal immigration, 11/15

JHA Council, 11/16
- continues discussion of draft framework decision covering definition of terrorism and thresholds for criminal sanctions
- Ireland and Italy block agreement on positive list of crimes covered by European arrest warrant, for which the principle of double criminality would no longer apply
- discusses contending approaches to harmonizing criminal sanctions for all crimes
- in preparation of the Laeken European Council, the presidency and Commission report on progress toward implementing the Tampere Conclusions, noting insufficient progress on asylum and immigration
- Italy floats idea for creation of a European border police
- agreement reached to increase frequency of JHA Council meetings to once per month
- endorsement of CEPOL Work Program for 2001

Hungary becomes first candidate state to close (provisionally) its chapter of accession on JHA, 11/28

December   **JHA Council,** 12/6–7
- final agreement reached on remaining aspects of Eurojust, including its data-protection bodies
- notes progress on thirty of forty-five items in the Antiterrorism Roadmap
- final agreement reached on framework decision on definition and sanctions for terrorism
- Italy continues to block final agreement on a European arrest warrant
- little progress made on draft framework decision on child sexual exploitation and pornography

Europol signs cooperation agreement with the United States, providing for limited sharing of information (not personal data) and exchanges of liaison officers, 12/7

Eight would-be illegal immigrants found dead in a shipping container near Wexford, Ireland. Five others found in serious condition in the container, which had arrived from Zeebrugge, Belgium, 12/8

After meeting with Belgian prime minister Guy Verhofstadt, Italian Prime Minister Silvio Berlusconi concedes on the issue of the European arrest warrant regarding thirty-two specified crimes, 12/11

Cyprus, Slovenia, and the Czech Republic close (provisionally) their chapters of accession on JHA, 12/11–12

Laeken European Council, 12/14–15
• "Laeken Declaration" calls for convention to prepare for next IGC on fundamental institutional reform
• affirms possibility that ten of the candidate states may join the EU by 2004
• affirms partial readiness of European Rapid Reaction Force to assume some crisis management tasks (e.g., disaster relief)
• receives reports from the Commission and the Belgian presidency on evaluation and implementation of Tampere Conclusions and the progress on the Antiterrorism Roadmap
• notes slow progress on immigration and asylum policy, endorses the Commission's new approach to illegal immigration, and sets deadlines for passage of new asylum measures
• orders study of ways to increase cooperation among national border patrols
• urges Council to examine Commission's green paper on a European public prosecutor
• heads of state and government fail to agree on permanent seats for seven new EU institutions, including Eurojust and CEPOL

Europol Information System (EIS) becomes operational for data exchanges on the euro in English

2002   (Spanish presidency)

January   Circulation begins for 15 billion new euro bank notes and 52 billion coins worth €649 billion, 1/1

Europol's mandate expanded to cover all forms of international crime listed in the annex to the Europol Convention, 1/1

"Consolidation of an area of justice" noted as one of original six priorities for the Spanish presidency

Spain proposes the creation of a European institute of police studies to promote consistency among new EU institutions on police cooperation (e.g., Europol, CEPOL, Eurojust, Police Chiefs Task Force, etc.), 1/8–9

February   Europol report to Article 36 Committee indicates that terrorism in Europe declined in 2001

Informal JHA Council in Santiago de Compostela, 2/13–15
• France, Belgium, Luxembourg, Portugal, and Spain announce agreement to implement the Euro-warrant no later than the start of 2003. Germany declares its intention to implement the warrant as soon as possible

- agreement on basic framework for negotiations with the United States on judicial cooperation
- agreement on common visa format and establishment of common consular offices
- Commission asked to study cost and logistics of EU visa database
- agreement reached on proposals to create joint investigative teams and to allow Europol to request that these are created
- Germany questions whether Europol is delivering value for the money
- agreement in principal on a new model for harmonization of criminal law

General Affairs Council, 2/18–19
- decision to create EU Police Mission in Bosnia and Herzegovina to replace the UN International Police Task Force on January 1, 2003

Commission adopts communication to address democratic deficit in Europol, proposing to create a committee of MEPs and national MPs, 2/26

European Convention established by Laeken Declaration under Valery Giscard d'Estaing begins work to prepare for next IGC, 2/28

JHA Council, 2/28
- holds wide-ranging televised debate on using external relations and international cooperation to fight organized crime
- approves "Global Plan" (i.e., action plan) to fight illegal immigration and the trafficking of human beings
- discussion held on planning for EU-U.S. judicial cooperation on criminal matters, including extradition
- approves supplemental spending of €3.1 million for Europol's 2002 budget to fund its new antiterrorism activities
- unanimous agreement reached in principal on framework decision to allow Europol to participate in joint investigations
- constitutional issues in some member states prevent final agreement on framework decision on freezing of criminal assets
- formal adoption by Ireland of some aspects of Schengen agreement on police cooperation (e.g., SIS), not including hot pursuit or cross-border surveillance
- decision on implementation measures for making operational the Eurodac database of fingerprints for asylum seekers
- agreement on Denmark as provisional host country for CEPOL's secretariat
- final decision setting up permanent Eurojust, provisionally based in The Hague

March   Europol signs a cooperation agreement with the Czech Republic, 3/5

Barcelona European Council, 3/15–16
- approval of Galileo satellite program and agreements reached on various economic reforms, including boosting competition in electricity and gas markets, raising the retirement age, increasing funding for research and development, and facilitating labor mobility

• representatives from the thirteen applicant states participate fully in a European Council for the first time
• thousands of police clash with antiglobalization protestors

The merchant ship *Monica,* containing 928 illegal Kurdish immigrants from Iraq, is towed into a Sicilian port, 3/18

Malta and Estonia close (provisionally) their chapters of accession on JHA. Romania's chapter of accession on JHA remains unopened, 3/21

April
General Affairs Council considers problem of illegal immigration and takes stock of progress on Antiterrorism Roadmap, 4/15

Romania becomes last of the candidate states to open its chapter accession on JHA. Lithuania closes, provisionally, its accession chapter on JHA, 4/19–20

Jean-Marie LePen of the anti-immigrant National Front Party takes second place in the first round of the French presidential elections, highlighting popular concerns over illegal immigration in Europe, 4/21

Euro-Med Conference held in Valencia passes action plan for economic, political, and social cooperation between the EU and twelve Mediterranean/Middle Eastern countries, including measures designed to fight terrorism, 4/22–23

JHA Council (Luxembourg), 4/25–26
• agreement reached in principle on minimum standards for reception of asylum applicants (e.g., provisions on housing, education, family unity, etc.)
• adopts conclusions calling for various measures on illegal immigration and human trafficking by sea
• political agreement reached on an action program for the Argo program, which cofinances administrative cooperation in the fields of external borders, visa, asylum, and immigration
• consensus reached on protocol to the Europol Convention to enable Europol to participate in joint investigative teams (excluding coercive measures) and to give Europol the right to ask member states to initiate investigations in specific cases
• adopts recommendation establishing multinational ad hoc teams for gathering and exchanging information on terrorism
• adopts decision establishing information sharing and national contact points for security at international soccer matches
• final authorization given to presidency to negotiate agreement on judicial cooperation with the United States, which may include extradition provided that it entails a guarantee on the nonimposition of capital punishment
• meeting with Russian ministers of JHA and agreement on joint declarations concerning information exchanges to fight organized crime
• conclusions adopted on the approximation of criminal penalties, replacing the minimum-maximum practice with four levels or ranges for sanctions

- in response to recent incidents in Europe, adopts conclusions on racism, anti-Semitism, and xenophobia
- continued disagreement on the framework decision on the sexual exploitation of children

May   **EU-U.S. Summit,** Washington, D.C., 5/2. Launch of negotiations on mutual judicial assistance, including extradition

Giscard makes speech in Stuttgart, calling for the European Convention to address the need for enhanced EU cooperation on JHA, 5/5/02

Assassination of Dutch anti-immigrant political leader Pim Fortuyn adds to the salience of immigration issues in European politics, 5/6

Commission publishes a communication on a new approach for managing the EU's external borders, including a plan for the creation of a "European Corps of Border Guards" to supplement, but not replace, the national border-patrol agencies, 5/7

Meeting between Blair and Aznar results in joint commitment to push for strengthened external dimension to EU asylum policy, 5/20

Commission communication aimed at European Convention proposes to eliminate the EU's three-pillar system, instituting the Community method for JHA and greater democratic oversight of Europol, 5/22

Ministerial Meeting, Rome, 5/30. Italy unveils feasibility study on controlling external borders, including common border police

June   Plenary session of the European Convention discusses reform of JHA procedures, 6/7

Latvia and Slovakia close, provisionally, their chapters of accession on JHA, 6/10–11

JHA Council (Luxembourg), 6/13–14
- formal adoption of final acts on the Argo program, framework decision on terrorism, the European arrest warrant, and the creation of international joint investigative teams
- discussion and approval of action plan for managing the EU's external borders
- agreement in principle on shorter, more concrete plan proposed by UK with emphasis on tightening borders and returning illegal immigrants
- adoption of Europol's *Annual Report for 2001* and Work Program for 2003
- agreement on Spanish initiative to set up police and judicial contact points to exchange information on terrorist investigations
- agreement reached in Mixed Committee on extending cross-border police surveillance under the Schengen *acquis,* on new requirements for the SIS, and on rules for Ireland and the UK to participate in the SIS
- approves regulation containing rules for internal functioning of Eurojust

- agreement on Dutch proposal to create a network of judicial contact points to share information on war crimes in support of the newly established International Criminal Court (ICC)
- adoption of recommendation intended to boost cooperation between national authorities responsible for monitoring private security firms
- failure to reach agreement on framework decision covering drug trafficking

General Affairs Council discusses external aspects of the EU's immigration and asylum policy, but fails to reach agreement on making developmental aid and favorable trade policy with third-party countries conditional on their cooperation regarding these issues

Seville European Council, 6/21–22
- goal of 2004 affirmed for EU enlargement
- discussion of institutional reform of the Council of Ministers and European Council
- lengthy and wide-ranging discussions on illegal immigration, asylum policy, and external border control

Agreements reached:
- adopt pending EU legislation on the trafficking of human beings
- establish joint operations at external borders and create liaison network of national immigration officers
- strengthen cooperation on migration flows and illegal immigration in EU relations with third-party countries
- adopt pending legislation establishing common asylum policy
- review the list of third-party countries whose nationals require visas to enter the EU
- to expedite policies and bilateral agreements on repatriation, especially with Afghanistan, and
- approval of draft declaration on the contribution of CFSP, including ESDP, in the fight against terrorism

(Danish presidency)

July   Europol assistance in "Operation Twins" contributes to the breakup of a major international pedophile network and the arrest of fifty suspects, 7/2

Denmark proposes protocol amending the Europol Convention, covering a wide range of issues, 7/2

Commission's proposed framework decision on the trafficking of human beings formally adopted by the Council (ECOFIN), 7/19

Poland closes (provisionally) its accession chapter on JHA, 7/30

August   Europol opens liaison office in Washington, D.C., 8/30

September   **Informal Meeting of the JHA Council in Copenhagen, 9/13–14**
- emphasis made that the full Schengen *acquis* will apply to the candidate states only after their accession to the EU and that they need further assistance to prepare for this

• progress reviewed on fight against drug trafficking
• instructions given to the Commission to draw up a repatriation program for refugees
• discussions held with U.S. Attorney General John Ashcroft on negotiations for judicial cooperation with the EU and to allow the exchange of personal data via Europol

October   Europol assistance in "Operation Sunflower" contributes to the breakup of major international human trafficking network geared toward the "sex trade," resulting in eighty arrests, 10/2

Commission recommends that the ten "Laeken" candidate states will be ready to conclude their accession negotiations by the end of 2002, 10/9

JHA Council, 10/14–15
• moderate progress achieved on most outstanding aspects of the Commission's proposed asylum package
• political agreement reached on framework decision on combating the sexual exploitation of children and child pornography
• political agreement reached on decision establishing a mechanism for the mutual evaluation of member states' legal systems in the fight against terrorism
• progress made on the framework decision specifying criminal sanctions for corruption in the private sector
• new procedures adopted for selecting members of Europol's directorate
• discussion held with JHA ministers from the candidate states on the implementation of the Schengen *acquis*, mutual recognition of judicial decisions in criminal matters, and the protection of commercial truck drivers against violent attacks

Ireland approves the Treaty of Nice in a second referendum, clearing the way for its entry into force and expansion of the EU, 10/19

Brussels European Council, 10/24–25

Intense negotiations result in landmark budgetary agreement to finance the cost of EU expansion through 2013, clearing the way for final negotiations with the candidate states

November   **EU-Russia Summit in Brussels, 11/11**
• agreement reached on transit provisions for the Kaliningrad region and movement through the future Schengen free-travel area
• joint statement calls for greater cooperation on terrorism, but the EU remains critical of Russia's policies in Chechnya

Tape-recorded message attributed to Osama bin Laden heightens fears of future terrorist attack in Europe, 11/12

JHA Council, 11/28–29
• general agreement reached on asylum reception conditions, but continued discord on asylum (Dublin II) and a common definition of "refugees"
• progress made on forging readmission agreements with several third-party countries

- adoption of general action plan for the return of refugees to their home countries, as well as a specific program regarding Afghanistan
- adoption of statement declaring that candidate states will be considered "safe" third-party countries concerning asylum requests
- formal adoption of the framework decision and related directive regarding the trafficking of human beings (i.e., the proposal related to the development of the Schengen *acquis*)
- failure to resolve remaining differences on pending framework decisions on racism and xenophobia and drug trafficking
- failure to approve supplemental agreement with the United States that would allow the sharing of personal data via Europol
- adoption of an act drawing up a protocol to the European Convention to specify the role of Europol in joint investigation teams

December   Council reaches agreement on asylum responsibility (Dublin II) by action taken in "silent procedure," 12/6

Copenhagen European Council, 12/12–13
- intensive negotiations result in agreement between the EU and the ten candidate states on the budgetary and financial aspects of their accession
- endorsement of plans for the ten candidate states to accede to the EU on May 1, 2004, and for Bulgaria Romania to do so in 2007. No firm date set for accession of Turkey into the EU

U.S. Secretary of State Colin Powell and Danish Foreign Minister Per Stig Møller meet in Washington, D.C., and note progress on negotiations toward agreements covering the exchange of personal data via Europol and judicial cooperation, 12/18

JHA Council, 12/19
- following resolution of concerns over legal liabilities and data protection, endorsement of supplemental agreement between the United States and Europol permitting the exchange of personal data
- agreement reached on general approach for text of the protocol to amend the Europol Convention concerning Europol's mandate, ability to manage and exchange data, direct links to national police agencies, and scrutiny by the European Parliament
- general agreement reached on framework decision, proposed by Denmark, on combating corruption in the private sector
- political agreement reached on the framework decision, proposed by Denmark, covering the confiscation of criminal assets
- agreement reached in principle to allow Europol access to some data from the Schengen Information System (SIS)
- Commission presents its biannual update of the JHA Scoreboard, noting good progress on many crime-fighting goals but continued delays on asylum and immigration matters, despite the positive impetus provided by the Seville European Council of June 2002

Signing in Copenhagen of supplemental agreement between the United States and Europol permitting the exchange of personal data. Optimism expressed for compromise on pending judicial cooperation agreement, including provisions to satisfy member states' interest in proscribing the death penalty when extraditing suspects to the United States, 12/20

Europol Information System (EIS) projected to be fully operational, including data exchanges on crimes in Europol's mandate, as well as automatic foreign-language translations, 12/31

Deadline for transposition into national law of common definition of and sanctions for terrorism, 12/31

2003   (Greek presidency)

Projected transposition into national law of common definition of and sanctions for terrorism, 1/1

European Union's Police Mission (EUPM) takes over the international police mission in Bosnia and Herzegovina, consisting of 900 police personnel, civilian experts, and local staff drawn from all fifteen member states and eighteen non-EU countries, 1/1

Eurodac database of asylum seekers' fingerprints becomes operational, 1/15

February   Treaty of Nice enters into force, 2/1

JHA Council, 2/27–28

March   **Brussels European Council,** 3/21

Veria, informal JHA Council, 3/29

April   **Athens European Conference,** 4/16
               • signing of the Treaty of Accession with the ten candidate states

May   **JHA Council,** 5/8

June   Expected conclusion of the European Convention

Thessaloniki, European Council, 6/20

Deadline for Multidisciplinary Group on Organized Crime to submit to the Council a comprehensive report on each recommendation in 2000 Action Plan, 6/30

(Italian presidency)

Expected agreement on agenda for next IGC

Deadline for implementation of European Arrest Warrant by all member states, 12/31

2004   (Irish presidency)

Expected start of next the IGC on institutional reform

May   Projected accession to the EU of ten new member states, 5/1

June   Elections for the European Parliament in twenty-five member states

(Dutch presidency)

2005   (Luxembourg presidency)

Deadline for European Council to receive general report or implementation of each recommendation in 2000 Action Plan, 6/30

(British presidency)

2006   (Austrian presidency)

(Finnish presidency)

Acronyms

AFSJ	Area of Freedom, Security, and Justice, or "area of freedom, security, and justice"
AHWGE	Ad Hoc Working Group on Europol
CEECs	Central and Eastern Europe Countries (also CCEEs)
CEPOL	European Police College
CFSP	Common Foreign and Security Policy
COREPER	Committee of Permanent Representatives
DG	directorate-general
EC	European Community, European Council
ECB	European Central Bank
ECJ	European Court of Justice
ECOFIN	Councils of Economic and Finance Ministers
ECSC	European Coal and Steel Community
EDIU	European Drugs Intelligence Unit
EDU	Europol Drugs Unit
EEC	European Economic Community
EJN	European Judicial Network
EIS	Europol Information System
ELO	Europol Laison Officer
EMU	Economic and Monetary Union
ENU	Europol National Unit
EP	European Parliament
ERRF	European Rapid Reaction Force
ESDP	European Security and Defense Policy
ETA	Euzkadi Ta Askatasuna (Basque Fatherland and Freedom)
EU	European Union
Europol	European Police Office
FBI	Federal Bureau of Investigation
FRG	Federal Republic of Germany

GAC	General Affairs Council
HLG	High-Level Group
IGC	Intergovernmental Conference
IGOs	intergovernmental organizations
INGOs	international nongovernmental organizations
JHA	Justice and Home Affairs
MEP	member of the European Parliament
MLA	mutual legal assistance
MP	minister of parliament
NSAs	nonstate actors
OECD	Organization for Economic Cooperation and Development
OEEC	Organization for European Economic Cooperation
PGE	Europol Project Group
PHARE	Poland-Hungary: Actions for Economic Reconstruction
QMV	qualified majority voting
RIO	Risk Immigration Operation
SEA	Single European Act
SIS/SIS II	Schengen Information System
TACEUSS	Transatlantic Consortium for European Union Studies and Simulations
TEC	Treaty Establishing the European Communities
TECS	The Europol Computer System
TEU	Treaty on European Union [Maastricht Treaty]
TFJHA	Task Force for Justice and Home Affairs
TNAs	transnational actors

Bibliography

Anderson, M. *Policing the World: Interpol and the Politics of International Police Cooperation.* Oxford: Clarendon Press, 1989.

Anderson, M., et al. *Policing the European Union.* Oxford: Clarendon Press, 1995.

Anderson, J. J. "The State of the (European) Union." *World Politics* 47 (April 1995): 441–465.

Baxter N. "Policing Maastricht." *The Police Journal* (January 1997): 49–53.

Benyon, J. "Policing the Union: European Supranational Law Enforcement Co-operation." In *Policing Public Order: Theoretical and Practical Issues,* edited by C. Critcher and D. Waddington. Aldershot, England: Avebury/Ashgate Publishing, 1996.

———. "The Politics of Police Co-operation in the European Union." *International Journal of the Sociology of Law* 24 (1996): 353–379.

Berthelet, Pierre, *Police and Justice in the European Union,* Working Document in Civil Liberties Series of the European Parliament Directorate-General for Research. Brussels, January 2001.

Bieber, R. "Links Between the 'Third Pillar' (Title VI) and the European Community (Title II) of the Treaty on the European Union." In *The Third Pillar of the European Union: Cooperation in the Fields of Justice and Home Affairs,* edited by J. Monar and R. Morgan, pp. 37–48. Brussels: European Interuniversity Press, 1994.

Biggo, D. "The European Internal Security Field: Stakes and Rivalries in the Newly Developing Area of Police Intervention." In *Policing Across National Boundaries,* edited by M. Anderson and M. den Boer, pp. 161–173. London: Pinter, 1994.

Boschi-Orlandini, F. "Europol and the Europol Drugs Unit: A Cooperative Structure in the Making." In *The Third Pillar of the European Union: Cooperation in the Fields of Justice and Home Affairs,* edited by J. Monar and R. Morgan, pp. 209–216. Brussels: European Interuniversity Press, 1994.

Breckinridge, R. E. "Reassessing Regimes: The International Regime Aspects of the European Union." *Journal of Common Market Studies* 35, no. 2 (June 1997): 173–187.

Caporaso, J. A., and J.T.S Keeler. "The European Union and Regional Integration Theory." In *The State of the European Union: Building a European Polity,* edited by C. and S. Mazey, pp. 26–62. Boulder, CO: Lynne Rienner Publishers, 1995.

Chryssochoou, D. N. "New Challenges to the Study of European Integration: Implications for Theory-Building." *Journal of Common Market Studies* 35 (December 1997): 521–542.

Commission of the European Communities. *Biannual Update of the Scoreboard to Review Progress on the Creation of an Area of "Freedom, Security and Justice" in the European Union.* Brussels: 2000–2002 (two updates each year).

———. Home page for Justice and Home Affairs: http://europa.eu.int/comm/justice_home/index_en.htm.

———. Home page of the Directorate-General for Justice and Home Affairs: http://europa.eu.int/comm/dgs/justice_home/index_en.htm.

Commission of the European Communities and Europol (joint report). "Towards a European Strategy to Prevent Organized Crime." Brussels, March 13, 2001.

Consilium. Registry of Public Documents of the Council of the European Union: http://register.consilium.eu.int/utfregister/frames/introfsEN.htm.

Council of the European Union. Home page of the Council on Justice, Home Affairs, and Civil Protection: http://ue.eu.int/jai/default.asp?lang=en.

Council of the European Union. *Action Plan of the Council and the Commission on How Best to Implement the Provisions of the Treaty of Amsterdam on an Area of Freedom, Security and Justice* ("Vienna Action Plan"). Brussels, December 3, 1998.

———. *Action Plan to Combat Organized Crime* ("1997 Action Plan"). No C 251/1–18. Brussels, April 28, 1997.

———. *Council Act Drawing Up the Convention Based on Article K.3 of the Treaty on European Union, on the Establishment of a European Police Office (Europol Convention).* Brussels, 1995.

———. *European Union Drugs Strategy (2000–2004).* Brussels, December 1, 1999.

———. *Europol Drugs Unit Work Programme 1998,* Brussels, 1998.

———. "Minutes of the Council Sessions on Justice, Home Affairs, and Civil Protection" (Press releases). General Secretariat of the Council. Brussels, 1993–2002.

———. *The Prevention and Control of Organized Crime: A European Union Strategy for the Beginning of the New Millennium* (Council Document 6611/00). Brussels, March 3, 2000.

den Boer, M., and N. Walker. "European Policing After 1992." *Journal of Common Market Studies* 31, no. 1 (March 1993): 3–28.

den Boer, M., and W. Wallace. "Justice and Home Affairs." In H. Wallace and W. Wallace, *Policy-Making in the European Union.* 4th ed. Oxford: Oxford University Press, 2000.

Dinan, D. *An Ever Closer Union: An Introduction to European Integration.* 2nd ed. Boulder, CO: Lynne Rienner Publishers, 1999.

Duff, A., J. Pinder, and R. Pryce. *Maastricht and Beyond.* London and New York: Routledge, 1995.

EUR-Lex. Portal to European Union Law: http://europa.eu.int/eur-lex/en/index.html.

Europa. Main home page of the European Union: http://europa.eu.int/index-en.htm.

European Commission. SCADplus. "Activities of the European Union" (summary of legislation on Justice and Home Affairs): http://europa.eu.int/scadplus/leg/en/s22004.htm.

European Council. *Presidency Conclusions,* various issues. Brussels: General Secretariat of the Council, 1993–2002.

European Parliament. Home page of the Committee on Citizens' Freedoms and Rights, Justice and Home Affairs (LIBE): http://www.europarl.eu.int/committees/libe_home.htm.

European Police Office (Europol): http://www.europol.eu.int/home.htm.

European Police Office (Europol). *Annual Report for 1998 (Report on the Activities of the Europol Drugs Unit/Europol 1998)*. The Hague, 1999.

————. *Annual Report for 1999*. The Hague, 2000.

————. *Annual Report for 2000*. The Hague, 2001.

————. *Annual Report for 2001*. The Hague, 2001.

————. *Europol Work Programme 1999*. The Hague, 1998.

————. *Europol Work Programme 2000*. The Hague, 1999.

————. *Europol Work Programme 2001*. The Hague, 2000.

————. *Europol Work Programme 2002*. The Hague, 2001.

————. *Europol Work Programme 2003*. The Hague, 2002.

Europol Drugs Unit (EDU). *Annual Report for 1996*. The Hague, 1997.

————. *Annual Report for 1997*. The Hague, 1998.

Fijnaut, C. "Policing Western Europe: Interpol, Trevi and Europol." *Police Studies* (fall 1992): 101–106.

————. "International Policing in Europe: Its Present Situation and Future." In *Comparisons in Policing: An International Perspective,* edited by J. P. Brodeur. Aldershot, England: Avebury, 1995.

Galloway, D. *The Treaty of Nice and Beyond: Realities and Illusions of Power in the EU*. Sheffield, England: Sheffield Academic Press, 2001.

George, S. *Politics and Policy in the European Union*. New York: Oxford University Press, 1996.

Gregory, F. "Policing Transition in Europe: The Role of Europol and the Problem of Organized Crime." *Innovation* 11, no. 3 (1998). 287–305.

Guyomarch, A. "Cooperation in the Fields of Policing and Judicial Affairs." In *New Challenges to the European Union: Policies and Policy-Making,* edited by S. Stavridis et al., pp. 123–150. Aldershot, England: Dartmouth Publishing Company, 1997.

Haas, E. B. *The Uniting of Europe: Political, Social, and Economic Forces 1950–1957,* 2nd ed. Stanford, CA: Stanford University Press, 1968.

Harding, C., and B. Swart. "Intergovernmental Co-operation in the Field of Criminal Law." In *Criminal Justice in Europe: A Comparative Study,* edited by P. Fennel et al. Oxford: Clarendon Press, 1995.

Hebenton, B., and T. Thomas. *Policing Europe: Co-operation, Conflict and Control.* New York: St. Martin's Press, 1995.

Keohane, R., and S. Hoffmann. "Institutional Change in Europe in the 1980s." In *The New European Community,* edited by R. Keohnae and S. Hoffmann, pp. 1–40, Boulder, CO: Westview Press, 1991.

Legislative Observatory of the European Parliament: http://wwwdb.europarl.eu. int/dors/oeil/en/default.htm.

Lindberg, L. *The Political Dynamics of European Economic Integration*. Stanford, CA: Stanford University Press, 1963.

McCormick, J. *The European Union: Politics and Policies.* Boulder, CO: Westview Press, 1996.

McDonagh, B. *Original Sin in a Brave New World: The Paradox of Europe.* Dublin: Institute of European Affairs, 1998.

Monaco, F. "Europol: The Culmination of the European Union's International Police Cooperation Efforts." *Fordham International Law Journal* 19 (1995): 247–308.

Monar, J. "Justice and Home Affairs." *Journal of Common Market Studies* 38 (September 2000): 125–142.

Monar, J., and R. Morgan, eds. *The Third Pillar of the European Union: Coopera-tion in the Fields of Justice and Home Affairs.* Brussels: European Interuniver-sity Press, 1994.

Moravcsik, A. "Negotiating the Single European Act." In *The New European Com-munity,* edited by R. Keohane and S. Hoffmann, pp. 41–84. Boulder, CO: West-view, 1991.

———. "Preferences and Power in the European Community: A Liberal Intergov-ernmentalist Approach." *Journal of Common Market Studies* 31 (1993): 473–524.

———. *The Choice for Europe: Social Purpose and State Power from Messina to Maastricht.* London: UCL Press, 1998.

Müller-Graff, P.-C. "The Legal Bases of the Third Pillar and Its Position in the Framework of the Union Treaty." In *The Third Pillar of the European Union: Cooperation in the Fields of Justice and Home Affairs,* edited by J. Monar and R. Morgan, pp. 21–36. Brussels: European Interuniversity Press, 1994.

Nelsen, B. F., and A. C.-G. Stubb. *The European Union: Readings on the Theory and Practice of European Integration.* Boulder, CO: Lynne Rienner Publishers, 1994.

Nentwich, M., and G. Falkner. "The Treaty of Amsterdam: Towards a New Institu-tional Balance." *European Integration online Papers (EIoP)* 1 (1997).

Nugent, N., ed. *The European Union, Volume I: Perspectives and Theoretical Inter-pretations.* Brookfield, VT: Dartmouth Publishing, 1997.

Partan, D. G. "The Justiciability of Subsidiarity." In *The State of the European Union: Building a European Polity,* edited by C. Rhodes and S. Mazey, pp. 26–62. Boulder, CO: Lynne Rienner Publishers, 1995.

Peek, J. "International Police Cooperation Within Justified Political and Judicial Frameworks: Five Theses on Trevi." In *The Third Pillar of the European Union: Cooperation in the Fields of Justice and Home Affairs,* edited by J. Monar and R. Morgan, pp. 201–208. Brussels: European Interuniversity Press, 1994.

Peers, S. *EU Justice and Home Affairs Law.* Harlow, England: Longman, 2000.

Rauchs, G. , and D. J. Koenig, "Europol." In *International Police Cooperation: A World Perspective,* edited by D. J. Koenig and D. K. Das, pp. 43–62. Lanham, MD: Lexington Books, 2001.

Regan, E., *The New Third Pillar: Cooperation Against Crime in the European Union.* Dublin: Institute of European Affairs, 2000.

Reichel, P. *Comparative Criminal Justice Systems: A Topical Approach.* 2nd ed. Upper Saddle River, NJ: Prentice Hall, 1999.

Risse-Kappen, T. "Exploring the Nature of the Beast: International Relations The-ory and Comparative Policy Analysis Meet the European Union." *Journal of Common Market Studies* 34, no. 1 (March 1996): 53–80.

Rosamond, B. *Theories of European Integration.* New York: St. Martin's Press, 2000.

Sbragia, A. M. "Introduction." In *Europolitics: Institutions and Policymaking in the "New" European Community,* edited by A. M. Sbragia, pp. 1–22. Washington, DC: Brookings Institution, 1992.

———. "Thinking About the European Future: The Uses of Comparison." In *Euro-politics: Institutions and Policymaking in the "New" European Community,* edited by A. M. Sbragia, pp. 257–292. Washington, DC: Brookings Institution, 1992.

———. "The European Community: A Balancing Act." *Publius* 23 (summer 1993): 23–38.

Schutte, J.J.E. "Judicial Cooperation Under the Union Treaty." In *The Third Pillar of the European Union: Cooperation in the Fields of Justice and Home Affairs*, edited by J. Monar and R. Morgan, pp. 181–192. Brussels: European Interuniversity Press, 1994.

Snyder, F. "Institutional Development in the European Union: Some Implications of the Third Pillar." In *The Third Pillar of the European Union: Cooperation in the Fields of Justice and Home Affairs*, edited by J. Monar and R. Morgan, pp. 85–96. Brussels: European Interuniversity Press, 1994.

Stone, A. "What Is a Supranational Constitution." *The Review of Politics* 56, no. 3 (summer 1994): 441–474.

Storbeck, J. "Europol: Probleme and Lösungen." *Kriminalistik*, no. 1 (1996): 17–21.

Treaty Establishing the European Communities (TEC): Consolidated Version, 1999.

Treaty of Amsterdam Amending the Treaty on European Union, the Treaties Establishing the European Communities and Certain Related Acts, 1997.

Treaty of Nice Amending the Treaty on European Union, the Treaties Establishing the European Communities and Certain Related Acts, 2001.

Treaty on European Union ("Maastricht Treaty"), 1992.

Treaty on European Union (TEU): Consolidated Version, 1999.

Tupman, W. A. "Supranational Investigation After Amsterdam: The Corpus Juris and Agenda 2000." *Information and Communications Technology Law* (June 1998): 1–15.

Uçarer, E. M. "Cooperation on Justice and Home Affairs Matters." In *Developments in the European Union*, edited by L. Cram, D. Dinan, and N. Nugent. New York: St. Martin's Press, 1999.

———. "From the Sidelines to Center Stage: Sidekick No More? The European Commission in Justice and Home Affairs." *European Integration Online Papers (EIoP)* 5 (2001).

———. "Justice and Home Affairs in the Aftermath of September 11: Opportunities and Challenges." *EUSA Review* 15, no. 2 (spring 2002): 1–4.

Urwin, D. W. *The Community of Europe: A History of European Integration Since 1945*. 2nd ed. New York: Longman, 1995.

Vermeulen, G. "A Judicial Counterpart for Europol." *UCLA Journal of International Law and Foreign Affairs* (fall-winter 1997–1998): 225–257.

Walker, N. "Policing the European Union: The Politics of Transition." In *Policing Change, Changing Police: International Perspectives*, edited by O. Marenin, pp. 251–283. New York: Garland Publishing, 1996.

Wessels, W. "The Third Pillar Plea for a Single Theoretical Research Agenda." In *The Third Pillar of the European Union: Cooperation in the Fields of Justice and Home Affairs*, edited by J. Monar and R. Morgan, pp. 237–236. Brussels: European Interuniversity Press, 1994.

Williams, P., and D. Vlassis, eds. *Combating Transnational Crime: Concepts, Activities and Responses*. London: Frank Cass, 2001.

Woodward, R. "Establishing Europol." *European Journal on Criminal Policy and Research* 1–4 (1994): 7–33.

Wright, J., and K. Bryett. "Multilateral Policing and New Conceptions of Security in the European Union." *Police Studies* 27, no. 4 (1994): 61–75.

Sources of News Articles

Agence France Presse (Paris)
Christian Science Monitor (Boston)

Daily Record (Glasgow)
Daily Telegraph (London),
Deutsche Presse-Agentur (Hamburg)
The Economist (London)
European Report (European Information Service, Brussels)
Focus Magazin (Munich)
The Guardian (Manchester)
Het Financieel Dagblad (English version) (Amsterdam)
The Independent (London)
The Irish Times (Dublin)
M2 Presswire (Coventry, UK)
New Statesman & Society (London)
New York Times
The Observer (London)
Press Association Newsfile (London)
The Times (London)
Vancouver Sun
Washington Post

Index

About the Book

Will the European Union soon have a policing agency similar to the U.S. Federal Bureau of Investigation? John Occhipinti traces the evolution of the European Police Office (Europol), bringing to life the core themes—the tension between supranationalism and intergovernmentalism, concerns over the "democratic deficit" in the EU, and the impact of enlargement—in the study of European integration.

Occhipinti draws from competing theories of European integration to explain the development of supranationalism in European police cooperation. Considering forces stemming from both within and outside of the EU and reflecting concerns over international terrorism and transnational organized crime, he explores the roles played by key actors and events at every stage of Europol's development, from the initial creation of the Trevi Group in 1975 to mid-2002. His work is a major contribution not only to the literature on Third Pillar issues, but also to an understanding of the deepening of European integration overall.

John D. Occhipinti is associate professor of political science at Canisius College.

Learning Resources
Centre